Facing Freedom

Solo Female Travel | Two-Plus Years | Five Continents

The Return to Self

Candy – Thanks so much for supporting me + my journey. Love meeting my autistic sisters throughout the world.

Live Love, Eryn

Eryn Donnalley

BALBOA PRESS

A DIVISION OF HAY HOUSE

1 Scripture, King James Version, The Analytical Study Edition

Balboa Press books may be ordered through booksellers or by contacting:

Balboa Press
A Division of Hay House
1663 Liberty Drive
Bloomington, IN 47403
www.balboapress.com
1 (877) 407-4847

The author has made concerted efforts to write with sensitivity and grace while maintaining the authenticity of this travel memoir and autobiography. In that light, certain names and locations have been changed or omitted to protect the privacy of others. This is a condensed recollection of events and true to the best of the author's knowledge.

Printed in the USA.

ISBN: 978-1-5043-8711-8 (sc)
ISBN: 978-1-5043-8710-1 (hc)
ISBN: 978-1-5043-8712-5 (e)

Library of Congress Control Number: 2017913182

Balboa Press rev. date: 10/27/2017

Contents

Part IV: Eclectic Teachings

Acknowledgments

It is with the deepest gratitude I thank a Source greater than myself for allowing me to experience this life-altering transformation and for all that has led me to this moment. I was provided with the perfect set of experiences and just enough tormented mental anguish to initiate the desire for radical change within myself.

I would be nothing without the spark of love that brought my parents together, and I am grateful for their union. I chose my parents for a reason, and they chose me in some cosmic way, and together we've struggled and loved, resisted and supported each other along this meandering path of life. To my father, who was plagued with depression for much of his life, and to my mother, who still battles her own, I wish you both peace of mind, and I dedicate this book to you. To my stepmother, who somehow always understood me and was an integral part in my life, I am eternally grateful for your support.

I pray that this book will be warmly received by all women, that it will aid in the process of healing and personal expansion, and most of all that it will inspire a deeper sense of worldwide compassion for all living beings, including ourselves.

The Call to Write

I've come to feel one has to be a bit mad to write a book. The amount of work that goes into a project like this compared to the probability of success, as most view it, is well, negatively weighted and unlikely at best. That leads me to tell you that writing this book wasn't done by choice, rather by necessity. It was a calling I couldn't ignore. Snippets and phrases and hundreds of thoughts spewed from my mind and oozed from my soul. A deep desire and subtle sense of obligation in my repetitive thoughts consumed me—but in a good, *this is your purpose* sort of way. I had to tell this story.

Ernest Hemingway once said, "There is nothing to writing. All you do is sit down at a typewriter and bleed." And that's how it happened ... I sat down and bled.

"I like stories where women save themselves."
—Neil Gaiman

Introduction

In March 2014, I made what many viewed as a questionable decision to leave the life I'd known in the United States. The walls of my world crumbled around me like a building's demolition. My three structural pillars—marriage, career, and homestead—were leveled, and I controlled the wrecking ball. When the dust settled from my life's destruction, I found myself lost in a land of unknowns with no blueprints for reconstruction.

I did, however, have this insistent force that kept gnawing at me, compelling me to drastically alter my course. I resisted and fought myself, adverse to the idea of change, but eventually I made an unlikely plan: pausing life as I knew it in America and resuming play in India. I had only two intentions when I left on my one-way flight, to find my highest self and a new creative path for my future.

Out of my twenty-eight-month healing journey across five continents came this book. Meant to be a healing text, sacred to me if no one else, I recount the transformative people and experiences that ultimately elevated me to a place of sustained contentment and true happiness. These were traits that had eluded me; their absence tormented me in the life I'd left behind. Only when I came to find a healthy version of myself did I fully realize how emotionally unhealthy I'd been, all while putting on a pretty face and functioning "happily" in society.

I've come to see there's a void we have, most of us—an emptiness and internal suffering we don't talk about at parties or even amongst our families and friends. We've become masters at filling this void and hiding from it so cunningly with food or TV, sex or relationships, shopping, working out, drugs, or alcohol, all high on the list of fillers.

Most of my life, I tried desperately to escape this void, clawing at life as the quicksand of negative inner dialogue, depression, and societal expectations worked to consume and suffocate me. I was surviving, yes, but gasping for air, never quite able to catch my breath. In all the energy spent on survival and personal destruction, I never considered the possible benefit of simply surrendering to the void and exploring it. My fears and insecurities held too much power over me then, and I'd been afraid of what I'd find.

Then one day in the foothills of the Himalayas, early on in my trip, I dove headfirst into myself and began an inward journey. It was uncomfortable and painful and confronting—but necessary and cathartic. This was the beginning of something, an opening. I began stripping away the layers of fear that had shaped the first half of my life, and I finally saw promise for the future. I began the reconstruction process, laying new foundations of love and compassion with walls of wisdom and emotional equanimity; day by day, country by country, I was building anew, traveling an unfamiliar path back to my true self.

The Purpose of This Book

The purpose of this book is to inspire you, to motivate you, to challenge and encourage you to find the best version of *yourself.*

I've structured the book in a way that brings you into the story of my personal evolution, through traveling, where I came to question nearly every aspect of who I was—my insecurities, fears, prejudices, and belief structures. These were the layers I needed to investigate to find my higher self. The true hope though is that it brings you to investigate the foundations of your own story and inspires you to elevate beyond it. We all have challenges and pain, perhaps trauma that's left us emotionally wounded, but it's how we rise above it that matters. In this rising up there is great power. When we choose the freedom of forgiveness and acceptance and *prioritize our emotional well-being*, we begin the healing process, and the past no longer dictates our future.

In every country, in every chapter, I learned something new about myself, and it led me to consider how I'd chosen to live my life. This book is part travel story, part lessons learned, and part free-flowing questions of self and American society as I roamed the globe. I've also included "expansion exercises" where I invite you to travel inwardly and think introspectively about your own life; how we form destructive patterns that don't serve us, to question our limiting beliefs that hold us back, and how we view our place in the world overall.

This is about how we value ourselves and how that dictates our lives. It's about finding purpose, regaining our personal power, and reclaiming our authentic selves. I've come to feel it's when these elements are out of alignment that we suffer the more outwardly noticeable symptoms of low self-esteem, depression, neurosis, unhealthy habits, and addictions.

I titled the book *Facing Freedom* after a practice I developed in month sixteen of my travels but also because I found such freedom in facing myself in full truth, both literally and figuratively. There were many immersive experiences I took part in overseas that were unique to my geographic location, so they're likely unavailable to you, but the Facing Freedom practice is a personal healing journey that can be done in your own home. The idea came to me one tumultuous night in north Thailand, and it had such dramatic effects I knew I had to share it with you. Ultimately, that practice is what led me to write this travel memoir with a healing theme.

I'll tell you about my own Facing Freedom transformation, in month sixteen, where I went from low self-worth with deeply woven threads of self-hate to radical self-acceptance and sustaining self-love. Then I'll give you simple instructions so you can navigate this immersive experience for yourself. Honestly, I didn't know a plateau of such inner contentment even existed, so I was surprised myself when I saw such a lasting shift.

This book was written with the deep belief that our people, our societies, and our planet are in desperate need of healing and positive transformation. When we rise up into our higher selves, we can then project love, grace, and compassion into the world instead of fear, greed, and skepticism. I believe this may be the greatest challenge of our time, to prioritize our individual shifts in order to propel a collective quantum leap.

Although this trip changed nearly every aspect of who I was and how I viewed life, I must admit there were really no striking discoveries or monumental treasures to be found on my quest. I see now, in all the lessons and expansion I was blessed to experience, I was ultimately *unlearning* and tearing down all the barriers I'd built up against my simplest, purest self. Finding the way back home to our true selves—this *is* the spiritual path.

Call to Mind

As we walk through life, we're presented with key moments or opportunities when we may choose a path that leads us toward personal growth and expansion or toward more of the same, whatever that is. Most of my life, I held myself in a state of inaction—more of the same—until one day I had a revelation. I came to see that my deepest source of unhappiness stemmed from the view I had of myself, and I grasped fully these two things: (1) this negative view was tainting every single aspect of my life; and (2) I came to know with full certainty that *I had the power to change it*, whereas before I thought, *This is just how I am.*

We're all living complex lives with a million different variables that affect, in countless ways, how our individual futures play out. No two lives are the same, and none of us know what lies ahead, but I do know this: we rarely, if ever, raise our consciousness by maintaining the status quo. Eckhart Tolle wrote in *A New Earth,* "There is only one perpetrator of evil on the planet: human unconsciousness. That realization is true forgiveness. With forgiveness, your victim identity dissolves, and your true power emerges—the power of Presence. Instead of blaming the darkness, you bring in the light" (Tolle 2005, pg. 160).

There are many avenues to raising our quality of consciousness and to finding inner contentment and meaning. I hope this book is one of many that will spark an awakening inside you. I've come to realize it will likely be a wide platform of resources throughout the course of our lives that will transform us in different ways; we must take them all in as they come, absorb them, and make changes as we can. This is the human evolutionary process.

As with most personal growth, I've found that a synchronistic combination of timing, interest, and desperation is often required to truly absorb information, to allow ourselves to be touched by it and motivated to make our own personal changes. I've also learned there is a vast difference between thinking something, knowing something, and knowing something deeply. We may read something meaningful in a book, and it may strike us in that moment as powerful, but unless we experience a profound shift directly, integrating the experience into our psyche somehow, it is unlikely to change us in any significant way. I'll remind you of this when we reach the Facing Freedom chapter where I invite you to confront yourself in a way that you may find challenging. The integrated experience, however, is critical to sustaining transformation.

This isn't a book about meditation; it's about elevating you to a place of love within yourself where you're willing to begin a discipline that sustains you. It's not about diet or emotional eating; it's about valuing yourself from such a deep place you no longer eat excessively to fill the empty spaces of your heart. And it's not about quitting an addiction or taking up jogging; it's about releasing habits that don't serve our highest purpose and choosing new activities that nourish us.

The Facing Freedom practice was a springboard, taking me to a place of inner acceptance where I valued myself so fully and so deeply, unhealthy lifestyle choices were simply unacceptable to me. And for the first time in my life, I was choosing a healthy life because I wanted to, not because my inner bully forced me to. I'd not known life existed without the inner bully beating me up in the playground of my mind. Now I am free—not perfect by any means but free.

I don't know why we're all sparked to transform in different ways and at different stages of our lives. I don't know why I was given this great gift of travel and the inner courage to take the drastic leap out into the world to find a better version of myself. I really can't answer those questions, but I sincerely hope this is the right time for you to pick up this book and that it resonates with you. If it inspires only one woman to navigate her own healing journey, it will have been worth all the effort.

Lao Tzu,[1] ancient Chinese philosopher, wrote, "If you want to awaken all of humanity, then awaken all of yourself. If you want to eliminate the suffering of the world, then eliminate all that is dark and negative in yourself. Truly, the greatest gift you have to give is that of your own self-transformation." Yes!

Know this, and try to know it deeply—feel it in your core. There is a power inside you that is unfathomable, a subtle power of truth and heart, not of pride or ego. Within that power is the real you—a happier, more carefree, content, and peaceful version of yourself that perhaps you lost long ago. It doesn't take a miracle to reclaim her. She's been there all along. We just need a few tools to help unearth the deeper essence of self, buried within.

Finally, if all my travel happenings and mystical musings are unsuccessful in the way of inspiring your own inward journey, perhaps you'll view *Facing Freedom* simply as the unlikely story of a woman who solo-traveled the world on the quest to save herself, from herself.

PART I

The Storms Before

"In a futile attempt to erase our past, we deprive the community of our healing gift. If we conceal our wounds out of fear and shame, our inner darkness can neither be illuminated nor become a light for others."

—Brennan Manning

CHAPTER 1

The Catalyst

All great change is preceded by chaos.
—Deepak Chopra

I lay on my yoga mat, flat on my back in the final resting pose, *savasana,*[1] and listened to the yoga instructor speak her words of wisdom. I didn't know it then, and she couldn't have known it either, but her words were about to awaken something inside me.

I'd only recently begun going to yoga class. I was one of those people that talked about going to yoga class, thought about going to yoga, and had even purchased a pair of yoga pants on the off chance I might one day actually go to a class, but in all the years of talking and thinking about yoga, I'd never attended a class—until now. Today some battle for betterment took place inside me. The good guys, supporting growth and expansion, won a narrow victory, overpowering the bad guys, representing depression and doubt. I put on my black stretchy pants and went to a class.

So I'm lying there on my mat—I know you want to know the magical words that changed me. The yoga instructor said softly, "Taking care of yourself doesn't mean just looking after your physical health; it also means taking care of your emotional health. We have to take responsibility for our emotional health." Tears welled up in my eyes and fell quietly from the corners, one by one into my hair. *We have to take responsibility for our emotional health.* The phrase paused in the screen of my mind just hanging there, not willing to move forward onto the next slide of thought. This was an awakening—a tiny opening of light that entered me. I knew in that moment I had to make major adjustments in my life to foster my own emotional health and stability.

It doesn't sound all that profound, I know. *You have to take responsibility for your emotional health.* It sounds rather an obvious statement actually, my emotionally healthy self, looking back at my unhealthy self. But this is how awakenings often happen. You're just going through life in a malaise, walking around, not really paying attention to the patterns of behavior that brought you there or the repeated times you ignored your instincts; you simply missed all the signals life sent you along the way, which we all do with heartbreaking frequency.

Then one day, something jumps up and grabs you—a symbol, a sign, a song, a quote, a memory, blades of grass in a sidewalk crack, a commercial, a coconut floating in the water, a gecko chirping, the way a leaf floats along effortlessly in the wind. Something happens, whether simple or profound. In that moment, you're struck by *something* that may have been there all along, but today you see it differently. The light blinks on in your mind like the Hot Now sign at Krispy Kreme, and you know you're changed in some unfathomable way. This was one of those days. *I have to take responsibility for my emotional health. No, Eryn, this doesn't mean fill the void with hot glazed donuts.*

I wish I could tell you after my stretchy pants awakening, all the answers suddenly revealed themselves. That I woke up one day soon after, magically realizing I needed to turn my whole life on its head and start over, questioning almost every aspect of what I knew to be "true," and that I was instantly able to change myself and choose a different path for my life. Unfortunately, it doesn't work like that. Usually our lives have to fall apart a little bit more (or a lot) before we feel compelled to evolve ourselves.

As for me, I feared change nearly as much as death, so it took several more years and a big internal push for me to jump from the precipice of my life—a crisis of the spirit, a crack from the self I'd known, a psychological fracture possibly? Technically I was within my faculties but on the verge of something—madness or transformation. I knew not which.

I'd later come to realize this was my "dark night of the soul"[2] experience, as described in various spiritual texts, but at the time I had no knowledge or terminology for this pivotal and painful turning point.

Offerings

I guess this would be a good time to back up and explain a bit about how I came to leave the States to begin with. You could probably guess. It all began with a divorce, which led to quitting work since my then husband and I worked together. I wasn't kicked to the curb, homeless, or jobless. It wasn't like that at all. I don't want to give you that impression. We were lucky actually, considering we were so inextricably linked in our personal and professional lives. If there is such a thing as a good divorce, then we had one.

Divorces are always terrible, and no party survives completely intact. It's as if a part of you has been surgically removed and placed in the currents of a river, an offering to the divorce gods, never to be seen again. It makes me so sad to think how we can treat each other in the times leading up to a divorce. Even when there's no hostility or major drama, there are so many months of passivity, silence, distance, and avoidance that, in hindsight, seem so confusing, cruel, and hurtful. Silence is death to a marriage. So much is said in *not saying*. It seems to me when we actively (or unconsciously) choose to avoid issues with our partner, we may as well start divvying up the furniture because that's the slow beginning of the end. But I still say we were lucky. There were no affairs or intentional gashes breeding animosity, and we chose to be civil and respectful in the midst of our pain. Maybe that's the best we could hope for.

Although we were both wearing our Olympic medals in the very popular divorce category and could've continued working together, deep down something told me I had to leave the company. In a way, it would've been the safer option to stay, but I felt I had to choose something different and find a new path for myself with a more creative element to it. The only problem was, with the emotion of the divorce, I couldn't throw myself into a creative endeavor. Although it had been my decision, I was still grieving terribly. Post-separation/pre-divorce mourning left me in a desperate state without inspiration or motivation—not ideal for the creative process.

This was all part of my not-so-minor freak-out that lasted about six months while trying to settle on a plan for starting over. I fiercely questioned my own decision to leave the marriage and rode the waves of sadness, anger, and regret all the way into the *dark night*. I was detoxing off the drug of codependency, and I resisted my inherent compulsion to find a new man. I somehow knew this was imperative at this stage in my life and something I'd never been able to do before. I was a relationship addict.

In the midst of my emptiness, side effects were severe: waking nightmares that left me sleepless and physically shaking in solitude; obsessive writing in the wee hours of the morning, trying to figure out where I'd gone wrong; heavy, frequent prayer and searching my neurotic mind endlessly for answers to why my life had dropped me off at the corner of emotionally induced starvation and despair. I was detoxing. My body and soul were withering into nothingness, and I began merging with the fibers of my mattress. *Damn you, life. How could you do this to me? I'm so over living … existing. God, just take me now! Please, just end it.*

I tried at times to rally myself. I had my plan A and plan B. I was a Girl Scout; I was prepared. But none of my plans were feeling quite right, and I promised myself I wouldn't do things that didn't *feel* right anymore just because they made sense. I'd tell myself regularly, *No,*

Eryn, don't fall into the trap of hamster wheel security. Search how you feel. I was extremely fortunate to have some financial flexibility and time to think while we worked to transition me out of the company, so I drifted on the raft of unknowns for a while until I figured out my future. *Where do I go, what do I want, what am I doing with my life? Aggggh!*

The Big Idea

In the midst of my panicked indecision, ranting madly one day on the phone to my good friend Aiden, he pitched a crazy idea. "Why don't you go to India and travel for a few months."

Screech, halt, stop ... what?

"Aiden, that's crazy!" I laughed hysterically at his ridiculous idea. I simply had no capacity to consider something so absurd. "What the hell kinda idea is that? Travel ... Who on earth steps out of their career midlife to travel? That would be completely irresponsible!"

My thoughts momentarily boomeranged out from the confinements of my narrow mind and out into the world, tiny snippets of thought flashing, *I'm not strong enough to do that. I don't have the confidence or know-how to solo travel. I can't go to India by myself. That's the most ridiculous idea ever.*

It was far beyond anything I would've ever conceived on my own. I never even *wanted* to travel like that; my dreams weren't even that big. All I ever really wanted was to live a "normal" life with a husband, house, and dog—standard ideologies of the American dream. And my idea of travel—which was really vacation, two very different terms I now understand—was flying to a Caribbean island (with a man of course) and drinking mojitos on a sunset cruise. I'd taken one trip to India a few years earlier with an organized yoga group, but that had been a complete fluke; after my stretchy pants awakening, some ethereal force changed the channel of my regularly scheduled thought program and propelled me to join that yoga retreat.

Aiden tapped the mic on his phone, intercepting my boomerang of erratic thoughts. "Eryn, you there? Where'd you go?"

"Aiden," I said in my sarcastic tone, "before today, I thought you were a pretty intelligent guy, but this is *the* most ridiculous idea I've ever heard. This just isn't even realistic! You should consider upping your therapy to twice a week. Call me back when you have some sensible ideas, please."

He called me again the next day, so persistent, reminding me what a unique opportunity this was—no job, no man, no house, no kids, and no responsibility for the first time in my adult life. "Ahhh, yeah, that's helpful. Thanks for reminding me of everything I don't have! Are you trying to make me cry? Seriously, I don't have time for this bullshit! I need real options here." I told him he was crazy again—and a complete ass—then hung up on him. Oh, I was really mad at him for suggesting something so preposterous.

I dismissed his idea completely.

Weeks rolled on with no new epiphanies striking me as to the perfect path moving forward, and despite my best efforts, my friend's traveling idea crept occasionally into my thoughts. I tried to consider this idea of *the world*, but I couldn't wrap my mind around the consideration of something so ... so crazy and seemingly irresponsible as taking an extended period of time off from my career. It was risky enough, the idea of choosing a creative path (for which I had no flowing creative energy), but to choose a traveling sabbatical? How would that time gap look on my resume, for goodness sake? That's like career suicide, jumping to my own death from the professional ladder I'd been arduously climbing for sixteen years—*especially* as a woman in the male-dominated construction industry. Oh, horrors no, we couldn't possibly have that! Extended leave is only permissible for birth or death. I couldn't see it then in that moment, but I was experiencing both.

Just to humor my friend, I printed out an inadequately sized 8½ x 11 world map and laid it on my desk, leaving it there to collect dust as I swirled on madly in my melancholy mania and my tornado of indecision. My internal doubt persisted, reminding me the best course of action would be to move to a new city and jump back on the hamster wheel of big business. *Keep climbing that ladder, Eryn. Everything will be better when you make it to the top. Go on now, keep going. It's the American way.*

I'd occasionally glance at it—*the world*—as I came and went from my apartment, surviving on my coffee and cheese toast diet, but a month went by before I actually sat down and looked at it. One day I walked by it, and … well, it sort of whispered to me in a way, "Come over here." I was in a hurry to leave and was actually annoyed at the world for continuing to taunt me. *Okay, okay, what do you want? Fine, I'll look at you!*

I sat and looked at it for a while, trying unsuccessfully to imagine what the world might *really* look like beyond the black squiggly lines delineating borders on my flimsy piece of paper. A repetitive thought circulated in my mind like a gentle current. *The world is in your hands, Eryn. How does that feel? Hmm, how does it feel? Fucking scary, that's how it feels!*

One dear friend had encouraged me to choose something that made me *feel* good, saying that if I followed whatever that was, everything else would fall into place. I liked the concept, but I wasn't quite sure *fucking scary* would qualify as a "good feeling" to follow into the next stage of my life.

I considered what travel might look like—a single, white American girl on a global odyssey—but my vision blurred, and the image became fuzzy in the construction site of my mind. All I saw were orange and white barricades blocking the idea. I couldn't deny it seemed like a better plan than my current trajectory of becoming one with my mattress, but I couldn't envision such a grand plan for myself. All I saw was fear. *Damn you, Aiden, for suggesting this! Grrrr.*

One day I finally brought it up, jokingly, to a girlfriend. I think I wanted to hear what it sounded like if I said it out loud to someone. Plus, Hayley was from the UK and the only real friend I had at the time from another country, so I considered her more knowledgeable and unbiased. I was pretty sure all my other friends and family would view it with complete skepticism and doubt. After all, that's how I was viewing it. Why would I expect anything different from them?

Hayley didn't think it was altogether a bad idea, but she did urge me, coming from her psychotherapy background, "Identify why you'd be going. Understand what it is you want to leave behind and what you want to move toward. Make sure you're not running from anything."

"Hmmm. Uh huh, uh huh, good point," I said, contemplating her comment. "Yes, I see where you're coming from there."

"But I don't think I'd start with India," she continued. "You wouldn't catch me there—no, no. One word for you, Eryn: parasites."

Later that night, I sat down with my map again, circling country names that sounded interesting—that is to say, those with names I recognized. I must've slept through geography class; my knowledge of the world was embarrassing, to say the least. I wasn't even *excited* about this self-imposed exercise of circling countries. It felt like one of those tasks you give yourself when considering a new career, including even the crazy ideas you know you'll never consider, like becoming an astronaut.

My mind was a rip current of thoughts; numbed by fear, grief stricken by my failed marriage, my life in shambles, the dark night swallowing me—I could barely breathe. Currents took me back and back and back to my conversation with Hayley. I asked myself if I'd be running from anything if I left the States. I pondered and questioned myself at length, trying to dissect my intentions. Then I went through the exercise again, my mind churning madly with ideas and possibilities and fear all turning into butter, clogging the arteries of my weary soul. *Security? Unknown? Security? Unknown? Take a chance on a new city unknown? Take a chance in the fucking scary world unknown?*

Tears filled my eyes, and I wept at the torturous state of my own indecision, drowning in question marks. I was lost inside myself, a one-finned fish swimming in circles. The divorce would soon be final. I was alone. I had no clear direction, and my mind was in a state of exhaustion after months of this vacillation and the preceding emotional turmoil related to the marital separation. I knew it wasn't healthy for me to continue wallowing in this indecision, and I had to choose *some* path for myself in the very near future.

At thirty-six, I shouldn't have even been asking myself these questions. I should've been happily married and possibly pregnant! *What am I doing with my life? Why have I always lived my life outside societal norms? What's wrong with me? Can't I just be happy for once? Why can't I have a normal life like everyone else? Damn you, Aiden, for suggesting this preposterous idea. I can't be an astronaut!*

Morning came—as it always does. I would've welcomed not waking up, but there ya have it … I woke up. We don't really get to choose these things, do we? I cursed the optimistic rays of sunshine that bounced into the windows of my apartment like sixth-grade cheerleaders. My crusty eyes blinked open. *Oh God, another day of self-torture! Noooooo, I can't take another day!*

A new thought arose; it was clear with absolute and unwavering lucidity, unlike all the previous mornings. My leaving the United States wouldn't be escaping reality or running from anything. My reality was over, the divorce papers were signed, the house was going on the market; all ties were broken, and my life was indeed now a clean slate. If I took this trip, I wouldn't be running *from* myself; I'd be running *to* myself.

Whoa. This is big!

In that single instant, it all made sense. All my life that led up to that moment, my mind's mixed-up Rubik's Cube clicked into the solved position. Here it was, the truth I could no longer hide from. I'd been running *from* something my whole life—me.

There were many layers to this I didn't fully understand at the time, but one thing was clear: traveling and leaving the only country I'd ever really known was somehow the most direct path back to my true self! I knew it with full certainty. In that moment, I realized I *had* to go. It was essential to my emotional well-being and personal growth. It didn't matter how scary, irrational, or seemingly irresponsible it was. I was going. I had a lot of work to do, just not in big business America or in any entrepreneurial fashion. This was the most important project of my life, and if I didn't work on it now, dissecting the patterns of my past, I'd repeat the same mistakes in the decades to come, causing myself and all those around me heartache and pain.

The Big Question

True to American form, I had certain goals and aspirations for myself when I left the States. I even, in my very type A personality, had a multi-tabbed Excel spreadsheet, detailing countries I hoped to visit, visa requirements, vaccination suggestions from the CDC, possible time line of travel, and danger zones and countries to avoid, but the most important thing was to consider Haley's question: why am I going? This couldn't be an elaborate extended vacation. This trip had to be more—so much more.

Reasons to Go

To get outside myself. I needed a new perspective on the me I'd known. The insecure, lost me. The overly busy and control-freak me. The type A, high-strung me. The depressed and out-of-control me. The emotionally exhausted me. I was sick of myself. Sick of my sadness. Sick of who I'd become—lifeless. Sick of being unsatisfied with life even though I knew I was so fortunate. *How dare I not be happy! Look at all I have!*

To regain purpose, create opportunity, and find inspiration. I was not satisfied with my career and knew I needed to find a creative path for my future. I'd always been artistic, but I'd not settled into what I would consider my niche. I knew I had to leave my old career to fully realize my potential, but I couldn't see clearly what my purpose might be. Surely the heavens would collaborate, clouds would part, and God would open his arms, casting down rays of light illuminating my life's purpose; isn't that how it happens?

Who am I? Because of psychological patterns that I'd already come to identify—specifically, associating happiness with having a man in my life—I knew it was imperative to divorce myself from my codependency character. I had the "need to please" syndrome coupled with an inability to be alone, and I defined myself through my relationships, so without a man, I simply did not know who I was. *Girl, this is a sad state of affairs. We gotta do something about this—pronto!*

To expand my horizons. When is that ever a bad thing? I'd lived my whole life in the South, complete with Christian upbringing and slight southern accent. I mean, y'all, I had coleslaw runnin' in my veins!

To find home. Why have I not felt at home anywhere since early childhood? Where is home? What does home mean? Is it sticks and bricks, mortar and furnishings? I'd had that, what most call a home, but I couldn't remember a time my heart felt at home. All my life, I'd heard, "Home is where the heart is." What the hell did that mean anyway? Is it with a person, like a partner? Is it with family so speckled from state to state? What if you're not at home in your own heart? I knew I hadn't been whole in a long time. I was shattered and scattered across the winds of time. *Hmmm, shattered and scattered. Yes, the latest offering for my Waffle House hash browns, replacing the very popular smothered and covered.*

With all this in mind, I reasoned that maybe having a nomadic existence would be good for me for a while. It certainly would cut down on the likelihood that I'd have a long-term boyfriend, and that was essential. I needed this forced independence. *Yes, I'll just move around the globe until I truly feel comfortable being alone and I have addressed this aspect of my flawed personality.* Considering I'd been attached to various men in long-term relationships for two straight decades, this seemed like a brilliant idea.

If I could manage emotional independence, it would be a

tremendous accomplishment. I had to do something drastic to arrest myself from my own repetitive, destructive patterns, and mending this part of my psyche was vital to my evolution. I couldn't maintain my current existence within myself any longer. I was forced to declare a state of emergency over the wake of destruction left behind after Hurricane Eryn. I could no longer hide from who I was or where I'd been. I had to face myself in total truth, organizing a quiet coup to overthrow my fears and the *less than* self I'd become.

CHAPTER 2

Just the Past

Until you make the unconscious conscious,
it will direct your life and you will call it fate.
—Carl Jung

I used to be a different person. You wouldn't think it if you knew me now, but it's true. I have to tell you about the darkness that came in the decades before I came to search for light.

<hr>

In the spring of 1985 when I'd just turned eight, my mom and I left my father to start a new life. We packed up everything and moved a six-hour drive away to another state. We left all our family behind, our church, my school, my friends, and the whole life I'd known as a child. *Bye, bye, Daddy.*

Not long after we settled, the pain began to invade me, envelop me, swallow me. *Screammmmm!* It was a deep and insatiable pain, like hunger but not. My tummy was full, yet there was a hollowness inside—the pain of a young girl who missed her father. I screamed a thousand silent screams only God could hear, pulling each pain from the corners of my heart, sending them to the heavens. I hoped He'd save me from my sorrow and protect my mother from my pain. He did nothing.

I hated everything about our new and different way of life. Small-town girl, now submerged in the inner city—complete culture shock.

Geography forced me to emotionally detach from my father, while unconscious blame led me to withdraw from my mother. All my physical needs were met, I was fortunate in that regard, but something changed in me that year, a splintering of the girl I would've been.

I realized food was quite comforting. I sat daily in front of the television with a block of melted cheese watching America's favorite happy family, the Cosbys. *Where's my happy family gone?* As it turns out, TV and high-fat foods were effective self-soothing distractions from emotional pain. This would be the beginning of emotional eating, self-judgment, and body dysmorphia.

At age nine, I found my first boyfriend. Holes of the heart will always look to be filled with something. It seemed pretty harmless then, but in hindsight, I realize that's much too young to be making out with boys. *Love me, love me.*

Mom sent me to a counselor when she realized I wasn't handling the transition well. After several sessions, the mental health professional told her I wasn't cooperating and she was "wasting her money." Mom and I made a silent agreement to sweep all the pain under the rug and carry on. *You tried, Mom. You really tried.*

When I was twelve, I started dating a seventeen-year-old. Can we really call it dating? He lived in my neighborhood, and I fell in love with him while sitting on the sidewalk watching him on his skateboard. He was black—African American. Perhaps now not the social taboo it was, but in 1989 in the South, let's just say it was difficult for my mother to accept. Her little white-bread Christian schoolgirl had adapted to multicultural inner-city life a little too much. *Look, Mom. I've adjusted. I finally like it here.*

I began sneaking out at night to see him, and my mother realized she no longer had control of her little girl. We fought and argued. I was rebellious and indignant. It was not a happy time for either of us. Fortunately the relationship ended when I wouldn't allow progression to intercourse. Crisis averted.

The school year ended, and Mom sent me back to live with my dad, who was stable now and had a new wife. *What? Nooooooo! You can't do this again. It took me four-plus years to like it here!*

I'd missed my father terribly, but after years with limited interaction—due to distance and finances, not his lack of desire to be a part of my life—a space had grown between us. The relationship was good; it was just different somehow. Daddy's little girl had changed a lot in those impressionable years away. I arrived wearing all black with dark painted fingernails.

Feelings of betrayal, internal loss, and anger toward my mother flooded me—a child between two homes. I didn't talk to her for a year. *It's gonna be okay. I still have cheese.*

One summer day, I stood in my father's kitchen and held a large kitchen knife to my wrist. I was thirteen. I contemplated life and death, feeling the cool blade on my skin, watching the blue veins pulse near the surface. I wondered what it would take to kill myself. *Is it just one cut across? Would that do it?* I didn't care if I lived or not. I just wanted not to *feel* anymore.

I didn't fit anywhere—not with my mother and not with my father and stepmother. As much as everyone tried, I was not at home anywhere. I didn't cut myself that day, but I wanted to. I wanted to end it all so badly. I'd become adept at turning the pain inward, so I carried on internalizing the emptiness, self-medicating with boyfriends and high-fat foods.

When I was fourteen, my father asked me what I wanted to be when I grew up. I told him I wanted to find a nice boyfriend, fall in love, and marry. This was the true extent of my potential happiness. He asked me again at age fifteen, and I told him I wanted to be an architect. I'd already found the boy I wanted to marry.

I was a freshman, and he was a senior. We loved from a place of truth and innocence, and I really thought I'd marry him. He went off to college in the fall, and I stayed behind. It was devastating.

I was shattered. It felt completely unnatural for us to separate; someone I loved, a man gone again from my life. The familiar hollow emptiness returned to my belly, the same one I'd felt when Mom and I left my father.

We grasped at long-distance love and hung from the cliffs of our hearts, scratching at jealousy, hoping and praying, and begging the young love gods to help us hang on. Year by year, the love was overcome by the fear of losing it. After three years and my high school graduation, I finally let go.

At high school, having long-distance love, I'd learned to disengage from the social scene, which meant distancing from my girlfriends. Yes, I was the girl who ditched her girlfriends for her boyfriend; I had little choice with his weekend visits. It had become a habit and my natural tendency to revolve myself around a man in the quest for wholeness.

Regarding female friendships, I seemed to regularly gravitate toward older women. Perhaps as an only child, I preferred the company of adults. Or maybe it was related to the unhappy mother/daughter dynamics and the longing for that relationship. *Cheese is the answer. Yes, I still have cheese.*

The summer after graduation and my high school breakup, I stumbled into a relationship with a married man. I was eighteen, and he was forty-seven, only a few years younger than my father. While working long days together at the cafe, he casually mentioned he was in the middle of a divorce. I was so naïve. I *never* questioned his lies. By the time I realized there was no separation or divorce in motion, it was too late. I was in love.

I was registered to begin a four-year university in the fall, but I dropped all my classes the first day. He never asked me to. He didn't have to. How would we be able to carry on with our love if I couldn't keep my full-time job working with my boss?

It became increasingly painful to be the other woman, not only as I was experiencing it as the mistress but to feel the weight of my actions against another woman and her family. Even when I tried to leave, he pulled me back again and again. I felt the inevitable demise of a dark star in the gravitational pull of a black hole as three months stretched into seven, then ten.

I don't remember how he introduced me to bondage. It wasn't so bad, most of it—maybe I even liked some of it. There were certain times … well … I'll just say I was bound in some compromising and degrading ways. Bondage—not really about love at all—more about power and control. But I never said no. I didn't have my voice then. I made the unconscious trade-off: if I do this, he'll love me more.

Alone one night at my father's house, I answered the phone. "Are you having an affair with my husband?" Finally, the moment I'd been dreading. I stood speechless waiting for the right answer to reveal itself to me. Chaotic commotion thrashed about on the other end of heartache, and the line went dead.

The phone rang again. "I need to know. Please tell me." I heard the desperation in her voice, feeling my part in her misery. Words are like daggers, the way they can stab and gash so fiercely. But there were no words. I had no words. Sometimes it's the words we *don't* say that inflict the most damage. I stabbed us both with my silence. Again, garbled, scratchy commotion and an abrupt disconnect.

I didn't understand what was happening on the other end of the line. Could the chaos and commotion hold a thread of violence? What if he hurt her? Or the children? I couldn't forgive myself if something happened to them. He'd never been violent with me, but when you back a man into a corner, you don't know what he'll do. You just don't know.

Twenty minutes later, I pulled into the driveway and found myself knocking on their door. So many emotions followed me there on the drive, but nothing in my eighteen years of life experience gave me the courage to speak. I stood on the doorstep feeling the enormity of it all as the door flung open. A split second stretched into a lifetime, two broken hearts now facing one another, confronting the truth from which we could no longer hide. She stabbed me with her silent daggers. I let her.

The shame, the embarrassment, the nauseating truth rushed me there on the doorstep, and I pushed it through my hair with my guilty hands.

"Where did you get that ring?" she said accusingly.

"Ummm, it was a gift."

"That's my ring! That's my anniversary ring! He gave you my ring?"

"Oh my God. Uhh. I didn't know. He gave it to me. I … I didn't know."

I took the ring from my finger and gave it to her as he came hurriedly to the door.

They swarmed off into madness, and I stood there at the threshold, the interloper looking into the life I longed for … well, a less dramatic version of that life. This was a life of madness— madness I had cocreated.

Closing the door behind me, I stood immobile in the kitchen watching them swirl about like tornadoes. What was I doing there? A referee? I can't really tell you.

She cursed him as he emerged from the bedroom. He said, "Let's go." In our separate cars, we drove away from unhappy suburbia, the shame and guilt following me. Unable to take him home to my father's house, we checked into a Motel 6. Not thirty minutes went by, and there was a knock at the door. "Police. Open up. Mr. _____, you're under arrest for domestic violence." They put him in handcuffs. "Young lady, you should go home and explain this to your father."

I wish I could tell you it all ended there. I wish I could tell you that, but that would be a lie, and I don't lie anymore. There's plenty more from the Jerry Springer drama that played out over the final few months. But this book isn't about sensationalizing the dramas of my life or those involved; it's about desperation and pain that causes us to act outside of our value system, and finally about recovery and healing, although that didn't come for two more decades.

When it was all said and done, I was half the person I once had been. And I already felt half to begin with, so maybe I was a quarter now. Depression is a patchwork quilt, hand-sewn over time with swatches of pain and fear, embroidered with threads of shame and inaction, a fringe edge of insecurity and regret. I'd been sewing for years now, finally stitching the last corners of my masterpiece.

It was freeing in a way to know the relationship was over; then again, it was empty and hollow—nearly the undoing of me—a deathless death, really. I was catapulted into the black hole of darkness … but I welcomed it. I deserved it. The dark angels of depression that had been hovering all around waiting for me to fall finally put me to bed and pulled the quilted cover of night over me. I opened my arms to the heavens and let the dark angels devour me whole—I mean my quarter self.

Not even cheese could save me now.

My father, not knowing how else to help me, set me up to see a psychiatrist, and I began a regular dose of Prozac and therapy. I don't really recall if the Prozac helped or not; I remember only numbness. On the other hand, when I stood again in the kitchen holding the same knife to my left wrist, I didn't kill myself when I so desperately needed to end it all.

It was a nice knife—cheery in a way with its bright sunshiny yellow handle. It would've just seemed so wrong to kill myself with such a happy knife meant for vegetables. I couldn't contaminate the sunshiny knife's existence like that or leave such a mess for my father and stepmother. I put the happy fucking cheery knife back in the drawer and opened a supersized can of chunky soup.

After that, it was like I wore the scarlet letter on my chest; married men were drawn to me, and, apparently, I to them. Some I resisted, a few I loved.

Finally, I met someone who personified the qualities I was looking for. He was close with his family, which I longed for, and he was kind, loyal, and single. I knew he'd never hurt me or lie to me, and I cared for him deeply, so I married him. All I ever wanted was a nine-to-five job and someone to love, but soon enough I felt the void once filled by his love starting to open again. He tried to love me, but I couldn't receive it. When we fill the void with external sources—whether love, drugs, alcohol, or food—it's never satisfied. All addictions are similar in this way.

I wasn't happy, but I couldn't tell you why—only that I felt empty. It wasn't my husband's fault though. I didn't know the love I needed didn't exist and could not be gifted from another. Maybe I believed myself unworthy of real love. Perhaps I'd been so scorched by love I just didn't know what real love was anymore; or maybe I never knew.

I didn't feel right. I didn't feel whole. I sat each morning in the shower, knees pulled to my chest, rocking under the flow of hot water, wishing to dissolve myself. Perhaps then I could swirl away down the drain, avoiding the hurt I knew I'd someday inflict on my husband.

I thought going back to school might be a good idea. *Yes, I'll fill the void with knowledge.* I began night classes in a civil engineering program while working full-time during the day. I was finally doing something good for myself. I knew I'd never be a licensed engineer or hold the coveted engineer's stamp—not from this junior college anyway—but at least it held the promise of a fulfilling career and better income. Then one day, I looked up from my blueprints and fell in love with a man who sat across from me.

Gradually it progressed into a full-on emotional affair that I somehow justified, reasoning that omission of sexual activity made it less than cheating. In this way, I tried to uphold my childhood Christian value system. Nevertheless, I was breaking vows I'd made to my husband and to myself. I ripped it all to shreds, ending the marriage. *Ashes, ashes, we all fall down.*

If only I'd come with a warning label:

Warning: This person assembled with broken pieces and may be hazardous to your health. Use caution when handling. Proceed at your own risk.

At twenty-two, I landed an interesting job with an engineering firm. It seemed a bit out of my league at first, but I was up for the challenge; inspector for taxiway and runway reconstruction projects at the regional airport. My personal life was always a mess, but I had a stellar work ethic. I came to excel in this position, and it would alter my life in many ways.

The relationship with the man I'd met in school was beautiful for a long while—until it wasn't. I wish I could tell you I honored the commitments I made to that man, but I can't. I had no willpower against my addiction to love. *Oh my God, I've screwed this up too!*

I was trapped in the cycle of pain, causing it and enduring it.

Once a man I loved, after receiving oral sex that he very much enjoyed, said, "Wow, that was better than I expected. I guess chubby girls *do* try harder." *Chubby girls try harder.*

No words. I had no words. What can be said, really?

One September day, planes flew into the World Trade Center and changed the trajectory of my life. What American was unaffected that day, and forever? Insignificant as it was to the tragic impacts, repercussions would soon ripple out regarding my career. Airfield construction ceased in the months to come, with all new funding funneled into new security measures. When my runway project was finished, so was my contract.

I thought I'd never leave my hometown again where my father lived, truly I thought I'd live and die there, but my company offered me a new position in another city, and just like that, at twenty-four, I was moving.

This was the perfect opportunity to start over. I vowed to myself that I'd take a break from men for two years so I could assess, reflect, and adjust, knowing the past years had been so dysfunctional. I saw the opportunity to change myself. I saw it clearly—the desperate need, the opportunity. Unfortunately, I didn't understand the nature of my patterned behavior and underestimated its power over me.

We rarely understand these sorts of things when they're playing out. Why else would anyone make any bad decisions—ever? In the end though, it was quite simple. When you're hungry, you eat; thirsty, you drink; these are our most basic needs. And when your heart is holey like mine was, you patch it with something—or someone. It was imperative to my survival. I was an emotional prostitute, giving too much of myself to receive love.

A few months after arriving in my new city, I fell for a not-so-recovered alcoholic. He wasn't married, thank goodness; at least there was that! I'd moved on to another form of dysfunction. *Oh, for the love of humanity, this codependent pattern to attach!* I could see it, but I couldn't stop it. Food, water, love … Sigh.

After this yearlong relationship, there would be another, and then another, and another. It was never about sex but about *the one* who would complete me.

In my incomplete state, emotional eating continued to be a problem. Amazing how you can still be so lonely while always having a man in your life. I used to think food and love were more subtle addictions than drugs or alcohol, but I see they can be just as dangerous because of their social acceptability. We *must* have food to survive, so we're left with only our willpower to choose wisely when confronted with an array of options. Arguably, we can avoid the drug dealer and the liquor store, but we can't avoid the grocery store. As for love … we're nearly dared to go through life without a significant other; American television, Hallmark card commercials, advertisements, and romantic dramas on every flip of the channel. It breeds the conditioned response; can any American girl *really* be complete without love?

I fell prey to the yo-yo dieting phenomenon with fad weight-loss plans. Back and forth I went, up and down the scale, ebbing and flowing with the waves of our media, following every new diet idea that washed onto my shore. Low calorie, low carbohydrate, high protein, low fat. You name it, I tried it.

Fitness commitments would prove to be impossible. Discipline like that requires strength of will and personal power; it takes a certain respect for self. I had very little of that left. I gave every bit of energy I had to my career and to whatever relationship I was in. I had none left for healthy disciplines.

As for my weight, I wasn't obese. I usually wore between a size 8 and 12, yet I saw only the freak-show circus-mirror version of my body, distorted and inaccurate. I silently hissed at other women who were beautiful and thin, secretly longing to be like them while simultaneously berating myself with near constant judgment and inner negativity toward my own chubbiness.

I remember a brief moment of elation where I finally fit into a size 6—the coveted milestone for any girl who struggles with her weight. I think I was twenty-seven at the time. I cried tears of joy in the dressing room at this momentous occasion. It didn't matter that I'd arrived at size 6 because I was emotionally drained and extended from overworking and the stresses of my current relationship.

I was unable to recognize incompatible men and unable to leave them when the relationship felt wrong. This is where the most damage occurred—my inability to leave, all symptoms of low self-worth. In this unwillingness, I silenced my own voice, staying until I simply could stay no longer. A friend once told me, "Humans will avoid change at all costs, until the fear of staying the same becomes worse than the fear of change." *Hmmm, yes.* I knew this sentiment well.

I developed hypothyroidism in my late twenties, a disease related to my lacking "strength of will and personal expression," says Caroline Myss, PhD (Myss 1995, pg. 99).[1] These were forms of emotional stress that led me to the decisions I made in life. Stress—a term so common and generic it's become meaningless, no? Intuitively I knew I was harming myself with the stressful life

I was leading, but if I *fully appreciated* the long-term damage I was doing to my body with my unconscious programming and habits, I would've been more dedicated to exploring the emotional causes much sooner. At the time though, I had no knowledge or awareness that I could change these aspects of my personality or that they were directly affecting my physical health.

Several career hops up the ladder, I was gaining optimal work experiences with an upwardly advancing salary. Even in my career though, I found I wanted validation. One day my boss, in response to a comment I made about his haircut, called me "an acquiescent sycophant." I had to look up the meaning of his words, but I knew I was being insulted long before I found a dictionary.

He wasn't wrong though. I was acquiescing to the wants and needs of others, not that he'd have any ability to fathom the details of my past that made me want his approval. I see now though, it had nothing to do with gaining his favor in hopes of professional progression, as he likely assumed, yet everything to do with the deep longing to be accepted as part of something.

Eventually I met a man who would become my second husband. He was kind and loving and generous, and we had a lot in common. I thought it would be forever. I so desperately wanted it to be forever. But it wasn't—because I was part of the equation, the only common denominator in all my failed relationships.

I prayed a lot during my marriage. I prayed myself to sleep every night begging God to show me a way through. I wanted to be content, to be happy. I didn't want to leave. I watched Discovery Channel shows where scientists were studying the nature of love— the variables and factors—what made lasting love and what kept you from it. I watched *Oprah* and *Dr. Phil*. I read *Psychology Today* trying to figure myself out within the marriage. I plead with God to show me a way to happiness. I begged for my own peace of mind and for that of my husband. But I didn't receive the answers I was looking for, and I didn't find peace. Instead I tossed and turned in my waking sleep, traversing the sleepy zones of consciousness through the night, receiving the consistent, unwavering gut-wrenching message:

> *You're not supposed to be here.*
> *You're not supposed to be here.*

Maybe it was God or maybe it was the seed of my intuition. Perhaps they are one in the same. It could've been self-sabotage, still feeling unworthy of a happy marriage, given all the damage I'd done to others before. Or maybe I was delusional. I'd not ruled that out, having recently learned details of my father's mental health history. I battled with God over His less than cryptic message regarding my marriage, angry with Him for not giving me a solution. I tried to negotiate with Him, fiercely debating back and forth in the night like Tibetan monks with their hand gestures and secret language. In the end, exhausted by the ongoing internal debates, I resigned myself to the message that wouldn't cease: *you're not supposed to be here.*

And so it goes ... separation, then divorce number two. I told you about this in the last chapter. At least I'd kept my moral vows, not allowing any emotional or physical affair. I couldn't hurt anyone again in that way. At least there was that. It's not much, but it was something.

I slipped further into depression. The dark angels rushed to my side, bringing my patchwork masterpiece to hold me through the *dark night.* I was drained and depleted with no purpose, no hope, no answers, and no devotion. I felt God had abandoned me with only half of the solution to my irrational equation. *You're not supposed to be here. But where am I supposed to be?* Maybe I abandoned Him.

My friend Aiden gifted me the grand idea of *the world,* and I began reducing life to one bank account and a storage unit. I wasn't excited about my new plan to travel. I was too scared and broken for that, still grief stricken and lost within myself. But it was the best option I could see to take control of my life, dedicating myself to the quest for my higher self. I had to go.

Still, the universe had one final test to make sure I was truly committed to my new plan.

A close friend of mine, in an attempt to keep me stateside, set me up on a date.

"No I can't go on a date. This is crazy, I'm leaving in four weeks."

"Okay," he said, "so you're leaving. What will it hurt then? Just have coffee with the guy."

Since the separation from my husband I'd been successful in dodging new relationships; my flight was booked and I was busy filling my storage unit. Maybe I let my guard down now that plans were steamrolling ahead and I was set on this plan of self-repair. *What can a cup of chai hurt, huh? Oh, go on.*

The first date turned into a second, then a third, then six, seven, eight across three weeks. *Girrrrrl, you're in trouble.* It's amazing how you can fall into the depths of someone in such a short amount of time. It doesn't take that long really. One minute you're minding your own business, and the next you're wondering how this person fits into your life, and you into theirs. Then again, what sort of decision can you make about a future with someone after knowing them only a few weeks? *Three weeks isn't enough, Eryn. Changing plans isn't an option. Don't do it, noooooooo!*

The last night arrived. I lay wrapped in his arms noticing how I just felt happy. Content. Tears silently fell across my cheeks as I quietly pondered the gravity of the situation. It'd been so long since I felt the intoxication of love I'd forgotten what it felt like. That in itself was a sad realization; I'd forgotten. It invaded me; the possibility and hope and beauty of it all coursed through my veins. He was heroin to my heart, and I liked it. I craved it. I needed it.

I wanted him to tell me that he'd miss me or ask me to stay. I wanted something from him, some signal, some *something* giving me an indication I should consider staying or coming back sooner rather than later. It would've been so much easier to stay. Embarking on this trip was one of the most frightening things I'd ever chosen to do. Staying would've certainly made a lot of sense. Then again it would've also meant one more time I'd change my life for the sake of a man, and I knew I couldn't do that. My mind begged me, *Stay on course. You must take this journey.* My heart responded to the mind, *But wait. What about love? What if he's the one?*

In the end, he said nothing. He wouldn't say what I so desperately wanted him to say. I don't think it was pride or ego or even that he didn't want me to stay—I think he did. But he was stronger than I was, and somehow he knew. He knew I needed to go.

Morning came, and I knew what I had to do. I withdrew the needle of his love reluctantly from my doped-up, love-longing arteries. We said goodbye, and I drove away.

To those I've hurt: I pray that you can forgive me for the pain I've caused you. Please know that I was coming from a place of deep pain within myself, and that precipitated my actions. For any heartache, disrespect, hurt, or long-term ramifications I had a part in creating, I am deeply sorry.

To those that hurt me: I have already forgiven you for any pain that you've caused me. I know you were coming from a place of deep pain within yourself, and that precipitated your actions. For any heartache, disrespect, hurt, or long-term ramifications you had a part in creating, I forgive you, truly.

Expansion Exercises

1) I invite you to journal your answers as we progress through the expansion exercises. Bringing awareness to your thoughts, feelings, and emotions is an important step in the process of healing.

2) Before we move forward in life, it's important to make peace with our past. How would you feel about taking an inward journey to recount any painful parts of your past? Place no judgment on yourself if you don't feel ready to address this aspect of your life. You'll know when the time is right.

3) Have you ever acted outside your value system? If so, can you recall why you didn't hold to your values? Dig deep.

4) Contemplate the idea of bringing compassion to yourself and others for any hurt that's been done. What would it feel like to forgive?

PART II

Shedding Fear

Months One to Twelve

CHAPTER 3

Week One—India

Jewels on the Ganges

The traveler sees what he sees. The tourist
sees what he came to see.
—Unknown

Forty-six hours of traveling brought me to the Niketan ashram[1] where I could finally rid myself of my cumbersome trekking backpack and the anxiety I was experiencing over my safe arrival. Now I could sleep. I didn't care what my room looked like or how alone I was; I could assume a horizontal position and close my eyes. This was all that mattered to me in this moment.

I'd been plagued with so many fears before leaving; I had to continually psych myself up just to board my flight. Before the moment I was strapped into my seat, I knew there was a high probability that I'd bail on the whole thing. See, making a plan to take a one-way flight to India and actually following through with it are two different things entirely. One requires choice, the other requires action, and I'd become really good at making plans but not so good at following through with them. Inaction—an unfortunate side effect of my depression.

There'd been plenty of reasons to stay but only one reason to leave—finding a better me. On that day, I combined choice with action and boarded the plane. My trepidations swirled madly, but when the wheels of the Boeing jet finally went up, a calm peacefulness came over me. I knew I was doing the right thing.

In the Delhi airport, I cautiously watched the Indian men as they stared at me, one of only two Western women in the domestic security line. Memories of nightly news told me their stares held the intent of malice, although my heart reminded me they were just curious. I couldn't decide which voice to trust, I really couldn't. But I watched them watching me, realizing how fearful I was, having not yet left the confines of the airport. I now stood in the moment of dread that I'd seen on my friends' faces when I told them I'd be solo traveling to India. I wondered how long I'd last out here in the world as fear of the unknown and my solitude swallowed me. Soon I'd be nothing more than a little speck of anonymous life floating amongst millions in North India. How would I survive? Fortunately, one friend sent me off with a self-defense magazine detailing, "How to inflict the most damage with a pen." I read it on the plane, hoping I'd never need to use these very specific and odd skills, yet fearing I might.

I awoke from my jetlagged slumber on the hard ashram mattress in a groggy state, wondering what day it was and how long I'd been asleep. I was now in a time zone nine and a half hours ahead of the life I'd left behind. Who even knew half-hour time zones existed? I opened my door and peered out to see if I was really in India or if it had all been a strange dream. Monkeys. *Yep, I'm in India.* They frolicked about in the garden outside my room, and the young Indian boy stood at the big brass bell in the distance ringing it loudly. Chai time. I'd been asleep for nearly twenty-four hours.

On my first day, I met George, a retired structural engineer from Switzerland. I couldn't believe it, a structural engineer right here sitting next to me with chai and cookies. Of all the people I could've met, the universe sent me someone I could relate to from my old life of construction back home. I never met a structural engineer I didn't like. We spoke daily about the ashram buildings, noting where they needed concrete repair and assessing their structural integrity. The idea of not working was foreign and uncomfortable, and I was already wondering if I could somehow put myself to work there at the ashram, my home for the unforeseeable future. George and I were fast friends.

The second day, I met Jagan, the Indian yoga instructor who taught morning classes at the ashram. An ashram, in case you're wondering, is a spiritual haven or long-stay retreat community common in India. Retreat, however, is a subjective term. My room resembled a sparse prison cell, although I did have my own bathroom—bonus. Jagan had a quiet, calm, reassuring way about him. I liked him instantly. "Morrre straight your back," he said in class as I took my first downward dog in the motherland of yoga. "Morrrre straight your leg." *All right, all right, I am morrre straightening my legs.*

Ashram rules stated that we were expected to join meditation and yoga at least once daily, and although the morning schedule was brutal, I preferred it. *I'm here to fix myself, dammit. I can't be sleeping in and taking the easy way out!* I cringed every morning at 4:30 when the big, clanky bell woke all who slept, but I loved opening my door to hear the Hindu *aarti*[2] hymns bouncing off the Ganges and up the hill to greet me with the smells that are so distinctly India: incense, burning debris, and butter lamps.

I dragged myself from the warmth of my bed and down to the meditation hall for the hour-long session beginning at 5:00. I sat cross-legged on a cushion in the dark room, feeling somehow I was taking my first step toward wholeness while simultaneously realizing I knew nothing about meditation. My mind screamed in a childish rant at my request for silence and stillness. My back revolted, my legs numbed themselves, and days passed within the hour. Finally, I was released from the unbearable seated position as my mind screamed expletives. Yoga followed directly afterward from 6:15 to 7:30, and then finally breakfast. *Yes, yes, finally food!*

George and a few others from breakfast invited me to join them for a special *satsang,*[3] which *Oxford Dictionary* defines as "a spiritual discourse or sacred gathering." When George invited me, I'd never heard of the word satsang or of this Mooji[4] fellow giving the satsang, but everyone seemed excited to hear him speak. *Sat—what? Mooji— who?* I didn't know what any of it was, but I was going.

That's when I met Siggy, as we were leaving the ashram to seek the wisdom of Mooji. It was my day five in India and coincidentally my birthday the day Siggy arrived. I hadn't planned on mentioning it to anyone. I figured it was birthday present enough to be safe and meeting people who spoke English.

I liked Siggy right away. She had a big, smiley, twenty-something face, Aussie accent, and long Pocahontas hair. She carried an air of innocence, but when she needed to store her bag in my room, I had to fight my cynical thoughts convincing me this stranger would transfer drugs into my bag and I'd end up in an Indian prison. What? I've watched *Locked Up Abroad*.[5] I know how this works.

New Job Descriptions

I was amazed, as the days passed, how my inner world began to change when I stepped out of my comfort zone and overscheduled daily routine, making the effort to simply open my mind to these new cultures. I'd been so neatly packaged up in my little U.S. of A box with red, white, and blue ribbon—and so conditioned to like it—I hadn't realized, or given consideration to what the outside world would provide: rich, meaningful, life-changing experiences and Mooji-infused musings.

It was a strange adjustment wandering the Rishikesh streets with no specific goals, aspirations, or to-do list for the day. Having worked full-time for eighteen years, at thirty-seven, I had to fight my beliefs that I was being irresponsible, maybe even lazy or selfish by choosing this path for myself, leaving the work world behind. Were these beliefs even mine, or were they the voices of societal conditioning? I could no longer determine the true author of this inner critical voice.

In a land so far away, I had to find my equilibrium in the nothingness of it all. I was searching for self, searching for truths. Searching the release of *doing* and, allowing that for myself, learning to *be* again. Maybe things would begin to naturally prioritize themselves and make sense if I could shed the perceived need to be *doing* all the time. I'd lost the ability, if I ever had it, to be with myself without the bombardment of noise, Facebook, or television; I'd become a master at filling the empty spaces. I guess that began way back in the Cosby years with a block of cheese.

Aside from my new aspiration of *being*, I fell into other forms of discovery once I set the intention to seek my highest self. The job description of a traveler, I soon realized, would be unlike any other I could imagine.

I was my own psychologist methodically exploring my behavioral pathology. Siggy and I took turns on the metaphoric couch in this internal detangling process. Was I clinically depressed? This seemed so definitively doomed to a life of dark angel fellowship. Was my internal angst causing my depression, or was my depression causing the internal angst? They seemed so inextricably linked and longstanding over decades. Perhaps I was chemically flawed and predestined for a life of premature unhappiness due to my genetic makeup and family history. This is what Western medicine would have us believe—that we're prewired, prescription drugs our only savior—and that's what I feared most, that it was beyond my control, which admittedly, to this point in my life, it had been.

I took on the role of historian, reviewing past relationships and mistakes I'd made, looking to uncover the true reasons I chose my partners and made certain decisions. I somehow felt that my deep longing to be loved and accepted was the single driving force that led to my pain. Ironic, how the desire for something so pure can morph into something so dysfunctional. What was it that led me to and kept me in incompatible relationships? Was I codependent?

I seemed to take naturally to philosophy, contemplating the depths of life over chai and dhal with fellow travelers I befriended.

What *is* the meaning of life? Why am I here? What is my purpose? What are my gifts that I can share with the world? What makes me feel alive? I was able to explore the nature of "Eryn" in a context that was completely free from judgment and structure. There was no *supposed-to-be* anything when sitting in a café in India. No business cards to pass out credentialing who I was. No perfectly decorated home to invite friends to. No one cared if I wore white after Labor Day (not that I would ever consider it!).

The anonymity of it all was a bit frightening at first—I had no identity—but then gradually and unexpectedly, it became quite freeing. I'd not realized the extra weight I carried from societal expectations alone. I was lighter in this freedom; my shoulders more relaxed; my jaw less tense and my forehead less crinkled. I knew no one, and no one cared who I was (or wasn't). This left me wondering. *I've shed every single label that defined who I was: wife, daughter, coffee drinker, business partner, emotional eater, construction manager, TV watcher, dog mom—all meaningless here. Who does Eryn want to be—who will she be—if the walls of society aren't there to confine her and suggest who she should be?*

My routines had been so deeply ingrained and my perceived obligations so vast I never had the capacity (or reason) to consider these things before. I felt intuitively though, in all this structure, I'd been completely missing the point of living. I'd become inauthentic, losing the potential long ago of who I could have been. Where had I lost myself exactly? I needed to understand this.

Jagan, the yoga instructor at my ashram, said to me one day, "Eryn, my friend, we are all like diamonds in the rough; only some of us will choose to chip away at the rock and the muck, polishing and sanding to reveal the hidden gem." *Ahhh, yes, you are wise, grasshopper.*

I contemplated the words of my yoga instructor. I knew this was the intent of my trip, although I'd not been able to express it so poetically to those who questioned my decision to travel. And although I knew with certainty that I had to leave, I still had no idea how I'd chip away at the rock and muck that had so cunningly encrusted me like barnacles.

The anthropological aspect of travel seemed to have great effect on me. Exploring and observing those around me—it all changed me. Exposure to the life circumstances of others, especially those less fortunate than I, turned my selfish internal world upside down and magically came to instill a deep, lasting sense of gratitude and humility that's hard to convey. On second thought, I don't think it was magic at all. I think it was simply allowing myself to *fully see* the lives of others, letting their pain sting me just a little (or sometimes a lot) before turning away. This provoked the rising of compassion within me over and over *and over* again.

So many times we turn away, shielding ourselves from the pains of the world, and it's easy to do when we're in our own bubble of modernized society. I'd been there too—in the bubble—but now I was here in India. I couldn't allow myself to be in these developing countries and then protect myself from the truth of it in fancy hotels or resorts. I needed to see it, to feel it deep in my core. So I let it. I let it invade me.

Mark Twain once said, "Travel is fatal to prejudice, bigotry, and narrow-mindedness, and many of our people need it sorely on these accounts. Broad, wholesome, charitable views of men and things cannot be acquired by vegetating in one little corner of the earth all one's lifetime."[6] That Mark Twain fellow knew a thing or two.

One morning I was walking along the Ganges[7] observing the routines of the locals, some bathing in the river, *swamis*[8] with their dreadlocks and saffron robes meditating under shade trees, and scrappy dogs cooling themselves in the shadows. A young girl came up to me and held my hand as I walked—she might've been seven or eight—the same age I'd been when I befriended cheese, although I knew instantly that comparing our lives was wrong. Her life was infinitely more challenging than mine had ever been.

She was trying to sell me flowers; I knew her game. You can't walk the streets of the city or the banks of the river without being approached. As we walked, I entered into the daily internal debate. *To give or not to give? Eryn, you can't save them all. Keep moving.*

Embarrassing admission—sometimes I ignored them. There are so many that approach you in a day, there's little choice. The harsh reality is I couldn't save them, and I knew it, but there's just something so … so, soul squashing in the reluctance to give when a child is begging. Sometimes all you can do is extend a little piece of your heart, sending them sincere, genuine blessings; Siggy taught me that. Other times my heart wouldn't allow me *not* to give, so I did. Every day was different, yet every day was the same. The magnitude of need cracked my heart open in a million little pieces and then hardened it in a protective shell the way hearts are so skilled to do.

I asked God repeatedly how He could allow this—some having so much while others so little—all because the seed of life birthed me in one country and someone else in another. It seemed so random and cruel. Is God random and cruel? My repeated inquiries to a higher power went unanswered.

This day when the girl grabbed me, her tiny hand disappearing into mine, I turned to meet her gaze; I was unable to look away. Her amber-colored eyes flickered with the naïve hope only a child can possess, before the hardships of life would stain her soul and hollow compromises would haunt her dreams. I was lost in her eyes, mesmerized by the glimmer of promise that I'd lost long ago. I saw myself in her eyes. I felt her stirring inside, penetrating me. We were the same somehow. I saw her, I saw me. I *was* her. She *was* me. Separate but not—the same beings of light, connected as one. We stood there for moments or minutes; time escaped me as the morning rush swirled madly around us. I was her, and she was me.

Other children noticed our exchange and swarmed around us with their excited voices and extended hands. We walked to the bank of the river and released a banana leaf bowl of fragrant orange blossoms together in an unspoken ceremony of union. She closed her eyes for a few moments, hugging me with her soft eyelashes, giving me a reassuring nod as if to say, *Our work here is done.* She squeezed my hand and disappeared into the crowd of children. I never saw her again.

I think of her often and wonder, when the flowers have withered and the years have passed, what else will she have to sell of herself to survive? I don't think I could bear to know.

Alan Watts[9] once said, "There will always be suffering. But we must not suffer over the suffering." It took me a long time to wrap my mind around this. My natural tendency was to lose myself in the vortex of inequity. As I traveled, confronted time and time again with suffering, I pondered his words, finally coming to realize he was right; we can't suffer over the suffering, but it got me thinking. If we turn our heads from inequity, as I'd always done, because it wasn't in my backyard, well, doesn't that create a different version of suffering within us here in the modern world? An affliction of affluenza[10] born from our excess? Where hearts are a little bit colder, protected by a thin layer of ice shielding us from our intuitive knowing that we have so much while others so little? I've come to feel deeply this is a factor in the pandemic of declined mental health that's befallen us in America. I have no formal data to tell me this is so, but the connection is now clear to me.

In the fullness of gratitude, the icy layers began melting from my hardened heart. And it made me wonder ... well, I wonder how the world might change if we all allowed ourselves to really *feel* the inequity.

Expansion Exercises

1) As you take on the role of inward traveler, might the job descriptions I adopted inspire you to look introspectively at your own life? Personal therapist or historian considering patterns from your past? What patterns have you already recognized?

2) What goals for personal betterment have you identified? Perhaps you've made the choice to pursue this goal. Have you taken action yet?

3) What, if anything, has prevented you from taking action toward this goal?

4) Have you identified your life purpose? If not, what are your natural gifts? What makes you feel good? What is important to you?

5) How would it feel to look beyond our own fences and our own borders to those less fortunate at home and abroad? Take a moment to contemplate the challenges of others still faced with basic survival needs. Might there be small things you can do in your own life that would make a big difference to someone else?

CHAPTER 4

Month One—India

The Path to Silence

Progress is impossible without change, and those who cannot
change their minds cannot change anything.
—George Bernard Shaw

Siggy and I became quite close during those two weeks in the
Rishikesh ashram. She survived a terrible bed bug infestation,
the nightmare of any traveler, and I survived the dreaded *Delhi belly*,
both hitting us the same day. We were forever bonded as soul sisters.

One day we were lying on the grass lawn, talking and watching
the monkeys misbehave, and she started telling me about a Buddhist
course she would be attending the following month in Dharamsala,
India.

Siggy excitedly said, "Ooh, ooh, you should do the course with
me. Yeah, it'll be great."

I thought for a second. "Nah ... I don't think that's for me. I
mean, I believe in their peaceful philosophies and all, but I don't need
a ten-day course learning about Buddhism. Plus, that's not why I'm out
here. I'm not exploring my faith; I'm just trying to figure myself out."

"Well, are you sure? It could really open you to something new."

"No," I said firmly, "it's really not for me. I'm strong in my
Christian faith."

She took the hint, and we dropped the subject.

I was closed.

Funny how I held this firm boundary based on my Christian belief system that would keep me from studying Buddhism, yet I couldn't hold to their ethical beliefs when it came to the days of married men in *The Past*. Our minds are tricky like that, the way they justify certain things and block others, a form of cognitive dissonance we humans can be so easily drawn into.

I've found it's good practice to call myself out on hypocrisies when I recognize them. If I bring awareness to experience, I then have the opportunity to make adjustments as to how I handle any given situation. These days it most often surrounds my snap judgments of others. It takes time to deprogram decades of habitual behavior, but bringing awareness to it changes everything; it's good for my soul growth.

Siggy and I decided we'd venture north and caught an overnight bus up to Dharamsala. We were on our way to visit the region known for its Tibetan influence where the Dalai Lama lives along with hundreds of thousands living there in exile. I don't know why exactly, but I was drawn to this mysterious region, although at the time I had little knowledge of the Dalai Lama or what he stood for.

On the bus ride, Siggy said, "Eryn, honey, you always have this look like you're unhappy or in a bad mood or stressed out. What's that about?"

I looked at her kind of surprised. "What? Do I? Well, I'm fine. I … I don't know what you mean."

I turned away and gazed out the window of the bus, pondering her comment as we passed mangy dogs and the corrugated metal slum city on the outskirts of Rishikesh.

I turned back to her. "Wait. Are you telling me I have bitchy resting face?"

She laughed. "Bitchy what? What's bitchy resting face?"

"You haven't heard of BRF? Bitchy resting face was this hilarious drug commercial spoof, showing people suffering from BRF—bitchy resting face. It's when you don't realize it but naturally wear an expression on your face of unhappiness and, well, bitchiness."

She laughed again in her adorable Aussie way, but then her expression changed to a sad puppy dog, head cocked sideways, eyebrows raised slightly. She put her hand on my shoulder. "Hon … yeah, you have bitchy resting face."

Is there a twelve-step program for that? "Hello. My name is Eryn. I suffer from bitchy resting face." Sigh.

In true American fashion, I intended to stay only a short time in Dharamsala, and then I'd move on to somewhere new. Siggy and I talked about going to Sri Lanka together, but I was already learning she was a free spirit, changing her mind with the wind and reluctant to make long-term commitments, long-term being anything beyond tomorrow. I, on the other hand, preferred the perceived safety net of obsessive preplanning with the idea that my controlling every detail would keep me safe and out of harm's way.

Siggy laughed at me when I wanted to prebook a room for us in Dharamsala. "Babe, we don't need to book ahead. Let's just figure it out when we get there. Then we can bargain for a room and walk away if they won't deal."

"Sig, we're paying five dollars a night for a room. If it's six dollars a night, what's the big deal?"

"Well, my budget is ten dollars per day," she said sheepishly.

I was gradually learning the art of long-term traveling in relation to both budgeting and booking, but my controlling mind fought me on many fronts as I observed Siggy, the seasoned solo traveler, in her blasé ways. It drove me a little crazy if you want to know the truth of it, but we were safer as a pair, and that's all I really cared about. I was happy to take a backseat role as the worrisome big sister. Plus, I had my pen defense skills, so I figured we were okay.

When we made it to Dharamsala, I assumed I'd stay only a week and would then feel ready to leave, giving me just over three weeks in India. *Surely that's plenty of time for anyone in India.* The universe, however, had another plan for me.

One morning, Siggy said, "Hey, I signed us up to attend a lecture this afternoon. Hope that's okay. It's only a few hours. If we hate it, we can leave."

"Yeah, okay, cool. I can do anything for two hours."

Siggy and I made our way to the Tushita meditation center and found a few seat cushions on the floor crammed in amongst a hundred others, patiently waiting to see ... well, I didn't know who we were there to see. I just hoped it was someone other than Mooji. I was maxed out from the mass Mooji exposure in Rishikesh.

Cave Dweller Inspiration

First we were shown a short movie, *Cave in the Snow*,[1] about a nun who spent twelve years in isolation in a remote tiny cave on the side of a frigid mountain in the Himalayas. I could hardly fathom such an endeavor. We were only in the *foothills* of this impressive mountain range, and I wore almost every layer of my travel wardrobe to sleep in each night—and I was still freezing! Twelve years of icy cave meditations, scarce food supplies, and inhospitable conditions? *Screech, halt, stop, whaaaat?* I sat nearly motionless, completely enamored, watching the story of this woman play out on screen.

After the movie, a woman in her seventies entered the room, with a shaved head and wearing the traditional Tibetan Buddhist burgundy robes. It was the brave woman from the cave, known as Tenzin Palmo. I must say I was a little star struck; she was like a Buddhist celebrity, although the term celebrity would *not* be in line with Buddhist teachings, I now know. I closed my eyes for a moment trying to envision this woman isolated on the side of a rock face in a Himalayan cave, and although I'd just seen the movie, I still couldn't imagine it. This dainty woman standing before us ... alone ... in a cave ... for twelve years!

My mind exploded a bit, little short circuits sparking off. I just, I just ... why would someone do that? Wouldn't she go crazy by herself in silence for twelve years in isolation? What kept her from freezing to death? What about food? Wait ... why on earth would someone do that? This just didn't make any sense to me—at all. Fourth of July fireworks carried on inside my mind with a grand finale of unanswered questions. I wanted to understand this.

Tenzin Palmo[2] began the lecture, speaking in her native British accent, talking a bit about her twelve years of "retreat," as she called it, then further to discuss how Buddhism and meditation can help us to "tame our wild minds," saying:

> The trouble that we experience in our life is mainly created by our unruly uncontrolled minds. We blame outer circumstances, other people, our families, our parents, our partners, our children, the government, anything, but ultimately the real problem lies within ourselves within our own mind. And the fact that our minds are so often controlled by negative emotions, such as our greed and our attachments and cravings; by our aggression and anger, frustrations, by our envy and jealousy of others good fortunes, by our own pride ... pride in Buddhism doesn't just mean we're better than others, it also includes thinking we are just as good as others or that we are inferior to others, because all of it is centered around me ... And the root of all these afflicting emotions that we have, our fears, our depressions, our anger our needs and desires, which disturb the mind and churn up the mind constantly, the root is grasping at the idea of a solid immutable independent everlasting *me* at the center of everything, so therefore, everything happens to me. And in order to make this sense of self feel comfortable, then we grasp at and attach ourselves to anything we think will give pleasure to me and get frustrated and angry and upset at

anything, which we think will give any kind of pain or displeasure to me. We do it constantly ..."
(Palmo lecture, India, 4.4.14)[3]

Wait, wait, wait, what? This is what Buddhism is about? Buddhism can help me with my mind? Really?

I'd witnessed in the past my own thoughts and emotions rocking me like an untethered ship in the not-so-perfect storm of my mind, with no one able to control the weather. I'd recognized that I was continually following an unhealthy pattern to prematurely attach to men, starting at a very young age, and I knew *that* was somehow driven by the mind. I also noticed a significant shift while immersed in my *dark night of the soul* months earlier, in that I was no longer blaming any outer circumstances that this nun now spoke of. I wish I could tell you that it had been a conscious choice on my part, to stop internally blaming the external x, y, z factors for my unhappiness; it was more like a long-held illusion that finally crumbled under the weight of its own inefficacy. It seemed obvious, at this stage in my journey that, simply put, *I* was the problem. Not my relationships or previous partners, not my parents, not my body, my arms, my legs, or any physical component but *my mind*. A truth I could no longer hide from. My mind was the gale force in the stormy sea of life, and I'd released the mooring of inner knowing long ago.

Four minutes into the nun's lecture, she had my full attention. Skeptical, questioning mental fireworks ceased. I quit fidgeting on the uncomfortable floor cushion, I reached out and held the hand of my soul sister Siggy, and I listened.

I felt as though this nun was speaking directly to me as she spoke with such serenity and firm knowing of their philosophies, drawing me into this idea that there really *was* a way I could help myself. I sat hanging on every word, entranced by her conviction that Buddhism *could* be used as a tool in figuring myself out. But it wasn't the type of conviction delivered with fire and brimstone and patronizing know-it-all direction; no, it was given with a soft, calm, gentle, and unwavering *knowing*.

I realized this woman *had* something that I didn't; she possessed something within that I'd never seen before. Whatever she'd sacrificed or given up those twelve years by leaving society and living in a cave, I intrinsically knew she'd gained some incalculable wisdom that was frankly unfathomable to me. I started to wonder if I should be enrolling in the retreat Siggy mentioned to me on the ashram lawn that was now on the horizon to begin next week.

I went back and forth with myself, considering my internal religious conflicts. *If I study Buddhism, does this mean I'm betraying God? Okay, there are definitely golden statues here; if I attend this class, does that mean I'm worshiping false gods or golden idols? Does this make me a bad Christian if I study Buddhism? Let's face it, Eryn. You've not been the model Christian anyway. Oh, go on.*

At first, I felt a bit uncomfortable in this monastic environment full of ornate gold décor and symbols all around so foreign to me. Everything was so different from the churches I'd attended back home. But I realized, now more than ever, religious wisdom didn't always come in a certain shaped package that looked like a church. Maybe great insights *could* be found in a temple that looked to be an Asian art museum. I dug down deeper and deeper within myself, questioning my resistance, seeing that I actually did feel comfortable there, even like I was meant to be there. It was merely a limiting belief telling me that this unorthodox path toward personal transformation and studying Buddhism would equate to turning my back on God.

I contemplated further … *Wouldn't God want me to find my highest and best self, even if it meant exploring other philosophies or religions?* I remembered something Dr. Phil[4] said on one of his shows: "So you've been doing basically the same thing over and over and expecting different results? How's that workin' out for ya?" *Yes, Dr. Phil, I know, I know, but …* I mean, how *do* you know what to do when you just don't know what to do anymore? I'd been in my *pause, reflect, and assess* mode, and that was a good start, but now I was presented with an opportunity that held potential for real understanding and betterment.

I was already of the opinion that Buddhism was less a religion and more of a philosophy, so maybe God would support me in this exploration of self. And wouldn't any progress help me to be a better Christian? Lord knows I'd made a lot of regrettable mistakes that were *not* in line with my values; I could hardly screw up life any worse than I had in *The Past*. Maybe this retreat could actually help me understand why I'd done what I did and make peace with it somehow. Perhaps it could allow me to tease out the threads of pain I'd so meticulously stitched in my patchwork quilt of depression, possibly to converse directly with my dark angels. I knew somehow they were all linked—the past, the present, the unforeseen future—but I couldn't figure it out on my own. I just couldn't. I'd never intended on being a bad person. It just sort of … well, you know.

The next day, I attended another Buddhist lecture where Glen Svensson[5] made an interesting point, "Bad people aren't really bad people; they're good people that don't know how to cope with the pain life has presented them" (Svensson lecture, paraphrased, 4.5.14). I certainly could relate to this sentiment based on my own life experience, knowing I'd not intended to hurt others. I pondered this statement in depth, and it allowed me to view the circumstances of others (and myself) through a more compassionate lens. We don't enter this world bad or evil or violent; no, we learn this behavior, or rather we *resort* to this behavior when we cannot cope with our own internal pain.

My father always had an affinity for the twenty-third psalm. In his pocket, he carried a small silver disk with the inscription etched so beautifully. "The Lord is my shepherd; I shall not want. He maketh me to lie down in green pastures: He leadeth me beside the still waters. He restoreth my soul: He leadeth me in the paths of righteousness for His name's sake."[6] I remember having to memorize this lengthy passage at my Christian school in kindergarten, although I didn't connect with its deeper meaning until decades later.

I'd held this disk in the palm of my hands, praying over my father when he left his physical form. It was special to him, so it was special to me, and I wore it around my neck when I left the United States, hoping it would somehow keep me safe. I had a sense Dad was up there in heaven eating Oreos and smoking a cigarette with God while watching over me and my intrepid adventure. *Look, she's gone to India, that crazy girl.*

I contemplated the passage, "He leadeth me in paths of righteousness for His namesake." *Hmmmm, maybe I was led here for a reason.*

And so it goes. Wisdom seeker became another entry on my traveler résumé, opening to the ideologies of a different faith in the quest for my highest self. I'd not planned to explore this aspect of life at all when I set out on my journey. I related the search for my highest self more to psychology than any form of spiritual path; they were separate in my mind. I'd never given consideration to any concepts outside Christianity and had no reason, desire, or interest in doing so. But if the universe or God or synchronicity brought Siggy to me on my birthday after she'd been turned away from three other ashrams—two strangers from different continents colliding in North India—then placed me on that cushion to hear the wise words of Tenzin Palmo, then maybe this was exactly where I was meant to be. *Or maybe the devil was testing me.*

The next day, I put my name on the waiting list for the Intro to Buddhism course, and the following week I entered my first silent retreat where I would begin studying the *nature of the mind,*[7] as the Buddhists call it. Siggy, ironically enough, decided that it wasn't the right time for her—she had a new boyfriend—so I happily took her place in this fully booked course, and she decided to attend later in the month.

Into Silence I Go

In a tiny little village in the foothills of the Himalayas, where I'd first encountered the cave-dwelling nun, I went into the temple of silence with high anxiety over this monumental endeavor. Ten days it would be with no phone, hugs from my soul sister, food or activities of my choosing, talking, music, laptop, camera, or other distractions, all while following a regimented schedule of meditation and teachings. *Eeeeeeek!*

I took to silence with all the others, eighty or so of us, to dig around and excavate in the trenches of our minds, trusting the guidance of those more knowing. We entered our individual inward journeys on a collective quest toward transformation.

6:45 to 7:30 a.m. Mindfulness Meditation

7:30 a.m. Breakfast

9:00 to 11:00 a.m. Teachings and Meditation

11:15 a.m. to 12:00 p.m. Walking Meditation

12:00 to 2:00 p.m. Lunch and Karma Yoga (chores to maintain property)

2:00 to 3:00 p.m. Discussion Group (We got to talk one hour per day. Yippie!)

3:00 p.m. Chai (Oh yes, chai, my only source of comfort for ten days.)

3:30 to 5:00 p.m. Teachings and Meditation

5:30 to 6:15 p.m. Guided Meditation

6:15 p.m. Dinner

7:30 to 9:30 p.m. Guided Meditation

I was a bit worried of what might happen when I went into this never-before-explored space of silence within myself. How would I handle it? Would I crack up and have some sort of breakdown given my predisposition to depression and my family history? These silent retreats are common on the travel circuit in India, I now knew, and

I'd heard of a few instances where people had severe breakdowns, having to leave their retreat. Essentially we're facing ourselves in full truth on all levels, and, well, sometimes we aren't quite ready to look at ourselves so deeply. This can wreak havoc with the mind. But I pushed my fears aside. Honestly, I was more afraid of continuing to live life as I'd done before. I was willing to try something completely different and uncomfortable in hopes of finding a better me.

Note to self: Notify Dr. Phil I'm finally trying something different.

I felt I was mentally and emotionally strong enough, quite possibly for the first time in my life, to handle whatever I'd find in the silence, although I'd never had to contemplate such a question until this moment. Come to think of it, I don't think I even knew silent retreats existed outside the monastic lives of monks and nuns until I made it to India. But here I was, now fully immersed in silence.

I found it fascinating to begin this internal dissection of the mind, observing the depth of the void within that led me to make certain decisions in my life. I hadn't realized one had the ability to explore the self in such depth without a psychology degree. As it turns out though, all we have to do is remove ourselves from the patterned behavior (relationship, alcohol, emotional eating, etc.) and our hectic environments (work, Facebook, TV, to-do lists, etc.) and look at ourselves introspectively in silence.

I feverishly took notes during the teaching sessions, soaking up their noble truths[8] and philosophies so relevant to our daily lives (I'll share some with you later), and I meditated. Geez, did I meditate. I didn't know one could meditate so much in a day, over ten days. I sunk into the depths of the guided meditations, finding unexplored caverns desperate for discovery. I searched myself. Seeking dark— finding the parts of my personality I wasn't so fond of, and facing them in full truth. Seeking light—searching to see if there was any light left to extract from within. And there was. Miraculously, by some grace of God, there was. We humans are remarkable and resilient like that, the way we persevere and overcome and rise up from the shadows. Amongst the pockets of pain, I found little embers of light dispersed all around. I gathered and assembled them on the projector of my mind to investigate, magnify, and rearrange them until they made sense on the screen of my life. I saw hope for a better me.

As the days passed, I shed layer upon layer of dysfunction, the rock and muck that Jagan told me about. Maybe this was what he meant by chipping away and polishing, although we'd not discussed any methods specifically. I investigated myself, my truth, my pain, my voids; day after day, I released the pains of life that led me to this cushion in North India.

By the end of the course, I felt I'd undergone six years of intensive therapy. Gratitude flooded me; grateful I'd found Siggy, for India, for the courage it took for me to get on that first flight and the circumstances that allowed me to take this trip, for everyone I ever loved and for those I'd love in the future I'd not yet met, for being led to this experience, and for the internal opening that propelled me into this course. There were even moments of gratitude laced with brief terror realizing I'd nearly blocked myself from this profound experience because of my Christian ideology. I saw instantly how religion—rather, humankind's interpretation of religion—although well intended, can limit and bind us to detrimental effect.

The dark angels that had been my long-term companions watched my monumental efforts from the tips of the distant mountaintops—still there but far away now, less ominous. Hope and love and promise blew in on the breeze through the Tibetan prayer flags, and I began stitching a new patchwork quilt, one that would nourish and comfort and support me as I traversed the globe and into the next phase of life.

I was learning how to breathe again.

Expansion Exercises

1) Can you make it a practice to bring awareness to your thoughts? When negative emotions surface, what has triggered them? What pains or unmet needs or expectations might be the underlying trigger?

2) From Tenzin Palmo's lecture, can you give consideration to the idea that we often "blame outer circumstances, other people, our families, our parents, our partners ..." when ultimately, "the real problem lies within ourselves, within our own mind"? Are there situations in your life where blame might be misplaced on outer circumstances? If so, place no judgment on yourself; simply bring awareness to your part and take note of them.

3) Based on Glenn Svensson's comment, "Bad people aren't really bad people; they're good people that don't know how to cope with the challenges life has presented them." Have you brought pain to another that's left you holding substantial guilt or shame? Can you bring compassion to yourself for the mistakes you've made? Can you feel compassion for those who may have wronged you?

4) Would you be open to reading more on key Buddhist principles that helped me view life in a healthier way, bringing me sustaining peace? If so, turn to page 283 under Petals of the Lotus in part IV, "Eclectic Teachings."

5) Are you willing to sit in silence, undisturbed, for ten minutes each day, simply focusing on your breath? Notice as your thoughts distract you; acknowledge them and let them go, bringing your awareness back to your breath.

Journal Entry
'Refuge'

CHAPTER 5

Month Two—India

I Climbed a Mountain

The best and most beautiful things in the
world cannot be seen or touched.
They must be felt with the heart.
—Helen Keller

After my heroic endeavor, internalizing, meditating, and exploring the depths of my soul for ten long, quiet days, I decided it was time for a climb. With my newfound emotional freedom and only a few weeks left in India, I could no longer resist the call of the Triund Trail, a popular overnight trek in the foothills of the Himalayas. It had started with a whisper, then a calm suggestion, finally a shouting demand. Climb that mountain! *All right already. I'll go, I'll go!*

Before the silent retreat, I'd met others who were making the trek, and I was invited to go, but I hadn't seriously considered climbing it myself. See, when you're pulling yourself from the pit of depression, wearing the patchwork quilt of pain, so heavy and burdensome, most nonessential physical exertion is inconceivable. But something significant had shifted during those ten days. I felt lighter, freer—more alive! Healed and more whole in some magical way, nearly a complete person again, finally regaining my sense of self, post divorce … post repeated life dramas … post the period of my life I will now refer to simply as *The Past*, a long-gone era only recognizable by way of radiocarbon dating.

I felt like maybe, just maybe I was beginning to rebuild my foundation again, reconstructing from the ground up with thick rebar and high-strength concrete instead of deconstructing the fragile house of Eryn that stood before.

I wanted to experience something spectacular—to immerse myself in the beauty of the snow-tipped mountains, to kiss the clouds and shout to the heavens. *I'm alive! I survived! I'm not self-destructing anymore!*

Unlikely Connections

It's strange how bonds can form so deeply between people in silence. Even when there were no words, lasting connections formed, and that's what led me to climb Triund with my new friend Breanna. We bonded during the silent retreat, strangely enough over angry monkeys.

I'd escaped the group silence one day during break time to sit in the woods and mitigate the effects of my internal implosion without disturbing the others. The silence of the meditations was intense, so it made the tears of recovery that much louder when they fell. Every time you heard a sniffled cry, you knew someone was releasing a heavy burden from their existence. We were all finding ghosts of the soul, sending them home to rest in peace in the graveyard of times past.

As I sat alone in the forest that day, I heard the frightened screams of a stranger in the distance. I looked over toward the stairs and saw a girl frantically running toward me through sticks and leaves of the wooded path. She showed no signs of slowing down as she approached, so I opened my arms to receive her. She plowed into my hug and continued crying.

"Are you okay?" I broke the silence.

"The monkeys, the monkeys, they're after me!"

I saw some energetic monkeys in the distant trees, but her screams must've scared them off. "It's okay, it's okay. They're gone."

We zipped our lips, reclaiming our silent vows, then found some big sticks and rocks to fend off the crazy monkeys as we made our way up the stairs back into class. Breanna always says I saved her from the monkeys that day. I don't think I ever told her, but she was the one who saved me.

Breanna and I set off for the Triund Trail, lighter versions of ourselves, carrying only the essentials for our overnight hike— blankets, snacks, and the all-important bottle of red wine. What? We were celebrating the survival of silence—and monkeys. You'd drink too! It was a crisp, cool, blue-skied April morning, a superb day for hiking.

I marveled at the trees, how they stood so tall and full of promise, stretching themselves, branches for arms toward the sun, miraculously growing from tiny crevasses of the rock face. *Ahhh look at that. Life always finds a way.* I was appreciating the simple beauties of life like never before. Every plant represented life; every bird, freedom; every moment a spectacular gift. Everything was beautiful again—everything. Rocks, ants, my new friendship … I was like a young child, mesmerized by the simplicities and wonder of it all.

Several hours into our hike, we came across a tiny chai hut that stood precariously on the steep slope of the mountainside, so we stopped for a rest. I come from the land of flat terrain; admittedly, my fitness life had primarily consisted of a few yoga classes and heavy lifting of my remote control, so although I was fairly thin because of the intense emotional dramas of the previous six months, I was not prepared for mountain trekking.

We sat perched on the rock bench, sipping our sweet, milky chai while perusing the snack offerings. Would you believe it, the hut in the Himalayan sky carried Oreos. Oreos! *Ah, a little piece of home in a cellophane wrapper. Yes please!*

Having spent five weeks in a culture so foreign, random unexpected reminders of home became such a comfort, providing massive nostalgic value, hence my excitement over Oreos. *Be honest, Eryn. Oreos excite you at any time.*

Pavier, the young shop owner, was excited to have American guests and serenaded us with his wooden flute, a *bansuri*. It was so beautiful. We listened in amazement to the Indian man's talented tunes, and I contemplated the wonder of Oreos while watching another man with two fully loaded cargo donkeys navigate the narrow path past us on their way up to the summit; a surreal moment. *Whose life have I been inserted into? Indian flute master, mountain trekking, Oreos, and cargo donkeys?* I had the acute realization I was oceans and lifetimes away from any home I'd ever known. I'd gone back in time to a distant, ancient land with only Oreos holding me to the twenty-first century.

Still far from the peak, we begrudgingly pried ourselves from the comfort of Pavier's hut and continued on the trail. The flute master continued with his magic melodies as we left him, and they carried all the way up the mountain with us to the final ascent as we moved in zigzag fashion up, up, up. We were close. So close. I was desperate to reach the peak.

Finally, we scaled the last boulder, and suddenly we were overlooking the most beautiful rolling green hills that extended far to the right and left on the crest of the mountain, with several blue-tarped, rickety structures dotting the landscape. Looking back to the south from where we'd hiked was the small town of Dharamsala. Looking north across the deep valley were the snow-covered Himalayas as far as the eye could see. Breathtaking!

I stood in awe, thinking of the many Tibetan refugees[1] who hiked these very mountains, far taller than the one we'd climbed. They trekked for weeks, sometimes months, taking only what they could carry, escaping the tyrannical Chinese to safely reach India. I'd heard stories of their heroic treks, but I had a new appreciation for their hardship as I stood overlooking the frozen mountain range separating India from Tibet. I contemplated the vastness of where I was, trying to comprehend how our world and its people could be so cruel. No sensible answers came to me.

An Indian fellow showed us to a tent. We threw our bags inside and went off to explore the oh-so-amazing mountaintop before the sun kissed us good night. We passed another chai hut and noticed several people sitting outside sipping tea, enjoying the warmth before the windy, frozen night set in. One man in particular stood out, the only non-Indian man I'd seen. He wore a navy-blue sweater and a mustard-yellow scarf wrapped tightly around his neck. He had brown skin and black hair with piercing eyes that told a thousand stories. *Whoa.* Our eyes locked, and I held his stare, my hazel eyes to his brown in a long-distance butterfly-inducing embrace while silently continuing past him. *Hello, Mr. Handsome.*

Breanna and I continued exploring, climbing rocks and taking pictures, laughing and running around like schoolgirls. Dogs slept lazily in the last rays of sun. Young boys played cricket. It was all just ... perfect.

Majestic beauty from all sides wrapped around me, and the enormity of it all hit me. I couldn't believe I'd actually left the United States with a one-way ticket and was standing here, glorious mountains all around cheering me. I realized what an epic leap I'd taken from the precipice of old into the world of new. I felt a huge sense of relief and some intuitive *knowing* that I was going to be okay.

This *knowing* was a new experience for me. I lived in skepticism and question marks before. I knew I'd done the right thing by leaving the United States, but I also knew I had to keep going. Who knew how the path would twist and turn as I traversed the globe? Appreciation flooded me, and I became overwhelmed with emotion, I brushed away the tears and hugged Breanna with the same intensity as the day we met over screaming monkeys.

We made our way back toward the tent to fetch the bottle of red, when I noticed Mr. Handsome sitting under a tree playing a bansuri.

Apparently we'd missed the wooden flute giveaway. Mr. Handsome *and* Pavier, really? My steps slowed to a stop, and I stood motionless, watching for a few moments as he sat there so peacefully with his melodies, unaware of my presence. I waited. I watched. The feeling was unforgettable. *You are meant to meet that man ... but not right now, Eryn. This is feeling a bit stalker-ish. Move along, move along. Hmm, do I believe in love at first sight? I don't know if I do anymore, but if I do, this is it.* It was kismet, fate, a serendipitous encounter with destiny. What chance did I stand against kismet?

I shed my stalker-like stares, running to catch up to Breanna. She went off to find a bathroom—aka, a big rock to squat behind—and I rummaged through our bags to find the corkscrew. I emerged from our tent to find Mr. Handsome walking toward me with slow, deliberate steps and a confident walk. His eyes penetrated and invaded me as I stood there speechless with the bottle of wine. *Whoa.* I took a step back toward the tent, hoping to brace myself against this force approaching me, feeling his arrows pierce the bull's-eye of my heart.

He had the most beautiful Israeli accent and flawless tanned skin with a heavy five o'clock shadow. We talked for a few minutes—about what, I don't recall. I was too busy holding my heart, keeping it from its instinctual urge to merge with this man. On the other hand, I wanted to voluntarily remove it from my chest and impale him with it before he changed his mind and ran away.

Breanna returned from her rock in her bouncy, energetic way, and we all huddled up on the hillside to philosophize about life and watch the sunset. The wine was terrible, but we didn't care. It was warm and made us giggly with the altitude. It didn't seem to help my headache though; the long day in the sun had taken its toll. Mr. Handsome said, "Come here. I will heal you." *Ohhhh yes. Heal me, Mr. Handsome.* I sat in front of him, and he stretched his legs out, one on each side of me, placing his hands on my back, applying perfect pressure so intently. My headache magically disappeared, as did my inhibitions, and I nuzzled deeper into him, leaning back against his chest. He wrapped his blanket around us both, and we all watched the sun fall in the distance, drinking the last drop of wine.

The temperature dropped quickly, and our bellies were growling. The Indian fellow called us over to the raging fire, and we feasted on dhal and naan bread, staples of the Indian diet. We huddled together on the tiny wooden benches, eating our dinner, talking with Breanna and Pavier from the chai hut, who'd come up from further down the mountain. I knew he had a crush on Breanna. *Awwwe.*

We listened to the enchanting melodies of the bansuri genius while Breanna made friends with the locals. She had this uncanny ability with her bubbly personality to fit in instantly to foreign cultures, feeling completely comfortable in her surroundings. As an introvert, I was amazed by her gregarious ways.

Mr. Handsome took my hand, and we left the circle of fire to talk for a bit. *Ohhh tell me all your stories, you gorgeous man.* I looked over to Breanna, still listening to Pavier, and gave her the *you okay?* look. She gave me an encouraging smile and a reassuring nod. *Yeah, go on.*

Only the moon lit our dark, shadowy faces as we became more immersed in one another and the magic of the moment, high on the frigid mountaintop. We huddled close on the cold, grassy earth, swapping stories, arms linked, my shoulder pressed against his, one blanket hugging us both as we extracted heat from one another. It was part fate and part chance, part past life reunion and part futures unfolding; our stories bouncing off each other like moonlight on the snow-covered mountains.

He told me of his life in Israel, and I told him of mine in America. Flashes of thought lit my mind like lightning, wondering if our lives could ever merge successfully with such cultural and geographical distances. *Hmm, could it be? Would it ever be—something?* I cast away my storm of forward projecting thoughts.

He said that he'd been camping here for several days and had planned to descend the mountain earlier that day. A mystical woman he met over breakfast made him rethink his plans, telling him he must stay and that he'd meet someone important. Reluctantly, he was convinced to stay another night in the harsh, frigid conditions.

"What, that's crazy. You made that up," I said, slapping him on the arm the way Americans are famous for. *Get outta here.*

"No, no, I do not lie about such things, darling," he calmly replied.

We covered lifetimes of stories and history and commonalities. I felt like I was falling into him, the light of love eclipsing the shadow of fear, pulling me in, receiving me, enveloping me.

Wanting to delve deeper into the complexities of Mr. Handsome but feeling like I'd abandoned Breanna at the fire with Pavier, I ran over to check on her to see how she was doing. "Breanna, how's it going? Are you interested in Pavier at all? Any love connection going on? He's so into you."

"Nah," she said. "He's nice and all, and we've been having a good time over here, but he's not for me. I'm going to bed soon. What about you? How are you and the Israeli doing?"

"Whoa. Breanna, something is really happening over there. Almost like … well it's like we know each other from another lifetime or something. I don't know if I even believe in that, but if I did, well, we were soul mates or something in a past life. I've never done anything like this, and I know we just met, but I think I'm going to spend the night with him. Is that crazy?"

"Aw, that's so sweet! Yeah, go for it!"

"It will be a frigid zero degrees tonight. What's a girl to do?" We both laughed, and she shooed me off.

I gathered a few things from our tent and went to find Mr. Handsome. He hadn't invited me to join him, but I somehow knew he wouldn't resist.

I held his hand as we left the warmth of the fire to find his tent in the dark. There were less than a dozen popped-up tents across the mountaintop, with hundreds of feet between them, but none were visible, as the clouds masked the moon. I followed with short footsteps across the rugged terrain, fully trusting this magical moment and the man I met just hours before. I'd never done anything so spontaneous. I hadn't decided yet if I'd make love to him or not, but I wanted to spend more time with him—to feel him next to me, his arms, his embrace, his breath in sync with mine. It could've been dangerous, I guess, but nothing in my life had ever felt more right, more natural.

Human nature that once begged us to layer our bodies with scarves and wool and blankets was now pleading with us to shed the artificial warmth in exchange for the magnetic heat emanating between us. Who am I to argue with the law of magnetism? Clothes were flying, arms flailing, lips colliding, our bodies seamlessly intertwining like rivers joining; the long-lost love I never knew reuniting after decades … after lifetimes.

He hung a tiny flashlight from the frame of the tent hovering above, saying he wanted to see me better. He gazed his dark angel eyes into mine, and I saw in a flash all his pain and all his sorrow. I held his hand and placed it on my heart. *I feel you.*

He stroked my hair, my face, my body, telling me I was beautiful. Rivers of doubt swelled the labyrinthine channels of my mind. *I'm beautiful? You think I'm beautiful? Really? He thinks I'm beautiful? Hmm, that's odd. No … really?* My mind continued its cynical anti-beauty campaign right there as I lay under Mr. Handsome. He just hovered there above me, under the flashlight, as if he were absorbing the depths of me. I thought to myself, *You've already got me in bed. You really don't have to say these things.* I smiled sweetly at him, trying to measure his statements, wondering where they fell on the scale of sincerity.

The funny thing was I felt and somehow *knew* that his words were genuine, and I would come to learn this was just his way, always speaking with honesty, passion, full disclosure of his feelings, and heartfelt expression. He didn't censor himself or carefully choose his words or hold back from his emotion. He owned them, and he aired them freely. I loved that about him.

Our opposing views of my beauty tumbled around in my mind like dirty laundry washing itself. I realized how disturbing it was that in this moment of all moments—where two souls had so unexpectedly collided on a Himalayan mountaintop—I was still creating negative labels of self-judgment, criticism, and fictional self-hate dramas in my mind. How dare I taint this beautiful experience! How dare I! In that moment, I swore I'd never create another false story of unworthiness, placing it between myself and a man. I sat up to meet him, kissing his full lips, immersing myself into him, receiving him into me.[2]

The brisk wind blew the tent all around us as we fiercely clung to one another, extracting and exchanging body heat, submerging, intertwining, and enveloping ourselves in euphoric energy. He was raw and passionate and intensely full of life; I was free and expansive and uninhibited.

We lay together curled up, the back of my body pressed to his front, two spoons nestled perfectly together, and began drifting off to sleep. I awoke suddenly realizing ... are you ready for it? I farted on Mr. Handsome. I mean it's India, and the food, well, sometimes ... my tummy ... it's, well, India. *Sigh*. I'm sure you understand. It wasn't loud or anything but still ... I farted on Mr. Handsome! I died a thousand embarrassing deaths, my eyes opening, somehow trying to determine if Mr. Handsome was still awake, although I couldn't see him in our spoon-like state.

I whispered, "Are you awake?"

"Yes," he said quietly.

Noooooooo! I started giggling. "Oh my God, I just farted on you. How embarrassing!"

"I know, I know. It's so beautiful, like you're blowing your love on me." He hugged me close to him and then started tickling me. We laughed and talked and made love again.

I wished I could've halted the progression of time, suspending myself like the flashlight, watching that moment forever where I lay, wrapped so peacefully and contently in the blanket of his love. All mental worries had subsided, and I was content with the fullness of life. If only we could suspend time.

Finally the golden rays peered over the distant mountain, releasing us from the grips of the frozen night. I rolled over and kissed Mr. Handsome on his forehead as he slept soundly and left him to his dreams.

Breanna was sitting on the hillside crocheting, and I joined her overlooking the snow-covered towers beyond the valley. The lovely Indian fellow cheerfully served us sweet chai, and we munched on peanut butter and bananas as we stretched ourselves across the rock face to receive the warm hug of sunshine finally greeting us.

Mr. Handsome emerged from the tent with a contented, cheeky smile on his face. My heart leapt from my chest in thumping rhythms as he walked slowly, coming closer to join Breanna and me with a chai. *OMG what if I'm not as cute in the morning sun? I don't have any makeup on. I didn't know I'd meet a man! Who brings cosmetics up a mountain in India?* I'd already forgotten the vow I made only hours before never to create fictional stories of unworthiness. I was good at breaking promises to myself. He snuggled up next to me, put his arm around my waist, and kissed my forehead. *Okay, whew. He's not repulsed by my just-been-loved natural morning glow.*

Breanna had an overnight bus to catch to Delhi, so we were eager to hit the trail. Mr. Handsome and I had only a few minutes together, but I gave him my number, a kiss on the cheek, and a big hug around his neck. "Hope we meet again," I whispered.

We grabbed our bags, I pet the cute, stray, mountain doggy on his head, and then I turned to blow Mr. Handsome a kiss. I felt a little twinge of pain with no guarantee we'd meet again, but I held it in my heart that we'd reunite in Dharamsala.

Breanna and I began our descent down the trail, and my mind replayed the previous night with Mr. Handsome and the possibility of a future. *Look at how the universe brought us together in the Himalayan sky. What if he'd left earlier? We never would've met. Maybe we were meant to meet and be together. Would I be willing to live with him in Israel? Or would he want to live in America with me? I wonder if we'd have children.* The stories continued excitedly swirling around in my mind. Some I shared with Breanna, others I kept to myself. Breanna told me about the boyfriend she'd left behind in the States, and we went on and on like schoolgirls talking about boys. *Swoon*.

I was aware the idea of a relationship like this working out was a long shot, and I wasn't even sure I'd be willing to alter my plans at this stage of my trip, not that I had many, but … I mean everyone knows you're supposed to fall in love *after* all the adventures and healing, at the end of the trip like in *Eat Pray Love*. It's not supposed to happen now! I hadn't really planned on falling for someone yet or having to ask myself questions like this. After all, one of the main purposes of traveling was to release the pattern to attach to men. That was the whole point of moving around—forced independence until I felt strong enough to use the drug of love responsibly. I knew I wasn't quite there yet. Then again, when do you ever really get to orchestrate the cosmic intelligence that blesses you with love? I mean it found me in the Himalayan sky for goodness sake! Who am I to question the fate that brought two strangers together on a mountaintop in North India? I was powerless to stop my mental projections of what might be.

Mr. Handsome reached out to me after that first encounter, and we spent much time together in the coming weeks. Our attachment to each other grew, as did our feelings of love, but there was another side to it—a shadow side. The dark angels I saw in his eyes that night, although passionate and raw, continued to come out again and again in other ways; he called it "his fire." I realized he hadn't yet found a way to escape his fire and was still battling the flames engulfing him. I'd just begun shedding my own dark angels. One by one I was telling them goodbye with each healing step I took on the streets of India, but I could sense them still watching and hovering in the distance, waiting eagerly to rejoin me.

I had a premonition of the future: my dark angels converging with his fire, swirling madly into the hell realm of love's darkness, destroying us both. I wasn't strong enough yet to help save him from his fire without igniting myself, risking an immolated death. I was barely strong enough to save myself.

I'd told myself after the silent retreat that I'd be open to exploring relationships on the road as long as I held the promise that I'd leave them if they weren't feeling 100 percent right. I knew my pattern was to compromise my needs and emotional health, molding myself to the other for the sake of the relationship, and I had to stop this cycle. I knew I could've loved him; it seemed I already did. My heart has a great capacity to give love—that I know.

Perhaps I could've supported him emotionally, drowning myself in his needs, but that would've been the old me. And this was the new me, or at least the beginning stages of the new me. A me that was a little bit wiser, a little more concerned about her own emotional stability, a little bit closer, one step at a time climbing the mountain to her higher self. I couldn't take the chance that I'd fall into the pit of his fire. I just couldn't take the chance.

Mr. Handsome decided to go into a Vipassana[3] silent retreat in hopes of dousing the spark of his flames, and we both knew that was goodbye. There was love on the mountaintop that cold, frigid night and forever in our hearts, but we saw the fated end to our love story.

Siggy was now also going into a silent retreat—the next session of the Buddhist course I'd recently completed—and I decided it was time to leave India, so we said our goodbyes. This is how you know when it's time to leave a place, when your heart tells you, not because of a prebooked travel itinerary. My heart knew it was time.

Many months later, Siggy and I were discussing the repeated sadness that comes in saying goodbye to those special people we meet on the road. Siggy said, "Once I feel that the exchange has been made between two people—the lesson learned—I just know it's time to say goodbye." She's so wise, that soul sister of mine.

I wouldn't have been able to grasp that concept fully or know it deeply then when I said tearful goodbyes to Mr. Handsome or to my soul sister. I couldn't have felt that truthful statement in my core like I do now, but I've come to know she's right. We can't hang on to everyone we meet—or everyone we love. We're not meant to. Sometimes the universe sends certain people to teach us. And somehow, in a strange way, I felt I was being tested. The universe was testing my pattern of attachment, tempting me with love, my most coveted possession.

I finished my last chai in the Carpe Diem café, left both my loves in silence, and boarded the overnight bus to Delhi. I thought of all the beautiful experiences that had unfolded with Mr. Handsome, and I knew … I knew everything was exactly how it was meant to be. I was his, and he was mine. It didn't matter for how long.

Expansion Exercises

1) What repeating patterns have you identified that don't nourish you? Perhaps in your relationship choices? Or in how you allow others to treat you? Or how you treat them? Lapsed commitments to yourself?

2) Do you have a tendency to compromise your needs for the sake of others? In doing this, how do you deplete yourself?

3) In prioritizing your own emotional health, what boundaries can you set to prevent this depletion? Consider that, in prioritizing yourself, you will be healthier and can then give more freely to others.

4) What repetitive negative inner dialogue do you notice within yourself? Perhaps relating to your self-worth? *I'm not enough.* Or body image? *I'm too fat.* Or career? *I'm not qualified for that position.* Can you recognize that these may be fictitious stories?

5) When have you "attached" yourself to a story where you projected an outcome prematurely? (Highly recommend reading on *attachment* in part IV, "Eclectic Teachings," on page 281.) In projecting an outcome, can you see that you take yourself on a roller coaster of emotions based on the success or failure of _____? How does riding this wave of emotions benefit you? How is it detrimental to you?

Journal Entry
'Desires'

CHAPTER 6

Month Two—India

Delhi Premonitions

We do not create our destiny; we participate in its unfolding.
Synchronicity works as a catalyst toward
the working out of that destiny.
—David Richo

I spent time in Delhi with my friend Sanjay, an Indian man I befriended from the silent retreat. He'd been telling me all about a book that I *must read* called *Power vs. Force*[1] by David. R. Hawkins, PhD, and was eager to get me to a westernized bookshop to locate a copy in English.

Sanjay flipped through the book, pointing out a few key pages that he thought might motivate me. I could tell he felt it was of utmost importance that I read this book. "Okay, Sanjay, I promise, the moment I'm settled enough and feel inclined to read, I'll start this book."

He looked intently at the spine of the book, tapping his finger on the printed emblem. I saw his mind percolating.

"Eryn, my friend," he said with his wobbly-head gesture the Indians are so famous for. "Do you know of Hay House Publishing?"

"No, I don't think so. Doesn't sound familiar." To this point, I hadn't been well read in the mind, body, spirit category, although obviously I should have been! I'd never heard of Hay House or even the infamous Louise Hay for that matter, but I didn't admit this to my friend.

"Remember that name, my friend," he continued. "I do believe that when you are ready to write your book, you will publish with Hay House. Yes, yes, I do believe it is so."

"Okay, Sanjay, but I can't even think about that right now. I don't even know for sure that I'll write a book or what it would be about, so publishing isn't even on the horizon."

"Yes, my friend, I understand. It is early in your trip. I see. But remember Hay House. I do believe it is so."

"All right, Sanjay, I'll remember."

"Eryn, my friend, do you drink beer?"

"Well, yes, Sanjay. Yes, I do."

"Good." He wobbled with a big smile on his face. "We shall have beers then."

And so it goes. Sanjay and I drank beer at the New Delhi Hard Rock Café. I'd long forgotten the conversation preceding our beer, but three-plus years later, I'm publishing *Facing Freedom* with Balboa Press, a division of Hay House Publishing.

We said our goodbyes, I promised him I'd read the book we searched out, and I made my way south to Sri Lanka for a short jaunt, then further east to Indonesia.

Expansion Exercises

1) Can you recall any time in your life when there was a great coincidence or synchronicity? If so, note them in your journal. Bringing awareness to these times will help you recognize them in the future.

2) In your daily life, look for any coincidences or synchronicities. What might they be telling you?

3) Envision making the conscious effort to slow your life down and bring recognition to the subtler side of life—coincidences, intuition, thought patterns (positive or negative), and emotional triggers. Would you be willing to make this a practice?

CHAPTER 7

Month Three—Indonesia

Narrow Minds

The enemy is fear. We think it is hate; but it is fear.
—Gandhi

Arriving in Indonesia, I found my prearranged taxi, threw my bag in the trunk, and jumped in the backseat. On Siggy's suggestion, I'd booked myself at a guesthouse in the Gili Islands that she'd visited before and I was eager to arrive at my secluded bungalow and relax for a week. India was unimaginably special but it was quite intense with its crowded streets and I always felt the need to maintain a certain level of vigilance. I was slowly finding confidence in this emotional and physical self-sufficiency, but it was exhausting at times, never quite feeling comfortable enough to let my guard down.

My taxi sped through the jungle on our two-hour drive toward the coast, and I tried to settle into the idea of being on my own again without Siggy. We'd been nearly inseparable since we met on day five of my trip, but now I was on my own again. I realized how much safer I felt as a pair. I watched the taxi driver carefully, giving serious thought to whether I was being kidnapped or not. Transportation alone, with a male driver, in the jungle, in a foreign land—ya never can tell about these things. You really can't. But I was tired from my delayed flights and multiple layovers, so I drifted off to sleep.

We screeched to a halt, and I was jolted awake rolling into the floor space of the backseat. I blinked my eyes open, shook myself awake like a cartoon character recovering from a crash, and sat up quickly to see where I was. The taxi driver opened the trunk to retrieve my bag, and I collected my things from the backseat to meet him and to assess my new surroundings. *Where am I? Am I safe? Any potential dangers here?* As a solo female traveler, these questions were always at the forefront of my mind. Nothing alarming stood out. I relaxed. It was nearly dark now, but I didn't think too much of it. I was so excited to be nearing my destination and eager to catch the final leg of my trip, a boat ride over to the island.

The nice taxi driver and I walked down the concrete boat ramp to the water's edge, and he pointed me to the captain. I climbed a rickety ladder to board the weathered teal wooden boat, and the taxi driver threw my bag up. *Whoa, it's like I've been inserted into an episode of* The Amazing Race. *How cool!* The captain and the taxi driver conversed for a few minutes in a very foreign language, and then the taxi driver asked me in broken English, "End work day. Okay-take-worker-home-island?" I wanted to accommodate the locals whenever possible, hoping to minimize the *I'm special* treatment that's oftentimes extended to the traveling American. I didn't want to be *that girl*, so I didn't think twice about it. "Of course, that's fine. No problem. Yes," I responded.

From under the awnings of two nearby buildings, men began walking toward the boat and scurried up the rickety ladder one by one. A dozen young men and one old couple boarded, and I scooched in closer to the captain, making room for everyone. They shuffled in, filling the entire boat, sitting across and next to me, as we pulled away from the shore at a tortoise pace in the underpowered skiff. We moved further from the shore into the still, dark waters as the sun sank behind the trees. That's when the flash of fear struck me. *Solo American girl in a Muslim country, on a tiny boat, in the dark of night, with no cell service, and I can't speak the local language.* Who would I call anyway if I was in trouble—911 Indonesia?

My flight had been delayed, which resulted in my arriving to the dock at sunset rather than in daylight hours as planned. I always made concerted efforts to arrive all the way to my guesthouse in a new country before sundown as a precautionary measure, but you know how air travel is; things don't always work out like we plan. Now that we'd be going to multiple islands to drop off the workers, I didn't even know which island I was to get off on or how long to expect the boat ride to be; this had all been prearranged by my guesthouse, and all I could do was trust—or freak out. So I freaked out. My pen defense skills wouldn't be any match for the group of strong twenty-something men, not that I knew where my pen was anyway.

The men all stared at me, this curious Caucasian person in their far removed homeland. I held eye contact with the older grandma woman, wondering if she'd wield her maternal influence over the young men if they tried anything. *Grandma will make sure I'm ok.*

Only minutes had passed, and the lights of the shore began to dim as we moved further from land. I could barely see the darkness of the tree line compared to the night's sky, and my mind began drowning me in the depths of fear. *Will they hurt me? Rape me? Kill me? Kidnap me and hold me in a bamboo cage until my family comes up with ransom money? What possible defense could I put up? Oh Eryn, please. They're harmless. Calm down. But there are so many of them! I wouldn't have a chance. They haven't done anything to you. You're fine! But … but there are so many of them.*

In my fluctuating panicky state, I thought of jumping off the boat so I could swim to safety. But where would I swim? It was dark, and I couldn't even tell anymore how far I was from shore. I thought I had this all figured out with my prearranged transportation, but after driving two hours through the jungle, I didn't even know where I was, except some cove of the Gili Islands in the South Pacific—I hoped that was where I'd been dropped off. Perhaps I wasn't even on the way to my guesthouse as I assumed.

My rational mind kicked in. *This is ridiculous. Why would you be jumping in to swim, Eryn? They haven't done anything. Calm down!* They continued staring at me and laughing like schoolboys. I tried to play it cool and talk with them, but the language barrier didn't allow it. The attempt only made them laugh more. I cracked a little smile and held one man's stare in front of me, trying to outwardly appear calm. I could only see the whites of his teeth and eyes, his shadowy figure bouncing with his laughter in the dark.

We pulled up to the first island, and the old couple got off. I looked at the captain with a questioning glance to see if this was my island. He shook his head, no. *Oh shit, now I'm alone with a dozen young men, on a boat, in the dark, in bum fuck Indonesia. No more grandma to protect me. Rape, murder, kidnapping—yep, this is it for me.*

Frantic thoughts continued. I felt nearly on the verge of a heart attack caused by my frenzied, out-of-control mind.

Random South Pacific Island Coroner's Office
Death Certificate: Eryn Donnalley
Cause of Death: Fear-Induced Heart Attack

We carried on in the tiny boat, and I tried to calm myself. *Okay, Eryn, breathe ... breathe. Do you really feel in danger? Do you feel negative intent from them?* I didn't think they were malicious laughs, likely just curious—probably not a lot of white American girls in this part of the world. Maybe they found it entertaining. I tried to feel into it, admitting to myself that I didn't feel aggressive or escalated energy from them; deep down I sensed they were harmless.

These guys were young, probably toddlers when planes crashed into our towers, and they likely had little access to television anyway; I was going to an island with no power for goodness sake! Maybe they didn't even know there exists an undercurrent of tension between Muslims and Americans in our post-9/11 world. My mind tried to reassure me, based on my intuitive assessment, of their innocent behavior, but I didn't trust my intuition yet. My intellectual mind screamed with preconditioned fears.

I'd never considered myself prejudiced before, but I couldn't deny that the Muslim/American element, along with being the only woman on board, heightened my fears. I wanted to trust my intuition over my intellect, but I couldn't. My mind—it was frantic. Fear won the internal battle that day, and I sat, paralyzed on the boat, waiting for something, or nothing to happen.

We pulled up to the second island. I looked again to the captain with anticipation. He shook his head, *no*. And then another island, *no*.

Finally, finally, years passed if not a decade of moonless nights, and we pulled up to the fourth island. The captain tapped me on the shoulder and pointed to the shore. *Oh, thank God, we made it!*

I jumped from the boat and felt the warm water on my legs, my feet burying into the sand under the weight of my body. *Finally I'm safe.* I felt relief as though I'd actually survived something traumatic and was just now, for the first moment, realizing I would be okay. A woman blinded me with a head torch before I'd even left the water's edge. "Eryn, is that you? We've been waiting on you for dinner. Come, come! Ratan will take your bag."

Instantly my fears subsided, and I felt a sense of calmness return to my body. Someone knew my name! I was where I was supposed to be. It had all been an elaborate fictional story I'd created. *Would they rape me? Attack me? Kill me? Would they ask a reasonable ransom amount to release me from the bamboo cage?* It occurred to me I was probably paranoid having watched too much crime drama television and nightly news, but I was powerless to maintain a realistic perspective in the face of perceived danger and my heightened fears of the world.

Ratan took my bag, and I followed him up to the guesthouse. I looked back once more to the boat pulling away. The young men spilled over the edge hollering and laughing while waving their shadowy hands in the dark at me. They were waving goodbye to their new American friend. I felt like I'd narrowly escaped death.

My shameful judgments and unwarranted fears crashed over me like waves, and I struggled to catch my breath. I cast my regrets out with the tide, hoping to reach the men, but they washed back in on me un-received, reminders of my ignorance.

The Trouble with Fear

This was the first time I had such a commanding realization of the true power of our thoughts. I'd studied and investigated *the nature of the mind* while in the Buddhism course, but that had been on a more personal, emotional level. Here I was presented with cyclical fearful thoughts convincing me I was in danger when, in reality, I was surrounded by goodness. As we walk through life, thoughts our constant companion, I see they'll either assist us in living life through love, growth, and expansion or they'll lead us astray to a life of fear, contraction, skepticism, and doubt.

"There are only two emotions: love and fear," says Elisabeth Kübler-Ross.[1] "All positive emotions come from love, all negative emotions from fear. From love flows happiness, contentment, peace, and joy. From fear comes anger, hate, anxiety and guilt. It's true that there are only two primary emotions, love and fear. But it's more accurate to say that there is only love or fear, for we cannot feel these two emotions together, at exactly the same time. They're opposites. If we're in fear, we are not in a place of love. When we're in a place of love, we cannot be in a place of fear."

We get to choose—love or fear—every single day, in every situation. We often don't realize we have the choice, so caught up in the unconscious madness of our own thoughts and the influences of media and our surroundings, but it *is* a choice. Although I wanted to believe in the goodness of people, I realized I'd slowly, across decades, lost the truth of the heart; what had replaced it was the falsehood of fear.

Expansion Exercises

1) Can you recognize, as Elisabeth Kübler-Ross states, that fear expresses itself in various emotions, including anger, hate, anxiety, and guilt? Conversely, that love shows itself as happiness, contentment, peace, joy, and acceptance? Consider whether you primarily live in love or fear.

2) Can you identify times when you prejudged another person, whether in your thoughts or actions, because of their ethnicity or cultural background?

3) Can you bring awareness to the idea that this is most often an unwarranted fear or misplaced judgment? Would you be willing to watch your thoughts and notice when you prematurely assess the *good* or *bad* of a person? Place no judgment on yourself in this process; only bring awareness to it.

4) Imagine a time with no television or media; if no one "informed" you, whom would you dislike?

5) Contemplate the benefits of choosing love over fear, both locally and globally, seeing all living beings as one human family.

CHAPTER 8

Month Five—Ireland

Pocket Watches

I know this transformation is painful, but you're not falling apart;
you're just falling into something different
with a new capacity to be beautiful.
—William C. Hannan

After my time in Indonesia, then visiting a few other countries, I made my way to the Emerald Isle. It was month five of my trip when I had an unlikely encounter with a stranger on the streets of Dublin. He was walking past a group of Czech tourists, and I was walking through them as they blocked the exit door to my hostel. In the commotion of it all, I bumped into a man carrying an Ikea-size bag of bread rolls.

"Oh, excuse me," I said.

"It's okay, no problem," he replied softly. "Would you like a piece of bread?" I declined his offer; he smiled and nodded his head, *suit yourself,* and carried on down the sidewalk.

I pulled out my map to figure out which direction I'd be heading. I was off to find the Guinness museum, a site of cultural significance—some might even call it a religious experience—not to be missed. I followed behind the man with the bread rolls to locate my bus stop headed in the same direction.

I caught up to him at the street corner as we all waited for the blinking green man to signal us to cross. Isn't it incredible that one little LED blinking man can direct us all so efficiently? Sometimes I think the whole of society might just crumble if we didn't have the structured direction of timed street crossings. At least we have the blinking man collectively holding us all together. On the other hand, maybe the green man is a tiny example of a forced structure that should be challenged. *Hmmmh.*

In Germany, for instance, I was surprised to see that no one, I mean no one, crosses the street without direction from the blinking man. Any other city I've ever encountered, people look both ways and cross the street without the green man's approval. There was something about Germany that felt so civilized and in order. I quite liked it. However, there was a time when many there followed direction or looked the other way in events that defy the very essence of the human spirit, so it begs the question: how do we know when to follow the order of society and when do we choose another path for ourselves?

I stood at the corner, contemplating the necessity versus limiting structure of the blinking men. I wasn't really in the mood for conversation, so even though the man with the bread rolls had an innocent, kind smile, I chose not to engage. The blinking man finally gave us his green blessing, and we all dutifully crossed.

I found myself lagging behind, hoping Mr. Breadroll wouldn't notice me, as we both carried on walking down the same sidewalk. Construction obstructed the path, so he crossed the road to the other side. I followed, and then we crossed back separately. I was starting to feel like a bit of a stalker as the main road became less trafficked and we were the only two people on this portion of the road away from the city center.

The sky grew darker with an ominous haze, and I knew the rains of Dublin would soon be falling, so it became more urgent to find my bus. There were no street signs, I was new to the city and my Zen navigation was failing me. *Grrrr.*

We were approaching another intersection, so I decided I'd just ask Mr. Breadroll if I was heading in the right direction. *He's harmless, Eryn. What—a hyper assault of bread rolls? Oh, go on.* There was something about being in a foreign country that put me on high alert, even in Europe. Normally I wouldn't think twice about asking a man for directions. Being a woman alone though in another country with no one to call if in danger, well, I was always on edge.

"Excuse me. I wonder if you can tell me if I'm going in the right direction."

"Well hello again." He smiled softly at me. "Wow, you look like a piece of art. What is this you're wearing around your neck?" he asked me.

I knew instantly he was harmless.

"Oh, well, this silver disk is the twenty-third psalm. It was my father's, and I wear it to keep me safe. This is a mandala I had made in India that says, 'You are your own refuge,' and it's really special. This is a key that opens the lock where I have my stuff stored at the hostel. I got it from an antique store in India."

He looked at each piece with such interest, admiring them individually in his quiet, methodical way. He wasn't in a hurry and seemed eager to engage.

"Hey, so where ya goin' with all that bread?" I asked.

"I'm delivering it to a homeless shelter. There's a bakery I visit each morning, and they give me their leftovers from the day before, and I take them to the shelter."

"That's very nice of you."

"Well, I sort of live there too. I can't say it's completely unselfish," he said sheepishly.

"Oh," I said, surprised.

He didn't appear to be what I envisioned a homeless man to be—not like any homeless person I'd seen in the States, anyway. He wore gray dress pants and a long-sleeve, burgundy button-up shirt (tucked in) with a houndstooth button-up vest and coordinating fedora. He even had a gold pocket watch he pulled from his vest occasionally to check the time. He said it was his father's and he carried it for good luck. *Awww.* Maybe the clothes were his father's as well—they were older than he was—but I didn't ask.

He had the air of an old wise man with his pocket watch and Morgan Freeman freckles dotted across his mocha-colored cheeks, but he looked to be about my age. His eyes, on the other hand, said he'd lived a thousand lifetimes with an ocean of sadness desperate to spill upon my shores.

I stood there taking in this new information, hoping he wasn't able to see all the preconceived notions scrolling my mind of what *homeless* looked like.

He carried on, "Well, I only live there sometimes. When the weather is nice in the summer, I just go to hotels and sneak up the fire escape to the roof and sleep there—until they catch me, and then I have to move."

"Hmmm, well that's creative," I said.

"Where are you from? What are you doing here?" he inquired.

I told him I'd been traveling for a while and my father had loved Ireland, so I wanted to visit. He'd attended Trinity College for a brief time in the late eighties when he was restarting his life, and I don't know why exactly, but I felt it was important for me to visit. I guess because Ireland had been important to him, I was feeling the need to retrace my father's steps in a way—probably because I was restarting my life too. Perhaps I just wanted to spend time in a place he adored so much. I liked the thought of my father being happy and enjoying life within a peaceful, calm mind, and I felt a lighter version of him all around me there in the streets of Dublin.

Atílio—that was Mr. Breadroll's name—heard me speak of my deceased father and the reboot of my life, and his look instantly changed, eyebrows peaking slightly in a dejected, defeated sort of way. "My father killed himself two years ago, and I just couldn't stay there in Scandinavia any longer," he blurted out with a relieved exhale. He set his bread bag down like it'd been filled with bricks of pain and he was finally releasing it for the first time. He continued,

"My life just didn't make sense anymore. Nothing made sense! I've just been sort of roaming around ever since."

My heart split wide open right there on the street corner as this homeless stranger spilled his story to me. I put my hands on my heart, feeling physical pain course through my body as his words invaded me. Life is so strange the way you can just be walking, minding your own business, looking forward to a pint of Guinness, and the next moment you're stormed with the collateral damage of another's degenerative mental health.

I gave him a hug, and we carried on walking and talking like we were long-lost friends. Cars and busses and people zoomed by us, on their way to work or school, to their lovers or mothers waiting, but we were there, two adult children suspended in time, tapping the keg of mental illness at the pub of paternal pain.

We finally came to the corner where I would go my way and he'd go his; he had bread to deliver, after all, and well, Guinness was waiting for me. I asked if he was on Facebook or if I could have his e-mail so I could check in with him and stay in touch. He said he didn't want to be linked into that world—not yet. We said a reluctant, brew-soaked goodbye. I gave him a prolonged hug and wished him well.

If it had been an old friend or a man I knew better, I probably would've spent the whole day with him. I couldn't have cared less about the Guinness museum, and he was obviously in need of a friend. As a woman in these situations though, I felt it necessary to pull myself back from certain connections with male strangers just to make sure I didn't get myself into trouble or give the wrong impression. These things can be tricky to assess. I found it to be a delicate walk I'd continually balance on the tightrope between my intuition and preconditioned fear.

I crossed the busy street to catch my bus, leaving Atílio behind. Thoughts of my own father pervaded me. He hadn't killed himself. I was lucky ... but his brother had decades earlier, not long after my birth ... and I knew my uncle and my father kept company with the same tormenting dark angels. Luckily, my father found a way to live with them—and fight with them—prescribed pharmaceuticals his weapon.

All my life, I'd seen the internal battles in the depth of my father's soulful, contemplative eyes, but he never told me his stories or that of the uncle I never met. *Daddy, what's wrong? What are you thinking about so heavy and deep, just staring at the trees? Daddy …*

I realized how fortunate I was that my father left the earth when his body gave out rather than voluntarily extracting himself from it. At least I had that. Atílio was left with unanswered questions and a pocket watch that only told the time of pain.

I had little understanding of my father's illness until after his death when I read his medical records. There'd only been the brief mention of depression amongst the family in hushed tones through the decades, but I always sensed there was more. Most of my life, I wasn't really sure there was anything *to* understand; it was just who he was—quiet, docile, and unusually calm. I didn't think much of it. It's not the sort of alarming behavior one would question or consider unhealthy if that's what you grew up knowing.

As I entered my late twenties and early thirties though, I began to wonder more about it, maybe because I'd felt on the verge of some mental fracture myself at certain times. I knew pieces of *my* puzzle were scattered in and amongst my father's past and these medical records, all tied up neatly inside the worn and yellowed envelope I received after his death. It looked so official with the United States Navy stamped across the front. *Private. Confidential.*

I suspected whatever happened that led to the stripping of his pilot's wings and subsequent medical discharge from service had been big enough that no one wanted to talk about it. Maybe they just couldn't bring themselves to discuss that period of their life—my mom or my dad. They made agreements long ago, whether silent or spoken, to scuttle the air-carrier of their past, sending it to the seafloor of the Mediterranean, hoping it would remain there unexplored for all of eternity.

Once I opened that envelope, I knew I'd be changed forever—to see what had shaped my father's life, and possibly his brother's—what had heavily impacted my parents' marriage and their divorce, ultimately altering my childhood, thus my adulthood.

Two years after my father's death, I was thirty-two at the time, I poured myself a fishbowl-size glass of red wine, buoyed the ship of psychosis from the seafloor, and read the transcripts of his mental illness. It had all begun when my mother was pregnant with me. I was born into pain—that of my father and therefore my mother. I sat at my dining room table for two days reading them, and I wept.

I began to understand the complexities of our family and the circumstances that changed our lives. Understanding somehow allowed me to reshape the pain of it in my mind and in my heart. The painful memories associated with the split from my father were still present but now with an element of acceptance that changed everything.

There's a quote from a 1990 *Oprah* episode I'm reminded of. "Forgiveness is giving up the hope that the past could've been any different."[1] This struck me in my teenage years when I first heard it—Oprah was my first real therapist—and I somehow always remembered it, but it wasn't until I read my father's medical records decades later that I was able to integrate that statement fully in my own life. Once I found understanding in the circumstances, I found true forgiveness, both for the actions of my mother and the inaction of my father.

Having reviewed and reflected on my father's life and my own mental health, it seems obvious to me much of the inner angst that plagued him was exaggerated, likely even propagated in repressing an early childhood trauma. It's in the misplaced internal shame and guilt, and containing it across decades, where much psychological damage is done. This is what I feel to be true. We all have pain. We all have trauma somewhere in our life that scars us, some far worse than others, yet we spend much of our lives hiding from the pain and repressing those skeletons that so desperately want to be unearthed, forgiven, and then laid to rest again. Joseph Drumheller explained in *Conscious Lifestyle* magazine,[2] "The definition of suffering is the avoidance of pain. Pain demands attention, and when it is avoided, it repeats itself over and over again. Suffering is the experience of the same repeating pain. Herein resides the grand paradox. In order to overcome suffering, you must experience your pain fully." As I was traversing the globe and confronting myself, I was starting to feel this to be true.

The separation from my father and the pain it caused me is far less significant than many. I know in the grand scheme of the world, my childhood trauma was negligible. Perhaps that's why I feel the need to share my story, *because* my trauma was insignificant and sadly common—a divorce and an out-of-state move—yet it splintered me. It sent me to a dysfunctional version of myself and to a path where I caused much pain to others and myself. Think of all the divorces today (among other traumas) that are likely turning little broken people into big broken people. And in our unwillingness to investigate the pain, instead turning to coping mechanisms, we increase the damage by resisting it. Then we carry it into all aspects of our adult lives and the next generation.

I've done a lot of thinking on mental health—lots of time for introspection when you travel alone. I've decided that, in relation to mental health issues, in my experience, even though we may have a genetic predisposition, it's the parts of life we run from that lead us to call down the dark angels of depression or sometimes to suicide. I've often wondered if the lives of my father and his brother would've been drastically altered if they'd only been able to communicate openly about their trauma or investigate their pain more thoroughly without societal stigma. Unfortunately, we'll never know.

I wonder … if we sought healing and understanding sooner in our lives, could we minimize the probability of genetic predisposition manifesting in us? All these thoughts swirled in my mind as I thought of my new homeless friend, Atílio, and the congruency of our lives, two adult children with questions of our fathers' mental illnesses. I made it to the other side of the street and looked back, seeing Atílio standing there on the corner watching me from where I'd left him. I put up my hand, waving goodbye, and smiled a somber half smile. He waved back at me, but his eyes pled, *Come back, come back.*

There was nothing more I could do. I turned away with a heavy heart and carried on walking toward my bus stop.

I waited … and waited.

The bus pulled up, and I stepped toward the door … but I couldn't get on the bus. I just couldn't. The bus pulled away slowly from the curb, and I stood there wondering why my feet had not been able to lift me and my artistic neck adornments onto the bus. I looked back to see if Atílio was still there. He was.

I crossed the street again, back over to see my new friend waiting at the corner of homeless bread rolls and battered brew. He waited there for me, his eyes lit up like Christmas.

"Listen, let me take you to dinner tonight, my treat—nothing romantic or anything, okay?"

"Wow, really?" he said excitedly.

"I'll bet it's been awhile since you've had a decent meal. I don't know the city very well. You pick—anywhere you want. Meet you here at 7:00 p.m., okay?"

"Yeah, okay," he said softly. His eyes smiled at me with appreciation and relief, like he'd been stranded on an island for years and was now for the first time seeing another human, another human seeing him … maybe it was.

I crossed the street again and caught the next bus, but I never visited the Guinness museum. It never rained either. I just rode around all day on the roof deck of the open-air bus wondering why the world was so fucked up.

We met at the corner at 7:00 p.m. and walked to a quaint restaurant not far down the road. We talked all night about the lives we left, the fathers we'd lost, and how the world would be so much better if we could all shed our pain, living in peace and harmony.

Atílio and I weren't all that different, both living our nomadic lives, trying to make sense of our past before carving out new futures for ourselves. He recognized that his life didn't make sense anymore and allowed himself the space and time to figure it out. He wasn't afraid to face the fear of the unknown. I really admired him in a way; he was so much braver than I was. I never would've ventured out into the world if I thought I'd have to sleep in homeless shelters or on Dublin rooftops; I would've stayed on the hamster wheel, running from myself.

When I left the hostel that morning, I couldn't have known I'd meet a homeless stranger and that we'd connect so deeply at the pub of our fathers' pain. Sometimes the universe or God or synchronicity—whatever you want to call it—places someone in our path because it's the right time for us to face something within that's desperate to come out, the things we'd rather leave hidden because they're dark and painful and murky.

If there's anything I've learned, it's that we shouldn't resist these things when they're brought to the forefront. We should embrace them, welcome them, and explore them—then take it further, immerse ourselves in them, become intimate with them, make love to them. Face it and face it and face it again until they lose their power over us. Only then will we find acceptance and forgiveness. In that space, we rewrite history in a way, shedding the pain we would've carried forward in life. In rewriting the past, we rewrite the future ... and then we are free.

Expansion Exercises

1) Can you review and note any emotional pains from your past that have gone unexplored? Perhaps from childhood? Or within your family? Old relationships?

2) Can you see the benefit of exploring these deeply layered elements of the past and that of your family? How might addressing and understanding your past bring about acceptance and forgiveness in your life?

3) What, if any, powerful, unspoken feelings are you holding about your family members? Friends? Relationships? Colleagues?

4) Can you put words to those feelings and write them down?

5) Envision what it would feel like to release these emotional pains or longstanding resentments. Put words to those feelings.

6) What would it look like to take initiative and broach the unspoken subject with your loved one?

Journal Entry
'Complexities'

CHAPTER 9

Month Six—Portugal

Half a Hippy

If you change the way you look at things,
the things you look at change.
—Wayne Dyer

A few weeks after my encounter with Atílio in Dublin, then circumnavigating Ireland, I hopped a ferry over to France for a reunion with Siggy. It'd been about four months since I left her in silence in India, and we were excited to reconnect. For the most part, I didn't have a plan of where I'd go or when; there were a few exceptions, but I was essentially floating where my heart guided me. I'd come to find, again and again, my heart always led me back to Siggy.

It gets lonely sometimes out on the road, always meeting new people and then saying goodbye. Ireland was especially solitary because I rented a car and toured the countryside on my own. It was the most breathtaking scenery, lush green rolling hills, huge cliffs that dove into the ocean, the incredible rock formations of the giants' causeway; it was beyond spectacular, but it didn't provide the same opportunity to meet people that I'd become accustomed to. I was sleeping in my rental car to save money, so I wasn't getting the regular commotion and interactions I would've had at a hostel or in the city. Like everything that played out though, the unexpected solitude served its purpose.

When I realized though I was only a ferry ride away from my soul sister, I cut my Ireland trip a few days short and made a beeline for the port city. Siggy's notorious for changing plans—a frustrating side effect of her free spirit—so although we discussed a month earlier meeting around this time in France, I knew that until I was actually there, standing in front of her, she was a flight risk.

We'd chosen France because she'd been in the country for a short period with her new boyfriend and wanted to head south through Spain and then into Portugal for a festival they'd purchased tickets for. Yes, it's true, Siggy had fallen in love after I left her in India, and her love led her to Europe. When we'd last seen each other, Europe wasn't in her budget, so when we said goodbye on the Tibetan flagged trail, we had no idea if we'd ever see each other again. You just never know when you say goodbye to someone you meet on the road; it's a big world out there, and solo travelers drift with the wind and the tides.

I was eager to meet Siggy's new love, curious to see what kind of a man my beautiful, carefree, full-of-life soul sister would choose for herself. Sadly enough, I barely got to know him at all; they broke up the day after I arrived, and he decided to leave France suddenly. Siggy and I tried to regroup and consider whether we'd carry on into Portugal or change plans entirely.

After much discussion—and brokenhearted wine drinking— we decided we were meant to attend the festival in Portugal and the now ex-boyfriend was just the catalyst to introduce us to it. Plus, we'd already purchased tickets to this eight-day camping festival, so we decided we'd carry on.

That's the cool part of long-term traveling. If you can let down your need to control everything (which was more difficult than I expected), *where am I going next, when do I go, is transportation booked, what will I do when I get there,* allowing the universe to lead you a bit, all sorts of interesting things happen. You meet people you never would've met and experience things you wouldn't have planned for yourself. You sleep in reed bushes in a two-person tent with a male stranger you've just met … Oh, that's just another crazy Siggy story. I'll save that for another day.

Siggy arranged for us to join in on a ride-share from France to Spain, then another from Spain to Portugal. She even found someone who was going to the same festival, so it was a relief to have transportation all the way to the camping grounds in rural Portugal. She's quite resourceful, my soul sister—a ride-share app, organized hitchhiking. Brilliant invention or convenient pickup for serial killers? It seemed safe enough with ratings and history to review the drivers, but in the end, we were still single women getting into a vehicle with strangers, traveling long distances in countries where we didn't know the language or where we were going. I was a bit nervous about the whole thing. Okay, okay, full disclosure: I was a frantic mess.

Siggy was the crazier of the two of us by far, completely comfortable piling into a car with strangers … maybe because of her age. I, on the other hand, had an exponentially larger viewing history of nightly news. I knew the world was a dangerous place and strangers were not to be trusted. *She's young and naïve. What does she know about these things?* I considered a twenty-four-hour drive with male strangers a risky mode of transportation at best.

It also didn't help that I'd just learned the full nature of this festival after hearing more about it from Siggy's now ex-boyfriend. The festival we were going to was a drug and psytrance festival. Psytrance is kinda like techno music on steroids—new information to me. And a festival where drugs are legal? I'd never heard of such a thing. I couldn't wrap my mind around this concept of legal drug use.

So here we are, Siggy and I waiting impatiently for our overnight ride-share to the drug and psytrance festival in the desert. Agonizing years rolled by, and finally a small, ancient RV arrived. It had a strange, yellowed exterior like the walls of a smokers' house, a rickety door that squeaked when it opened to reveal the slight stench of mold from its first microorganism infestation in 1972. Four young men exited the RV to greet us.

My mind furiously battled itself considering the dangerous possibilities of this scenario. *You've got to be kidding me. No way. People get kidnapped in campers like these, never to be seen again! We're gonna end up buried in a sunflower field on the side of the highway in the Spanish countryside.* Siggy hopped around in excitement at the idea of riding in an RV to this BAM festival in the desert. I now wasn't even convinced I wanted to attend.

I contemplated the situation. The muscles of my bitchy resting face tensed as I sulked about this less-than-ideal situation. Mostly I was angry with myself for not being clear with my own limits of what I considered safe transportation. I was supposed to play the big sister role; I'm the one meant to keep us from doing stupid things. I realized in that moment how I traveled so differently (more cautiously) on my own versus when I traveled with Siggy. The RV, for some reason, seemed infinitely more dangerous than if we'd been riding in a standard car or SUV. My favorite crime drama investigator stood in the corner of my mind shaking his head, *"Bad idea, Eryn. This is a bad idea."*

With reluctance, I reasoned that if I was meant to die that night by whatever incident one prematurely dies of in a 1972 RV with four male strangers on an overnight journey to a drug and psytrance festival, well then, I figured it was just my destiny. I put my trust in God and stepped into 1972. *If it's your time, then it's your time. Oh, go on.*

I prayed a lot that night, laying awake, "protecting" Siggy, aka useless obsessive worrying and keeping watch to make sure the guys weren't rummaging through our bags. Siggy slept like a baby, that trusting soul. I was awake all night.

I'm happy to report we survived the overnight journey, arriving safely to the Portuguese desert. There were no major incidents, incursions, or attacks. We weren't raped, robbed, or buried alive in a sunflower field either. And ya know what? I even liked the guys we rode with, three Italians and one Dutch. They were good people. I felt guilty for thinking so negatively about the whole situation, but well, when you're scared, your mind will, when left to fend for itself, create elaborate fictitious stories. *Look at all these misplaced judgments, Eryn. Didn't we learn about this in Indonesia?*

I write so in depth about fears, because, well … there was an ever-present level of emotional stress that came when every person I met was new and likely of another nationality and therefore unfamiliar; every city, every country, every plate of questionable food, every road, jungle, bus, café, taxi, and guesthouse was a multilayered chasm of unknowns. Even when I presumed I was relatively safe, there was something mentally challenging that came with the sheer vastness of unfamiliarity solo traveling brought, month after month. This is why I have gray hair now. I'm sure of it.

Something monumental happened though as I continually stretched and pushed (sometimes pulled by Siggy) beyond the walls of fear. I saw my own vulnerability exposed, realizing the people that had the opportunity to harm me didn't. Not in hometown America but across the world. Siggy and I were nothing but a speck, a dot, two pixels of life inside an RV roaming on a desert road, plotted on a map, in the country of Portugal on the continent of Europe, far away from her home country and mine, but we were safe.

Despite my own skepticism, with each successive "survival" across India, Sri Lanka, Indonesia, Israel, Italy, Ireland, France, Spain, and Portugal, something inside began to fracture and crack. The encultured paranoia and fear that had been infused into my psyche over thirty-seven years gradually began dissolving. I realized *I* was the one bringing fear to each situation. Me! Not them. I could no longer maintain these walls that had been unconsciously constructed around me. In the wake of these repeated fractures, a different version of me was emerging, a version that knew humanity at its core was good. Light and love were slowly eclipsing my own fear and darkness.

BAM Festival

Here I am at the eight-day drug festival—me, the girl who's never even been high before. I was a little in shock at first; it's a drug festival, a foreign concept to me in all ways. I mean I come from the country where we have a whole war on drugs. Entire shows dedicated to drug busts! A never-ending loop of the "Bad Boys" song ensued ... *Bad boys, bad boys, watcha gonna do, watcha gonna do when they come for you.* A drug festival ... legal ... who knew?

All my life, I'd been programmed: drugs = crime. Remember the antidrug campaign:[1] this is your brain (picture of egg), this is your brain on drugs (fried egg on pavement), any questions? Effective deterrent, I must say. Plus my father had warned me how drugs would ruin my life. I determined early on in my teenage years my life was challenging enough with the unhealthy relationships I kept getting myself into, so I didn't think it was a good idea to push my luck by adding a drug habit.

I didn't smoke my first joint until I was thirty-two but felt nothing except the buzz I was already experiencing from my Cruzan rum and Coke—I mean my fourth rum and Coke, but who's counting? Me, at an eight-day drug festival with 40,000 others? It didn't add up, and I felt a bit out of place. How did I let Siggy talk me into this? Then again, everyone was really nice (stoned), and I was trying not to judge anything too quickly. I pushed aside my preconceived notions of what a drug festival might entail and decided to make the best of it. I did, however, jot down the number of a taxi I saw leaving the compound ... just in case.

I was surprised to see such a variety of informative seminars offered: permaculture, sustainable living, future economics, adobe clay house making, geo-engineering, and conscious democracy to name only a few. These expansion opportunities were unexpected and quite impressive, I thought, for this twenty-four-hour-a-day music festival. I think I left that part out before; yes, blaring psytrance music played all day and all night. There was even thumping in my dreams—or maybe that *was* the psytrance—oh, I don't know. I couldn't tell if it was the hard ground or the heavy beats that kept me up all night.

One lecture in particular caught my attention, psychedelic science and the alternative therapy, aptly named psychedelic psychology. I'd never considered that scientific research was being conducted using drugs proactively in the name of mental health. Pioneering Czech psychiatrist Stanislav Grof was quoted by the Dutch lecturer, Joost Breeksema, saying that, "Psychedelics, used responsibly and with proper caution, would be for psychiatry what the microscope is for medicine or the telescope for astronomy."[2] Joost would carry on to discuss growing evidence that supports psychedelics being helpful with patients who suffer from depression and PTSD. *Hmmmm, really? Really?*

Would I consider doing drugs in the quest for mental health? This question took its first of many loops around the racetrack in my mind.

Acid ?

Internet service was pretty shoddy in the Portuguese desert, so I reached out to my friend Aiden back home. His task was to research the short- and long-term side effects of LSD, the substance discussed at the lecture for possible alleviation of depression.

I hadn't experienced depression since leaving the States. I'd had somber times, sure, excavating the emotions of times past, all the way through death meditations in the Buddhist retreat, but these were momentary. Nothing like the dark angels that had flown with me before, or the heavy burden of the patchwork quilt I'd grown so accustomed to wearing. Perhaps it was because my mind was constantly occupied with new things.

I've come to think that maybe it's the hellacious monotony and stagnation of life that's so damn depressing. It's the carpools crushing us, the debts destroying us, the mundane maddening us, the cubicles confining us. We're not meant to live our lives in these three-walled prisons—I mean cubicles. When we choose careers that pad our bank accounts without nourishing our soul, how *could* we have any other response than mental health decline?

Whatever the reason for my newfound emotional freedom, I wasn't naïve enough to think I'd shed my deep, relenting dark angels. I assumed they'd be back. Perhaps they were napping in the far corners of my mind; I'd worked them pretty hard over the previous twenty years. Even dark angels need to rest.

Aiden got back to me with possible side effects of LSD: Short- and long-term memory loss possible. Occasional reports of people with mental health issues coming back from the high, never the same again. Like a switch turned off in the state of the high, never to be turned on again. *Hmmmm, what causes that, I wonder? Ummm probably a predisposition to mental illness, duh!*

LSD seemed risky, but I was intrigued by the idea that it could be another avenue toward sustained mental health. I knew my father had unwillingly suffered from hallucinations before I even said my first word, and he probably wouldn't understand my voluntarily inducing them. On the other hand, emerging scientific studies are showing it could be of benefit … *Hmmmm.*

BAM offered free onsite drug testing, ensuring the substances purchased were of the purest form. Drug testing for free! They also had a twenty-four-hour onsite psychedelic emergency care clinic to handle any major medical issues. These people were serious about safe drug use! If this American girl was ever gonna partake in a pioneering quest for mental health using LSD, well then, this was the place to do it.

I talked to Siggy about the seminar I attended and my family's mental health history. Psychedelics would be new for both of us, so she couldn't offer any experiential knowledge, but she said she'd support me either way. Dare I tempt fate with my own mental health by trying LSD? I asked myself one final question: *self, do you ever plan on running for public office?* I couldn't start a campaign on lies, and

American voters wouldn't understand this. I got a quick, undeniable internal response, *Hell no.*

"Okay, Siggy. Let's go buy some LSD."

"Whoa, really? You sure, hon?"

"Yeah, let's do this."

We made a cardboard sign that boldly said, ACID?, then made our way to the dance floor of the main tent. We'd seen other people use this method to find a dealer in the days before. What? We didn't know how to buy drugs. I was still singing the "Bad Boys" song, imprints of fried eggs on my brain. I'd never before had to consider how to buy drugs, and they didn't have a psychedelic pharmacy Walgreens pop-up tent.

We decided Siggy would wear the sign. (1) Because I was chicken shit and she wasn't, and (2) because I had a credit card and could bail Siggy out of jail if we were caught up in a drug bust. I felt inevitably the DEA people were hiding out somewhere waiting to swoop in. Decriminalized drugs;[3] I still couldn't believe it.

We entered the dance tent, me scanning the outskirts for undercover DEA agents. *Bad boys, bad boys, watcha gonna do? OMG we're buying hard drugs, we're gonna be in jail soon.* Three minutes after stepping onto the dance floor with our ACID? sign, a woman approached us. We bought three tabs, one for each of us and one to test. Not one DEA agent swarmed in on us—not one! I'd entered an alternate universe.

Tests showed our LSD to be "pure," whatever that means, so at least we knew it wasn't laced with destructive chemicals. We took our tabs and went to find a quiet place on a nature trail, far away from the crowds. In a festival of 40,000 people, quiet places were few and far between. We had a short meditation and blessed our LSD, praying for a positive trip, feeling if we went into the high with a positive intention, we'd be more likely to have good experiences. I realized in that moment what a hippy I was becoming—a drug festival where I'm meditating before my LSD trip? Where had my type A Excel spreadsheet self gone? Perhaps with all this peace, love, and kumbaya influence, I was morphing into a hippy. Okay, okay, maybe only half a hippy.

I wondered if I'd experience any adverse psychological effects. Siggy knew the history of my father and of my concerns, so we promised we'd stay together for the entire trip. I held the tab in my hand, contemplating it one more time. *It's a gamble, Eryn. Could be good, could be disastrous, could be neutral. Only one way to find out* … We clanked our little tabs together like beer steins, *cheers,* placing the tabs under our tongues.

We held hands and walked back toward the festival, sitting on swings dangling from a big oak tree that beckoned us. We rocked back and forth on the swings that held us like arms, waiting for the high to take us—where, we didn't know. The swings released us from their embrace, sending us to a nearby tent where we draped ourselves across an oversized hay bale. An extreme heaviness came over us that made it imperative to be lying horizontal … so we did. We lay like lovers facing each other, staring for eternity into each other's eyes, lost in nothingness. I stroked Siggy's Pocahontas hair, wiping a tear away as it dripped from the corner of her eye. We spoke no words.

Eventually we were shooed out of the event tent for a workshop to begin, and suddenly we were full of energy. I felt so alive and free—like anything was possible. We ventured further into the chaos of the festival, and that's when I began to realize how difficult it would be for Siggy and I to stay together. There seemed to be an internal pushing and pulling that worked to propel us both in different directions, like two blobs of seaweed floating in the ocean, opposing currents pulling us. Everything was so colorful and spectacular. "Look, there's a bird. Siggy, where'd you go? Siggy!"

"I'm here, I'm here," she said.

"OMG look how the sun shimmers on the water. Look, Siggy, look! Siggy, where are you?" I'd hear her faintly in the background of some distant land while standing right next to her, yet unable to find her. *Where are you, Siggy?* Not long after, I wandered off in search of the porta potties, and she came and found me waiting in line, scolding me for leaving her. "Okay, okay, I had to pee. Sorry." It was beyond our control. Leashes. Yes, leashes would've been useful.

Trip Assist

In true American fashion, I had a brilliant business idea during my LSD trip. Lizzy, a friend of Siggy's from Australia, saw us floating around in our Technicolor dreamland and came to check on us. It was good timing too because I'd taken a dark turn as nightfall approached, panicking now at the thought of Siggy and I losing one another.

My mind was agitated because I didn't understand the nature of the high. I still wanted to control it but found myself powerless. Had I hit the plateau and I'd maintain this level of high-ness for the remaining seven hours or would I be spiraling more out of control? Would it be like a roller coaster, with varying degrees of fucked-upedness? The fear of falling further frightened me, and I hadn't thought to ask this question of anyone before we took our tabs. I was coherently aware of these thoughts and questions, but I was unable to articulate them to Lizzy. I descended into a state of fear that churned and shook and whipped around inside me. *What's gonna happen to me if I lose Siggy? Am I gonna end up passed out in a bush with a stranger? What if my mind snaps and I'm lost and alone in the dark amongst 40,000 people? Who will help me? Will I be able to find our tent in the tent-city madness?*

I was scared and anxious and tired of my dirty feet! I missed clean feet! I was tired of this semiarid desert life. Dry, lifeless tumbleweeds rolled by me every single day! And I couldn't take it anymore! I wanted a real bed. I was exhausted after six nights of camping on the hard earthen floor with the constant thumping of psytrance. I was tired of plywood porta potties and outdoor showers, but most of all I was worried something terrible would happen to one of us if Siggy and I lost one another.

Was this the beginning of a trippy, uncontrolled, downward spiral into a dark hole? I became fearful and paranoid—also symptoms of psychosis my father had experienced. But it was too late now. I was trapped inside the high. Resigned in my fear, looking for comfort, I curled up inside a big, dusty, prickly bush, her twiggy arms holding me as I sobbed. *I hate Portugal! They don't even have soft, fluffy bushes to sit and cry in! I don't want to be high anymore. I want macaroni and cheese. I miss my dog!*

Siggy and Lizzy stood there in front of me, both concerned about my deteriorating state. I saw the look on their faces and the questions in their minds. *Seven more hours of this or should we haul her off to the psychedelic emergency care center?* Siggy left the serious contemplation with Lizzy, yet still trying to help in her own trippy way, skipping circles playfully around me and my bush of despair.

Time escaped me as I sat curled in the bush; it could've been five minutes or an hour. Lizzy said with exaggerated cheer, "Hey, ya know what we do when we get upset?" She wore a big smile on her face.

"I don't know. What?" I whimpered with my trembling lips through my streaming tears.

"We change scenery!" she said excitedly with a clown-like expression. She held out her hands to take mine, pulling me from the briars that possessed me. "Hey, let's go on an adventure. Whadda ya say? Look, there's a cool rock!" She pointed over to the shores of the lake and a big stone a few hundred feet away.

I couldn't deny the rock was pretty intriguing. "Whoa, you're right, that *is* a cool rock!" I said with the sincere, excited interest only a high person would understand.

Lizzy skipped off toward the lake, and I followed her. Siggy finished her last circle around the bush of despair, the three of us now skipping merrily toward the lake. I'd forgotten about the *very exciting* rock by the time we arrived to the shore, but my tears had dried, and my temperament completely changed, and that was all that mattered.

I could see it clearly; I'd been tricked out of my sadness and fear, with something as simple as changing scenery, but I'd not been able to do it on my own. And that later got me thinking … maybe that's all we need in life sometimes, is to change the scenery, either literally or figuratively in our mind. If only we can catch our fearful thoughts before they lead us into the prickly bush of despair, we can course-correct ourselves.

That's when the brilliant business idea hit me. "Lizzy you're our *Trip Assist*! Helping others safely navigate the world of psychedelic tripping." Trip Assist … I saw it lit up on the worldwide web of my mind. "Lizzy, I'd rate you five stars and give you a stellar write-up."

As Siggy and I sat on the shore, now in a calmer, serene high, we watched the trees in the distance across the lake. They were breathing, their trunks exhaling oxygen. I watched in amazement. *Whoa.* Their branches for arms reached to the heavens, begging in unscreamed pleas to be understood and valued, *help us, please, help us,* questioning how those on earth could poison them with the arrogance and disregard of chemical poisons and pollution. Although Siggy and I were surely experiencing it differently, we both marveled at the organic *aliveness* of the forest as the trees moved in unison, *inhale, exhale, inhale, exhale,* their breath so perfectly timed with the others. *Whoa, trippy.* The message was clear. We must save them.

By 3:00 a.m., nine hours after placing the tabs on our tongues, the effects were finally wearing off. Siggy and I cuddled on Astroturf grass like koala bears in a BAM desert café. We gorged ourselves on high-calorie comfort foods, celebrating our survival. We'd survived the hallucinogenic trip into the unknown, now returning to our roots here on Mother Earth.

Conclusions

I don't believe there were any lasting effects, positive or negative in the way of my mental health in trying LSD. There was nothing glaringly evident of benefit, so I would consider it a neutral experience, feeling incredibly fortunate that I can say that. It could've taken me to a dark place from which I couldn't return.

Generally speaking, I've come to think it's best to live our lives and find healing in our natural, unaltered states, without the use of any drugs, prescription or otherwise. Looking back at my old life, I wasn't a part of any drug culture, but I was using outside sources as numbing agents; alcohol, excessive television, food, and sleep were some of my favorites. No one is perfect, and moderation is important in all aspects of life, but I think if we take drugs or eat excessively or watch seven seasons of *Dexter* in three weeks (I did this!), then perhaps we should explore our internal environments that are propelling us toward these habits that, ultimately, keep us from full and abundant lives.

Upon reflection, I see in my old life I was missing a deep, knowing sense of self-love and self-respect. This was the root of all my pain and the coping strategies I adopted. In my *not* acknowledging this, I turned away from my own problems, individually and in my relationships, distracting myself with these external fillers. I think many suffer from this low-level sense of unworthiness, an unexplainable void. I'm starting to wonder if it's inherent in all of us as humans, an existential loneliness. This causes us to reach out in various unhealthy ways, even when we know we're damaging our bodies with our habits, sometimes our soul with our choices. I wonder … Are we all just trying to fill the deep longings of the soul with external sources when we should be looking inward to our intuitive, deepest knowing?

I find lessons now in *all* I experience, and in this LSD trip, I came to see clearly several things. Firstly, if I'm overwhelmed in emotion, I'll make efforts to change the scenery in my mind, which could include physically changing locations or perhaps finding a quiet place to meditate and recalibrate my thoughts. Secondly, we must protect our earth home. We have been given this beautiful gift to inhabit, and humankind is systematically destroying it with our ignorance, arrogance, and disrespect. If each of us makes small changes in our lives, we can, and we must, make a difference. Finally, although I don't want to promote drug use and my publisher has advised that I caution you against it, if you're going to venture into the realm of hallucinogenic drug use, find yourself a good Trip Assist. Just in case. Never underestimate the power of a good Trip Assist!

I do feel it important to mention, I was surprised to see that over the entire eight days at BAM, with 39,999 other people, sharing outdoor showers, porta potties, long lines for food, and tent cities one on top of the other, not once did I witness any fighting or aggressive behavior … not once! I doubt the same could be said for a rock concert, let alone an eight-day festival where alcohol was the primary stimulant. On that note, I think I'll go pour myself a glass of red wine while I ponder the next chapter. See, another hypocrisy. I'm not perfect; I'm just observing the world.

Expansion Exercises

1) In the height of an emotional response, what can you do to change the scenery in your mind? Would you consider removing yourself for several minutes to calm yourself before reacting? Perhaps even changing physical locations if necessary to calm your emotions? Would this allow for a more rational response?

2) What other effective strategies can you use to remove the heat of your own emotion from a difficult situation?

3) When you feel an emotional response rising within you, can you bring awareness to that feeling while it's happening? Work to find the root cause of the emotion?

4) Environment: can you bring awareness to the idea that the earth is a precious place and that we would be wise to respect and take care of it?

5) What steps would you be willing to take in your life to support the repair and continuation of a healthy planet?

Journal Entry
'Trippy'

CHAPTER 10

Month Eight—Brazil

Quantifying the Immeasurable

For those who believe, no proof is necessary.
For those who disbelieve, no amount of proof is sufficient.
—St. Ignatius De Loyola

Interesting how this trip unfolded for me, choosing locations based on feeling and intuition rather than a well-thought-out pre-organized trip around the world. I'd not yet considered visiting South America and truthfully hadn't felt *the call* to go there at all, until one day, well, it called me.

About six months into my trip after spending a month with Siggy, I was exhausted and eager to be in one place for a while, so I decided to visit my friend Hayley in London. She's the friend I met before leaving the United States who encouraged me to make sure I wasn't running from anything by choosing to travel, if you remember. Now she was home living in London, and I was never so excited to visit someone I knew and unpack my bags for a few weeks. We made dinner together and listened to music. I relaxed on her couch like I would've in my own home long ago. Traveling was great. Meeting new people from all around the world was amazing. Exploring unfamiliar territories and cultures was incredibly expanding, but nobody tells you how hard it is. The guesthouses, strange food, uncomfortable beds, carrying everything you own on your back, and moving around in unfamiliar places. After a while I just wanted to have a meaningful conversation with someone I'd known longer than an hour and cook something delicious in a real kitchen. I made myself at home.

One morning I awoke from a dream, sitting up in bed with this intense *knowing* that I was supposed to help a family member back home. He'd been on my mind lately, with his increasing disabilities that left him now nearly full-time in a wheelchair. Concerns were mounting because their current rental house couldn't be modified to accommodate a wheelchair, and life was becoming increasingly difficult. The family wanted to purchase a house but was struggling with the down payment. Let's face it, coming up with substantial sums of money is challenging for any family, but with ongoing medical expenses and surgeries, it was seemingly out of reach. In my dream though, an idea came to mind; I could start an online fundraising site to see if we could rally others to help raise funds.

The site went live, and within three days we'd raised $3,000. Every morning, I woke, eager to see if we'd raised money overnight; and each day we did. I wept in Hayley's dining room seeing the plan was actually working. Within no time we were up to $15,000. Hundreds of people came together to help this family in need—all stemming from a simple dream. It was no big deal, really. All I did was set up a page on a website, but well … I'd spent much of my life held in the cycle of inertia—a depressive's way of coping, inaction. I'd been distant from this part of my family, both geographically and emotionally, since childhood, and it just felt good to have an idea, to act on it (for once!), and in the process connect with family that I'd long ago drifted from. Soon after, they purchased a home that suited their special needs.

This happening during my visit to Hayley drew her into their story, leading her to say, "Well, if you really want to help him, you should take him to see John of God in Brazil."

"John of who?" I asked.

Hayley began to tell me of the times she'd been to see a healer years earlier and that he was performing miracles. I hadn't planned on visiting South America necessarily; I mean I'd hardly planned anything, so it hadn't crossed my mind. I felt fortunate to have made it out of Asia safely and was happily adjusting to European travel. I didn't want to push my luck, having heard so many dangerous stories from South America.

Hayley carried on about her experiences with the spiritual healer, and although I trusted my friend, I was extremely skeptical. A man with a second-grade education who supposedly channels spirits from deceased doctors, healers, and saints was bringing real-life healing to people in need? I discarded the whole idea, unable to believe in something so outlandish, but it continued to nag at me, *what if, what if*? I wanted to believe my friend and her fantastic story, but a legitimate spiritual healer? Really? I couldn't comprehend it on any tangible scale.

I took to the Internet, finding that Oprah had been to see John of God in Brazil, and Wayne Dyer[1] claimed to have been healed remotely by the same man. Remotely? I'm embarrassed to admit this, but my friend's words weren't enough to convince me; I wanted a renowned Western figure to show me this healer was legit.

I was so skeptical I even organized a phone consultation with my American doctor[2] back in the States. He's an integrative medical doctor focusing on holistic healing, so he's not your typical American MD. I was curious if he'd ever experienced any sort of energy healing and what his thoughts might be. Surprisingly he told me that he *had* participated in energy healing and had an extremely positive experience. He cautioned me though, telling me that energy work initiates healing of the *whole person,* including mind, body, and spirit; it may or may not show itself in the physical sense. *Uh, huh, uh huh … I think I understand … Umm, maybe not. Huh?*

There were two people in my life who were struggling with physical disabilities and illnesses, so I was holding them both in mind while considering Hayley's suggestion to visit Brazil. To be honest, I wasn't even sure either person would be open to my exploring this on their behalf; I hadn't brought it up to them yet, fearing their skepticism might persuade me. By this stage though, I'd done so much research on this man, the healer, I was intrigued by what I was reading and out of sheer curiosity was now feeling compelled to go. Plus, I was traveling anyway, so why not visit Brazil? I wouldn't have a chance of persuading them to join me if I didn't see something miraculous first. I would've felt it irresponsible to even suggest it. Their lives were challenging enough without an unnecessary trip to Brazil. But now I was feeling the pull to go … just to see. If I happened to get any sort of healing in the process, then that was a bonus.

I planned five weeks in Abadiania, Brazil, thinking I'd investigate and observe the first two weeks. If I saw anything miraculous, I'd try to persuade my loved ones to join for the remaining three weeks. I knew still that would be a long shot, not only from a logistical standpoint but also in the way of belief. It was possible, even probable, they wouldn't consider it. Most of us are strongly fixed to our belief systems, and my visiting an energy healer in Brazil? I knew that was taking people way beyond their comfort zones when it came to beliefs.

I considered my timing to end my European travels, cancelled the monthlong silent retreat I'd signed up for in the Nepalese monastery, organized a *pousada* (guesthouse), and booked a flight for month eight of my trip; then I told my loved ones I was going on their behalf.

The Concept of Beliefs

I thought a lot about my beliefs during this portion of my trip— and the general concept of how one comes to take on beliefs. I was forced to really. I'd been placed (and voluntarily remained) inside the box of Christianity from such a young age, I couldn't even allow myself to believe in this unfathomable healer that I was now speeding toward on the wing and a prayer of a Boeing 777.

My mind went through an unending loop of skeptical and sacrilegious thoughts. *How can you allow yourself to believe any man has the ability to heal? He's a snake oil salesman at best, exploiting the sick and dying at worst. How can I possibly believe in this? This goes against all logic and sensible thought. This will likely be a total waste of money and time!*

Then I remembered watching the Wayne Dyer video before my visit, listening to his experience. He was quite convincing … and I feel he's credible and knowledgeable as one of our twenty-first-century spiritual gurus of the West. When Wayne Dyer said he was healed remotely and it was orchestrated by John of God—not even in Abadiania, Brazil—at his home in Hawaii, well I couldn't turn away from that.

Beliefs—where do they come from? I began dissecting and probing at this question. We usually don't give much thought to why we believe certain things. We simply believe what we believe, usually feeling with our full self that it's the truth, whatever *it* is. Most of the time, we're brought up in a family, household, culture, or religion that instills in us as young children our beliefs. We adopt certain prejudices, rituals, superstitions, our dress, diet, and nutritional habits. We take on all of these characteristics, mannerisms, and "truths" from our early environments, and just like that, our belief systems take root.

Caroline Myss, PhD,[3] renowned best-selling author, medical intuitive, and mystic, writes, "It is extremely challenging, and often very painful, to evaluate our own personal beliefs and separate ourselves from those that no longer support our growth … These points at which we must choose to change or to stagnate are our greatest challenges … The process of spiritual development challenges us to retain the tribal influences that are positive and to discard those that are not" (Myss 1996, p. 110).

Until traveling, I never cared to explore or research other belief systems, especially when it came to religion. Generally we gravitate toward reading or involving ourselves only in that which expands on or consolidates what we already believe. Rarely do we want to embrace an idea or belief that challenges our own because we have a fear (whether conscious or unconscious) that it might undermine our deeply held beliefs that bring us comfort or solace. This is why I resisted so fiercely in my first month of travel the idea of studying Buddhism. "I'm strong in my Christian faith," I said to Siggy. Yet here I am in month eight on my way to consult a variety of healing entities working through one man, a spiritual healer, in the middle of nowhere, Brazil. I decided not to prejudge the trip and to remain open to whatever experiences lay ahead of me.

At the time I visited Brazil, I was clinging precariously to the cliff of Christianity, yet afraid to let go because it was so fundamental to the way I made sense of the world and myself. Without Christianity, what foundation was there? Although I hadn't attended church regularly or Christian school since childhood, the God-based bedrock I stood on was firm … firm, in its own shaky, dysfunctional way. My traveling to Brazil, though, left me questioning everything. How could I believe certain immeasurable ideas to be true while dismissing others? Some may want empirical evidence before believing in God; others don't need that. So, how do we determine which unquantifiable beliefs we'll give credence to and which ones we won't?

I considered the limitations of my own beliefs—of all beliefs. I considered love, intuition, fate, God, a higher power, the devil, miracles, psychics, angels, the power of prayer, heaven, hell, karma, religious texts, ghosts, luck, past lives, and aliens; and how many of us believe wholeheartedly in at least one of these immeasurable phenomena with no proof of existence?

When I began questioning my beliefs, I felt deep inner resistance to my own questions. I was defensive even. I wanted so badly for my beliefs to be "right." But what if I allowed the possibility, for example, that there was a simple man in central Brazil healing others and having a palpable, tangible effect? If I believed this truly, my whole worldview would have to change; and how could this fundamental belief change so dramatically without my very self-identity cracking and changing too? But look at me; I've gone astray skipping like a stone across the choppy waters of *belief* ... I digress.

The Man behind the Healing

João Teixeira de Faria[4] is internationally known as John of God, or João de Deus—a name given to him, not one he assigned himself. At sixteen, as the story goes, Joao left his poor family to find work in a nearby town but was not successful. He sat by a creek and was greeted by a spirit whom he later determined was Saint Rita of Cassia. The spirit instructed him to go to a church in town where people would be expecting him. Young João didn't understand the meaning or why he should go, but he went anyway and found that church members were, indeed, expecting him. He then lost consciousness and woke several hours later, apologizing for passing out from hunger.

To João's surprise, a senior member told him he had not merely passed out but that he had incorporated the spirit of King Solomon and that over his three unconscious hours, he had healed people and performed amazing surgeries. João had no recollection of the three hours and naturally thought it was a mistake. Afterward, he was given a meal, and more discussion took place between him and the clergy, and João began to reflect on the possibility that it could be true (johnofgod-healing.com para. 5, 6, and 7). This was the beginning of his career as a healer, and he's been performing healings consistently over the past forty years. It's reported that John of God is considered by some to be the most powerful unconscious medium alive today and possibly the best-known healer of the past two thousand years.

João says openly, "I do not cure anybody. God heals, and in His infinite goodness permits the Entities to heal and console my brothers. I am merely an instrument in God's divine hands."

Physicians have been to visit John of God to determine the whys, whats, and hows of the healing interventions that happen at the Casa de Dom Inacio. Most leave there perplexed themselves, struggling to quantify what they've seen. Dr. Jeff Rediger,[5] licensed physician, board-certified psychiatrist with a master of divinity from Princeton, traveled to Abadiania as a complete skeptic. He said, "I went to collect lab reports and radiological exams, photos of people that report to be physically healed and to see if the reports can document that. If it is true, it is a world view destroyer for me because it means that things are happening that I don't know how to explain."

I'd read all the articles, watched the documentaries, seen the testimonials, and done countless hours of online research … the jury was still out.

How It Works

Healings are free. That's everyone's first question: how much does it cost? Susan Casey, journalist, editor in chief at *O* magazine, and author of *The Wave,* visited John of God, reporting, "He says a real healer cannot charge. If you charge for something that is not yours (because it's not him that's doing the healing), that power goes away. It's not yours to charge for."[6]

Healing sessions are held at the Casa de Dom Inacio[7] three days a week, and I estimated about 1,200 people per day saw him, and this is how the man dedicates his life, every week of the year. The entities working through Joao often prescribe herbal remedies, simple passiflora capsules that have been made more potent with specific healing energies. This remedy is sold to those who can afford it for about $10 per bottle and is given to those who are in real financial hardship. Like any town though, there are gift shops, places to indulge yourself, and a few high-end guesthouses, so if you want to spend a lot of money, you certainly can. I had a private room and bathroom in a clean, well-kept guesthouse nestled on the edge of the Brazilian plateau, owned and run by Austrians. From my balcony, I lay in a hammock inhaling the clean, warm air and listened to the whirring, chirping, and buzzing of nature all around me, all for twenty dollars a night and less than ten dollars a day for food—very inexpensive cost of living.

The first day, I wanted to observe my surroundings and see if I could figure out what was happening. Videos I'd seen showed visitors having their eyes scraped with scalpels or forceps forcibly shoved up their noses, among other procedures … all with no anesthesia. I was not excited to know I'd soon be witnessing all this in person. No longer was I protected by the safety of distance, watching from behind my laptop. Here I was, now at the casa, seeing the small stage in the front of the gathering hall where it all happened. It suddenly became very real, the gravity of what I was about to witness, substantial.

I took a seat in the middle of a row, midway back from the stage. I didn't know how it worked, but I didn't want to be selected from the crowd to have a physical procedure. I was safer farther from the stage. *No way you're picking me out of the crowd, mister!* Of course I'd come to see that no one is singled out. It doesn't work like that. People volunteer, but I wasn't sure of anything at first, and I wasn't taking any chances he'd want to shove that sharp, pointy thing up my nasal cavity and into my brain. *No, no, no, no, nooooo.*

Many visitors had the good sense to hire a guide, because it's quite chaotic, but I decided I'd go it alone since I had ample time to check it all out. In each session, morning and afternoon, people volunteered to go up on stage and receive physical "surgeries" from John of God—rather from the *entities* working through John of God. Terms I'd never used before like *entities* and *psychic surgeries* would now become everyday topics of conversation here in Abadiania.

I watched in amazement and disbelief as eyes were scraped, bodies were cut open, and, yes, forceps were shoved up noses. All this was done with *no anesthesia or sterilization.* My mind kind of exploded a bit as I watched people stand on stage, calmly receiving their "surgeries" without so much as a flinch, like they'd become entranced, entering an altered state of consciousness. Something inexplicable was going on.

Dr. Rediger, doctor and theologian mentioned before, witnessed similar physical surgeries and talked to patients during and after surgery. He saw firsthand people being cut on with no flinching or any pain whatsoever. He said, "I've heard some people use the term spiritual anesthesia. I have no way to understand that."[8]

It was a chaotic environment with people of all ages packing every inch of the small, open-air gathering hall. Men, women, children, mostly European and a few Americans, were in attendance; I'd guess about half were foreigners, and the other half were Brazilians who'd bussed in from different parts of the country. Every seat was taken, and every inch of floor space held a person eager to soak up any healing energy that emanated from this man. Much of what was said was in Brazilian Portuguese, so we'd sit sometimes for an hour not understanding a word, but eventually a translator would take the microphone and direct us or share their testimonial. Many of the casa workers were previous patients that had been healed and had now come to volunteer or work as guides.

Surrounded by so many who were here making this profound effort to prolong their lives, there was a sense of heaviness and urgency. The sad reality was that almost everyone there was suffering from a debilitating disease, psychological disorder, or nearing the end of life. Women with shaved heads sat beside me, presumably going through chemo, a man with Tourette's syndrome regularly blurted obscenities while standing in line, people pushed their loved ones along in wheelchairs. Desperation was all around. Despite this, most were amazingly calm and patient, even with the sheer volume of people spilling outside the building onto sidewalks and benches. We all moved around one another in relative harmony, hoping for healing.

Although my doubts remained, it became evident that if I was going to participate in what was happening—whatever *it* was—I'd have to drop down from my analytical mind and settle into the heart space, allowing myself to enter the unknown. I remembered what my friend Haley said, "Try to have faith and remain open. This healing is miraculous and will change the course of your life, if you have the courage to allow it. Surrender your ego and surrender to divine will, and, in time, you will receive your blessing and your healing."

In the second half of day two, I checked out from my skeptical mind, opened my heart, and joined the others waiting in the "first-time line." I followed hoards of people into a back room eager to see what happened beyond the closed blue doors. Framed pictures of Jesus and other saints hung all around on various walls. All who entered treated it as a sacred space, shuffling slowly forward in silence past hundreds of seated people, eyes closed, meditating in the current of energy.

John of God sat in a simple, oversized wooden chair with cushioned arms at the far end of the largest "current room." It wasn't opulent or extravagant, but he was slightly elevated as you might expect if you were coming to kneel before a priest. I watched the others before me pass in front of John of God, each encounter lasting only seconds. I inched closer to the front and finally stood before him as he held his hand out to hold mine. I looked into his eyes as I'd been instructed to do. A translator stood by, yet no words were spoken. His eyes, although intently held with mine, were foggy and distant, like he was lost in another world. I stared deeply into the pale gray fog looking for answers to questions unknown. I was sizing him up.

He released my hand, scribbled something illegible on a scrap of paper, and handed it to me. I was politely dismissed and followed the others out of the room. *What, that's it? Three seconds? No shining lights coming from above? No spasms of my body indicating an internal shift? That's it?* The paper was my "prescription" for an herbal supplement, which I purchased at the casa "pharmacy".

The morning of the third day, I entered what's called the "second-time line" that would lead me to John of God again. I couldn't report back to my loved ones if I hadn't immersed myself in the happenings of the healings myself. I listed my top three ailments I hoped would be healed, including:

1. Heal my hypothyroid condition
2. Cure my longstanding depression (even though I hadn't felt it in ages, I assumed it was lying dormant and would return)
3. Provide complete emotional healing from childhood traumas and *The Past*

When I passed before John of God, I gazed again into the gray fog of his otherworldly eyes and handed him my list that had been translated into Portuguese. He gave me another scrap of scribbled paper that the translator told me was for psychic surgery. *Say whaaaaaat?*

The afternoon session of the third day—the last opportunity for healing that week—I entered the psychic surgery line, and we all followed along into the same back room I'd entered before. My flowing white skirt trailed the tile floor, and I stared down at my sandaled toes in solemn contemplation, walking slowly behind the others. Was something monumental about to happen to me in this event I could hardly comprehend, a psychic surgery?

We were directed to an area beyond John of God's oversized chair and took our seats in church pews. I was alone as I could ever be, eight long months on the road, now here in small-town, Brazil, knowing no one yet connected to a hundred others of varying nationality with the common thread of hopeful healing.

I took a deep breath, closed my eyes, and sat quietly holding the intention of healing in my heart. *Ground control to Major Tom ... deactivate the analytical mind, drop into the heart space, commence healing.*

John of God walked around us speaking his native Brazilian Portuguese, blessing us while the entities performed their healing. It was a surreal experience, not knowing what he was saying, or what, if anything, I was supposed to feel. We just sat receiving—what exactly, I wasn't sure.

After "surgery," we were all escorted to another room where a prayer was recited and we sat meditating for fifteen minutes. Then we left the room and were told to follow the specific post-surgery instructions. These included complete bed rest for twenty-four hours; we were not to use phones, read, use the Internet, or leave our rooms and we were to sleep as much as possible. The guesthouses were set up for this, and meals were provided in our rooms, along with anything we needed for twenty-four hours after surgery. I slept, I ate, I slept, I ate, and I slept some more. Whatever he'd done, although I couldn't define it, had severely taxed my body, and I slept as if heavily sedated.

Dr. Rediger experienced something quite inexplicable when he was at the casa. He spontaneously began bleeding from an incision on the left side of his chest one day while walking down the street—it seemed to appear from nowhere. He said, "I've been to seminary, medical school, residency in psychiatry, and nothing had prepared me to understand (this incision)." He had *not* had physical surgery. No surgery! Spontaneous incision and bleeding! *Say whaaaaaat?* He later said, when asked about that particular incident six years later, "I have no idea what happened there. I mean, it changed everything in my life, but I don't understand it yet ... I don't have a medical explanation for it. My life has been turned upside down in many ways. It changed many things for me. I'm a different person now."[9]

After my psychic surgery (I can hardly believe I so freely use this term), the time came for me to call my loved ones in need back home. I'd come here for them, but there was nothing definitive I could tell them. I'd not seen anyone leave a wheelchair to walk. I'd seen people cut on and stitched up with unnaturally little blood loss right there on stage. Surprisingly, I was now eager to sit on the floor directly in front of the stage to see better what was happening. Still, I couldn't determine if miracles were truly taking place, although I felt like something tangible was happening in an intangible way.

Grrr. My intellectual mind desperately grasped for ways to define this. I wanted to talk to those that had physical surgeries, but they were wheeled away to a back room for recovery. It was impossible to find them again with so many people, all wearing white.

I spoke to my loved ones in America for whom I'd made the trip to Brazil. One said it was too far beyond what they were able to consider and that it went against their beliefs as Christians. They decided they wanted no part in it. I respected their decision, but it led me to think again about beliefs, wondering how someone with such a desperate physical condition could turn down a potential healing opportunity (that could be done remotely) because beliefs held them so firmly to disbelief and fear of sacrilege. I understood it in a way, as I'd had plenty of my own looping skeptical thoughts before arriving in Brazil. And geez, I even resisted studying Buddhism in month one of my trip, the most peaceful and innocuous of all religions, so I knew this was a stretch. On the other hand, not trying seemed unimaginable too. The second loved one *was* open-minded to energy healing and happy to travel with me into the bizarre healing journey of surrogate psychic surgeries. *Surrogate what?* I know, I know. I can't make this stuff up.

The following week, I participated in another psychic surgery. This time it was on behalf of my loved one. I would be the conduit in Brazil for my friend in the USA to receive psychic surgery just as Wayne Dyer had received healing remotely in his home in Hawaii. My friend and I talked extensively about issues related to her rare health condition, and I had them translated into Portuguese as I'd done the week before for my issues. Once again, I meditated in the current room, holding my friend in mind and heart with the intention to be a channel for her healing. I still wasn't quite sure how to be a channel for her healing or what it meant exactly, but I was quickly opening to these ideas that were once foreign to me. The Brazilian cast his healing prayers over me while my friend simultaneously rested in her home to receive healing in the States. Then we both followed the strict postoperative guidelines for twenty-four hours.

When the twenty-four hours was up, I talked to my friend back home to see how she was doing, if she felt any effects. Nothing to report.

We followed the same surrogate surgery routine the week after. This time something miraculous *had* happened. Since early childhood, my friend had been blind in one eye, and after the second surgery, now she could see! *Whaaaaaat? No ... really?* From thousands of miles away, she explained all this to me. I listened with my astonished ears, crying together our long-distance tears. Something *had* happened.[10]

Dr. Rediger wrote of his overall experience, "My interpretation of what happened to me is this. In short, we all matter, far more than we typically have a clue about and love is what is real. We tend to believe in what we can see and touch, and believe that the world as it appears to be, is the real world. On the basis of my experience I've come to believe that reality is both revealed and concealed by the world we see with our eyes and that none of us are who we appear to be ... There's something that settled in my heart that I feel like I know something true. I think what I really believe is that we really do matter more than we have a clue about; every one of us does. There's something unrepeatable and good about who we are. There's something mysterious about being human. I believe that our suffering comes in some way from *not getting it* about the dignity and goodness of what our individual life means and I believe that we also may often feel alone. We're not alone in any way like we believe we are. I think we are more connected. There's a dignity and goodness that we bring into the world and the point of our lives is to get it about that."[11]

I've come to feel Dr. Rediger is right; there's something we're *not getting* about the preciousness of our own lives and the depth of our own meaning. When I take a moment to really contemplate and integrate that sentiment, recognizing the insignificance of the minutiae we typically fill our lives with, it propels me to make deep and lasting changes. It makes me want to be a better person.

It bothered me immensely to know that some people would experience remissions and recoveries from healings at the casa while others wouldn't. It vexed me and perplexed me; saddened and maddened me. Why wouldn't everyone be healed? My heart searched and searched for answers that would satisfy my analytical mind; they battled one another furiously over this question, why some but not others?

Looking back, knowing more now than I knew then when in Brazil, I believe we all carry deep emotional, psychological, and spiritual wounds that can play major roles in the manifestation of physical diseases, shaping our individual futures. We aren't giving enough credence or recognition to our internal suffering, and this precipitates many of our physical ailments. I'm certain now, for example, that I created my thyroid disorder—I feel it deeply. I know it to be true. Years and years of internal angst and pain, inauthentic living and suppressed feelings, how could it not express itself physically? I wasn't listening to the cries of my soul, and eventually it screamed out in physical expression of disease. There were physical signs early on, even in my teenage years, but I didn't recognize their importance. I didn't understand it then. So in relation to why some heal and others don't, if emotional stress is the root of our disease, it's reasonable then to propose that we cannot experience physical healing of our ailments until we forgive, accept, and dissolve away the old wounding. I now intuitively feel this to be true and have personally experienced it.

Caroline Myss, PhD, writes in *Anatomy of the Spirit*, "During the past four decades an enormous amount of information has become available on the role of the mind in health. Our attitudes play a tremendous role in creating or destroying the health of our bodies. Depression, for example, not only affects our ability to heal but directly diminishes our immune system. Anger, bitterness, rage and resentment handicap the healing process, or abort it entirely. There is great power in having a will to heal, and without that internal power, a disease usually has its way with the physical body. With all these new realizations, the power of consciousness is being given an official place within the medical model of health and illness … Healing requires unity of mind and heart, and generally it is the mind that needs to be adjusted to our feelings, which too often we have not honored in the daily choices we have made." (Myss 1996, pg. 244 and 245)

If there's one recurring theme I come to again and again as I travel inwardly and outwardly, it's that the mind is far more powerful than most of us believe and the state of our mind has direct effect on the body. When we take steps toward healing wounds of the emotional and spiritual realms of self, we will then have a better chance at naturally regenerating our bodies.

What of the healing I requested for myself in Abadiania—hypothyroidism, depression (and fear of its return), and complete healing from emotional wounds? Although symptoms didn't magically evaporate into the tropical Brazilian air, I was led to further experiences in my trip that brought about complete healing of all my emotional wounds, leaving no scars (i.e., my past no longer dictates my behavior that defines my future). I have full knowledge that I am master of my destiny. Whether I slide back into depression or not, that *will be in my control.* "One is one's own refuge,"[12] as the Buddha said in the Dhammapada. I take that to mean I can choose to be a haven for myself, mentally and physically, or I can create a degenerative environment within. I take it to mean I can save myself! *Yesssss.* I am in the final stages of healing my thyroid naturally,[13] now stable on only one-sixth of the thyroid medication that I'd been taking for the previous ten years. This is extremely rare to succeed in drastically reducing thyroid medication. I continue making efforts toward healing and hope to come off medication completely. Would all this be true had I not visited John of God? Who can say?

My new and dear friend Christian, a third-time visitor to Abadiania, told me once in relation to John of God healings, "We're talking about things happening beyond our comprehension and on a whole other dimension than what we can fathom." It took me time, but eventually I came to feel Christian's sentiment. Perhaps there are certain things going on in this world that we simply cannot grasp with our intellects yet may still be true; maybe it's even arrogant of us to think we *should* be able to understand and quantify all truths. Finally I settled into a place of peace about it, realizing we're not *meant* to understand—not at this stage in our human evolution anyway. Maybe it was never my place to try to quantify the immeasurable.

~ Rest in peace, my dear Christian. You are not forgotten. ~

Expansion Exercises

1) What do you believe? This could relate to what you believe about yourself. *I'm not good enough.* It could relate to your values. Or your religious beliefs.

2) Why do you believe in each? Where do these beliefs originate?

3) Are these beliefs authentic to who you truly are, or are they deeply ingrained from childhood and societal conditioning?

4) Why do you give credibility to one belief while dismissing another? Could this be a limiting view? Dig deep.

5) In dismissing an idea or concept without exploration, could that be holding you back from new experiences and expansion?

6) What would it look like to open your mind to new concepts and ideas that you would've previously dismissed? Even seeing a movie you wouldn't normally see or reading a book you wouldn't typically read?

7) When we automatically dismiss something, does this stem from love or fear?

Journal Entry
'Beyond'

CHAPTER 11

Months Ten to Twelve—Tanzania/Rwanda

Detour to Humility

I believe that to meet the challenge of our times, human
beings will have to develop a greater sense of universal
responsibility. Each of us must learn to work not for his or
her self, family or nation, but for the benefit of all mankind.
— His Holiness the XIV Dalai Lama

After my time in Brazil, I hopped my return flight to London
so I could spend the holidays in comfort with my friend
Hayley while I figured out my next move. Brazilian visa requires
that you have an exit ticket before entering their country, so I
couldn't take my one-way flight, figure-it-out-later approach, as I'd
become accustomed. Truth be told, I was also feeling the pull to
return to London for the possibility of a romantic connection with
an Englishman.

I'd met him long before actually, on a ferry in Indonesia early
on in my trip, but he was returning home shortly thereafter, so we
had little time to connect. Through the magic of Facebook though,
he noticed many months later that I was in London (the first time
before Brazil), and bing, bang, boom, we found ourselves on a date
to visit a donkey in an old English pub in the country. *A donkey in a
pub, say what?* I know, I know. I saw an article in the paper one day

while riding the London tube and knew I had to visit. I'm a sucker for all things furry—it was my idea. Pair a cute donkey in a pub with a pint of cider and an English gentleman, and you've got yourself a beautiful day.

When the Englishman picked me up to go visit Becky the donkey, he said, "You look so ... so alive." I melted a little in that moment, I really did. *I look alive. Wow, I do? I do! I feel alive!* I think it might have been the nicest compliment anyone has ever given me. I felt alive. Like I'd somehow revived myself from the dead and was taking my first breath of new life; dug myself up from six feet under; jolted my heart back to life with electrical currents of growth and cathartic healing. I was alive!

He couldn't have known the power of that compliment or how important it was that I *felt* alive. He couldn't have understood how incredible it was that my *aliveness* was visible to the outside world when before I'd been a mere shadow of myself. I'd been living for decades, but rarely had I *felt* alive. I was regaining my sense of self with every step on foreign soil, and he saw it in me. And so it goes, the Englishman and I began something that day—over beer, a feisty donkey, and being alive. Then we continued the connection via Skype across continents during my time in Brazil. The beginnings of, or at least the possibility of love was sprouting like buds on a long-abandoned railroad track.

At month nine of my travels, I felt emotionally grounded enough (finally!) to take the idea of a new relationship s-l-o-w-l-y, without too many forward-projecting attachments or expectations. I'd never been able to do that before. There'd always been a force emanating from inside, propelling me toward attached relationships that I didn't understand or have control over. I couldn't risk falling into the abyss of love's doped-up addiction so quickly and irresponsibly like I'd done so many times before, having lived most of my life from the grips of an attachment disorder. Eryn + Man = Happiness. I was grateful to have mended myself, detaching from my propensity to attach. *Go, me! Emotional independence.*

That said, I was excited at the prospect of a new relationship forming, but I also knew it was about time to give real consideration to the second and very important part of my journey—finding a more purpose-driven creative endeavor that I could immerse myself in, forging a new path forward. I'd been away so long already I couldn't just float around anymore; I'm too American for that. Now that I was feeling more whole and healed, I needed to find purpose again. I thought that would come in the form of writing a book, but I didn't have any fully formed ideas yet as to what I'd write.

The convergence of these two concepts—possible relationship and a new path—led me to question all sorts of things. Would I be open to settling in Europe for a while if there was the possibility of love? I assumed after the holidays I'd be heading to a low-cost Asian country to extend my budget while forging forward on my new creative endeavor. If I'm honest though, I always knew I'd be open to love. If it felt right to settle with someone abroad, I'd go for it. I could write a book anywhere as long as I was emotionally grounded, yet it was *far* too soon in the relationship to consider that possibility. We'd only been out a half-dozen times. It was just too soon.

Then one day the Englishman proposed an interesting idea. "You should come to Africa with me in January. I have a wedding to attend in South Africa, and then I thought I'd travel Tanzania and Rwanda for a few months. What do you think?" *Whoa! Africa!*

I pondered the possibilities. Am I willing to postpone my creative project for three months in Africa? If the relationship worked out, would I move to Germany with him as he planned to do after traveling? If it didn't work out, I risked everything, fearing most that I'd be thrown off my own course to write. My mind ran off, attaching fictional stories to both the success and failure of a relationship that had barely begun. Sigh.

I remembered struggling with creative ideas when I separated from my husband, and I couldn't go back to that state of mind at this point in my trip—in my life. I *had* to dive into a creative path and carve out a new life for myself so I wouldn't have to return to construction management. This was my chance—to shed my old self and then to turn that transformation into something more authentic, more passion and purpose driven. This was my chance!

When on the road, I knew there were endless possibilities that could permanently derail my plan. *What if I contract a strange illness and need to return to the U.S.? What if something happens to my mother? What if, what if, what if?* I felt I was working against some invisible time clock that told me I'd spent enough time on the healing part of the journey and needed to get started on the working aspect of it. If I was feeling the pull to write and then postponed it—well, like I said, it was risky.

Then again there was the chance of love … and let's face it, love leads us to decisions that defy all rational logic and reason.

I weighed the pros and cons on the grand scale of my life. And then I said yes. Of course I said yes! I had the chance to explore the opportunity of love *and* a faraway land unknown to me. Who says no to that? I guess I'll always be one of those people that will take a detour for love. *Or maybe this was still part of my pattern. Hmmm.*

I sat in the tiny Adlestrop church in the English countryside and prayed about the journey we were embarking on toward love. I was so scared. I knew once we went to Africa, life would be different somehow. Not only with whatever I'd experience of Africa, but when traveling with someone—I don't mean a two-week vacation but travel—there's a bond that develops that's intimate and enduring. I'd found it with Siggy and had witnessed it in others. I already knew I'd love him—maybe I already did in a way—and what scared me most was losing my newfound equanimity and the objectivity of my solitary existence in the free-fall of love that would surely find us somewhere between the beaches of Zanzibar and the hills of Rwanda.

The problem with the drug of love is you can't really ever quit it completely. I suppose you could if you wanted to imprison your heart, locking it up, never allowing it to be held by another. But if you're going to walk around in the real world opening yourself to relationships, there will always be the propensity to lapse into addiction. It had been my weakness, my addiction, my vice—the cocaine of attachment, the meth of codependency, the heroin of my heart. I had to trust myself to *use responsibly*.

I asked God to help me maintain perspective as we set out for our African adventure. *If this is love and everything about the relationship is feeling right in my core, then send me onward to Germany with a full heart, ready to take on a new future with him. But if there's a force bubbling up from the spring of my soul whispering, "Something's missing here," then give me the strength to say goodbye before turning it into a long-term relationship predestined for doom.* I sat in that church on Christmas Eve day, so far away from the life I'd left in America and everyone I knew, feeling my aloneness and vulnerability in this vast world. Tears fell across my cheeks, and I begged God to help me maintain clarity as we traveled. I knew my weaknesses, and I prayed for strength to combat them.

Africa Bound

January came, and the Englishman and I set off with our one-way tickets to Africa. The Englishman was excited to plan our adventures, reviewing his guidebooks and mapping out our travels. I was excited to let him. At my month ten of being away when we arrived to Zanzibar, I was suffering from travel fatigue. Vagabonding for so long on my own, drifting around and submerging myself in all these immersive experiences, a heaviness had settled over me.

Traveling alone had been extraordinary on so many levels, yet the continuous hardship of self-sufficiency was exhausting over time. I've come to believe a life well lived can be measured by the experiences we have, not by the possessions we accumulate. Traveling is like an experience explosion; new sights, sounds, and cultures impaled me like shrapnel and fireworks at every turn. Absorbing it all, primarily alone, took its toll while simultaneously expanding me in unimaginable ways. But with my Englishman, although I'd known him only a short while, I trusted him completely.

He was a good man. It was a relief to be able to lean on someone again, emotionally, mentally, and physically—to have someone else witness a part of my journey, allowing me to witness his. I wasn't alone in the world anymore.

We spent a few weeks of near vacation-like travel on the island of Zanzibar, and then we transitioned into "hardcore traveling" as I call it, moving west across the southern part of Tanzania, the lesser-known part of the country few from the developed world will ever see. My Englishman was an adventurer, preferring the road less traveled. I loved that about him. It was rugged and challenging, confronting and exhausting. It would come to change me in ways I wouldn't fully understand until many months later.

Buses in the Dark

Starting from the coastal port town of Dar es Salaam (Dar), Tanzania, we hopped our first bus heading west. I'll never forget the bus station at 5:30 a.m., a dark maze of madness, dozens of men swarming, trying to persuade us onto their bus. We had a flashlight and our bus tickets and were trying to find the bus we'd been assigned, but the tangle of men surrounded us and moved with us as we walked the dusty dirt lot. Strangers in the night tugged and pulled and shouted in their feverish auction for us, the loudest bidder getting the *mzungus* (Swahili term for white Westerner).

Adrenaline flowed to my extremities as fear rose from within, preparing my body for its instinctual fight or flight—not that I could've found any speed with my heavy backpack. My mind was surprisingly calm though, looking the men in the eyes, assessing if they were potential dangers. It can be hard to read the intentions of men, but I'd had plenty of perceived "survivals" where things turned out okay. I was learning to trust my intuition and read the energy of others, and I trusted my Englishman. With him, I was safe.

We picked one man from the frenzied crowd to converse with that spoke a bit of English, and he quickly announced himself to the others as our guide (not that we needed one, but with the determined chaotic crowd, it seemed we had no choice). The other men quickly dispersed, and our man led us, trying to put us on several buses that didn't match our ticket. We argued and persisted, eventually ending up on, what we hoped, was the correct bus.

As we settled into our seats on the bus, my adrenal system relaxed. I thought about the desperation of the crowd of men. It was madness. But I saw instantly that they didn't want to be aggressive; they *had* to be aggressive. Their survival depended on it. I was beginning to view things through the lens of love and compassion instead of the lens of fear. In that, the true nature of their reality became clear.

We watched as our bags were thrown into the undercarriage, hoping they wouldn't then be removed and shuffled off to never-never land. I held the hand of my Englishman, relaxing into our blue fuzzy seats that would be our home for the next eight hours. We pulled away from the Dar dirt lot, the sun rising behind us, and we started our journey westward, far from the city and into rural Tanzania.

Through the Eyes of a Female Traveler

I need to talk about solo traveling as a woman versus my observation of men who solo travel. They seem to be vastly different experiences, and in pondering this, along with the Dar bus terminal experience, some interesting thoughts are rising up in relation to prejudice, violence, and labels. Bear with me in this digression.

I've come to feel it requires equal parts courage, strength, endurance, and naiveté for a woman to travel extensively and alone. Men when traveling alone seemed carefree, relaxed, and confident. Perhaps they have concerns over being scammed or robbed, so they're cautious, but generally I noticed they were calm and collected. I, on the other hand, was constantly on guard, concerned I could be in a situation—nearly any time—with the potential of sexual or physical danger.

Whether in developed or developing countries, I began witnessing my judgments, dissecting the near xenophobic fears that plagued me. I understood they were born of ignorance and mistrust, and I wanted to dismiss them, yet they persisted. At times I berated myself, feeling the poison of prejudice had infected me, when in a crowd of Indian, Muslim, or African men, for example. I didn't want to profile them in the way my mind seemed so inherently inclined to do, but when concerned for my safety, my mind deceived me a million times over.

Now that my exposure to various cultures is more extensive, I've come to see it's not a cultural, ethnic, or racial prejudice at all—rather, a fear of men, justifiably so, I'm afraid. It's not about black or white, American, African, Brazilian, Indonesian, European, or Australian; it's not about Christian, Muslim, Jewish, Hindi, or atheist. The common denominator underpinning my fear and the vast majority of inappropriate sexual and violent action in the world is *gender.*

It's an obvious observation, really, but when I only knew my own country, it was easier to direct certain judgments in the secret spaces of my mind toward minority, ethnic, or racial groups. It's our human nature to isolate something unfamiliar and gravitate toward what we know. This makes it easy for many to label some of our recent violence in America, for example, as an ethnic, racial, or Muslim issue, pointing the finger toward a minority group that stands out. The reality is, though, we're far more likely to be killed by white male extremists in America than radical Islamists[1] ... but they don't talk about that on the nightly news.

This all got me thinking about how we come to form prejudices and more importantly how to release them. We release them by bringing awareness to their inaccuracy.

In stepping away from my own country and observing myself in the world, the reality became clear; generally speaking, men are carrying out gun violence in America, men are gang raping in India, men are pirating ships in Somalia, fraternity boys are raping female college students in America, terrorist attacks are typically carried out by men in all countries, and male priests are raping children in the Catholic Church. Nearly all violence is perpetrated by men; ethnicity, race, and faith are only convenient labels to distract us from the true commonality: gender.

I'm not man bashing here; I want to be clear on this point. I *love* men, really, I do. The vast majority of men walking this earth are decent, generous people, and I've been fortunate to cross their paths and blessed to have many in my life. And of course we can't rule out women entirely; we're not perfect, and we surely play our part in the madness of the world. Historically speaking though, I think most would agree, women are rarely at the root of violence.

Not once when approached by a group of women from *any country* was I concerned for my safety. In fact, it was quite the opposite. I felt my heart opening to women. I felt their pain, their need, their despair, and it shattered my heart to feel their suffering. With men, I kept my guard up, feeling the potential threat of danger was more imminent, and that left me questioning what *that* is. What is it, besides testosterone, that drives men to behave irrationally and sometimes violently? Looking through the lens of compassion, I see that both men and women in developing countries are struggling for survival, but the men express it differently, displaying a more dominant energy, like at the Dar bus terminal.

Are we looking in the wrong direction when we look at an ethnic group or designate judgment based on *any* cultural classification? Maybe we should be investigating one layer deeper into what drives any extremist behavior in *men*. What's at the root of any mental affliction that allows one human to harm another? I'm considering the Buddhist lecture I heard in India by Glen Svensson when he said, "Bad people aren't bad people, they're good people that don't know how to cope with their own pain." Perhaps it all comes down to suffering, oppression, and inequality, and this is what drives violent action.

The magnitude of all this is beyond me, but I ponder the statement made by the Dalai Lama at the 2009 Vancouver Peace

Summit on the important role of women, "The world will be saved by the Western women."[2] Maybe hearts of compassion are the only cure for this global disease. True or not, there is much work to be done to inspire empathy, equality, and peace worldwide.

The Road Less Traveled

You see a lot of a country and the lives of its people when you take a bus; it's a window into another world if you're willing to look at it. Since the age of sixteen, I'd driven my own car, so I'd not spent a lot of time on buses looking peripherally to the lives of others. Riding local transport in rural Tanzania though, I found a new perspective beyond the dashboard and highway ahead. That's true of life too, I suppose; if we're hell-bent on progressing forward, we steamroll through the good, the bad, and the ugly, giving little acknowledgment to what's happening around us.

We stopped in various towns, staying a week or more in some, others only a night or two. We explored small towns, searched out decent chai, and wandered dirt roads to nowhere. With nothing to do but observe, I lost myself in contemplation, watching the lives of others stand still as we passed them. All a country's beauty and all its hardships are there, positioned next to one another; tall wispy grasses waving in the wind and lonely clay dirt roads as far as the eye can see, unknown tree species and mud brick houses with corrugated metal roofs. Woman lined the sides of the roads under tarped, rickety structures selling their wares and breastfeeding children held close to their bodies in cloth slings. I watched as the women worked. Some sold food and drinks at the bus stops, balancing goods on their heads, many rushing the bus windows to sell to us as we pulled in; some were seamstresses; others, who knows what they sold? I saw the men too, of course, but I *felt* the women. I felt an indefinable link that bound me to them. Town after town, day after day, the Tanzanians were going about their lives, and I was observing, absorbing them, and receiving them into my consciousness.

I considered how our lives were different, thinking how grateful I was for all the choices I had in my life they likely wouldn't be blessed with. How could I have been so concerned with choosing the perfect rug for my living room when they couldn't ensure clean drinking water for their children? Why was I given so many choices and they so few? The question tormented me; truly it did. If you can spend time in rural Africa or India, Israel or Indonesia without questioning your faith, then you're a better person than I. I questioned it daily, begging to know why being born in America gives us opportunities others won't experience. That's the gut-wrenching truth of it. They were no different than I. I was no better than they were. But I was born in America, and they were born in rural Tanzania; that was the only factor separating us. *God, why? What sort of nationwide karma blesses one and challenges another so fiercely?*

It seemed to me that the roadside women of Tanzania wouldn't have the opportunity to climb a corporate ladder or have financial independence. Living in a society where men were still considered superior, many of their gifts and talents would go unexplored. There'd be little possibility of divorce or freedom of choice. I wondered if they had the heart to have ambition or if it was an unlikely dream they dare not consider. I was reminded of this with heartbreaking frequency as we rolled on the wheels of gratitude further into the central east African countryside.

One girl really struck me on the way to Sumbawanga, this barefoot beauty, as we waited on the dirt road in front of the tin shack shops. She looked to be maybe sixteen; beautiful skin, sharp facial features, hair cut very short, wearing a clay-stained white skirt that fell just below her knees with a tattered T-shirt and bare, dirty feet. She sat on a large sack of grain watching me watching her. We held eyes for several minutes, connected in cross-cultural contemplation as I tried to read her, absorb her, and understand her … somehow I wanted to know her. She looked away.

I thought of myself at sixteen. I was dropping baskets of french fries in a vat of grease at Arby's, thinking to myself, *Is this it?* Luckily for me, my teenage fast-food gig was only the first stepping-stone in employment jumps; the sky was my limit as to how I would spend my career days. This girl led a very different life though, and when she asked herself, *Is this it*, I'm guessing she came back to herself with a different answer.

On the instruction of a man, she lifted a sack of grain onto her left shoulder, carrying it off into the distance. My eyes followed her through the crowd until she was out of view. She had arms of an Olympian—impressive really—but I knew she'd not seen the inside of a Gold's Gym. Her muscles were born of labor and sweat and necessity, a career path I've not had to endure.

The bus roared its engine, and my heart sank at the thought of not seeing her again. I knew I couldn't do anything, but I saw something in her: hope and promise wrapped in hardship and obligation. How could I save her? Would it even be right to save her? Is that the view of an arrogant Westerner to think of saving her? Maybe she was happy. Did she even need saving? What to do? I could do nothing.

The barefoot beauty returned and perched on another sack of grain, immediately searching me, the only white face in the bus window, locking eyes with mine once more. The wheels of the bus began to turn, and I put my palm on the window, trying desperately to reach the girl I knew I'd never reach. I pulled a smile from the depths of my heart and asked God to send her a happy life. She held up her hand and smiled.

Liemba Bound

We made it to the end of the road, our destination, the farthest southwest point of Tanzania and the township of Kasanga, nearly a thousand miles from the hub city of Dar where we'd departed weeks earlier. Kasanga is a tiny coastal town on the southern tip of

Lake Tanganyika at the northern border of Zambia. We were there to catch the MV *Liemba*,[3] an old German warship, now a passenger and cargo ship sailing northward twice monthly. If our bus journeys had delayed us, we'd be stuck in the tiny generator-powered town for two weeks. My Englishman timed and planned our journey well.

I'd taken to cutting the Englishman's hair. I don't know what made me think I knew how to cut a man's hair, but as it turns out, I did. It was all very *Little House on the Prairie*-ish. Such a nurturing and caregiving act to cut someone's hair—someone you love—like cohabitating dogs or cats that lick one another in a cleansing ritual of possessive nurturing. A small intimacy, yes, but perhaps my favorite part of our African adventure.

Lake Tanganyika is the world's longest freshwater lake and is said to be between nine and thirteen million years old. It's shaped like a green bean, lying between the Democratic Republic of Congo on the western long side, Tanzania on the east, Zambia to the south, and Burundi to the north. Tanzania and Zambia were considered safe to travel, unlike Burundi and the DRC.

The Englishman and I embarked from the Kasanaga port and threw our bags in the first-class cabin. First-class travel in western Tanzania is much different from that in America. Shared bathrooms were filthy, the floors always wet with I don't want to know what, and freaky fluorescent blinking lights that reminded me of a horror film. The first night on the ship, I locked myself in a bathroom stall. The latch jammed, and I nearly gave myself a heart attack imagining I might have to sink down to the wet floor and crawl under the door. I slammed my hips against the door trying to free it, but it wouldn't budge. After a few minutes of panic, a large, bare-breasted woman magically opened the door from her side. I smiled a big smile at her and said thank you in Swahili (asante sana, asante sana!). I didn't shower once while on the boat and made attempts to limit fluid consumption so I could minimize trips to the bathroom. Luckily we had a small sink in our room, so we could brush our teeth and have makeshift splash showers in our room. I thought I'd shed my desires for sparkly, clean bathrooms long before in India, but they snuck up and stung me again like the Clorox I longed for.

The *Liemba* stopped for passengers and cargo frequently, day and night, over the course of four days. Each time a muddle of activity approached the boat, loading and unloading oversized bags of maize, people scaled the sides of the boat from their small fishing vessels to pull children and bags from our ship. Fish, ears of corn, live chickens, and plastic buckets among other things were sold and thrown up to passengers eagerly waiting with their hands reaching out from the sides of the boat to catch their goods.

It was such a mad, hurried, and chaotic endeavor for the men in their small boats to reach the *Liemba*. It seemed at times we were being pirated and the ship taken over, but we quickly realized the necessity of it. Whoever got to the ship first and yelled the loudest usually got the luggage and therefore the person and the fare for the short boat trip back to shore. It was like the Dar bus terminal but on a lake. Necessity and survival depended on their frenzied display.

With only a few first-class cabins, many slept in the belly of the ship in second class, with third class sleeping on the decks. By day, breastfeeding women, men, and children sat on the decks outside our room waiting for time to pass in the hot sun. Children played and danced about. Men huddled in groups playing cards. Muslims gathered regularly, laying out their mats to pray. In the distance, to the west, beyond the hazy sky, we could see the far-off hills of the Congo, to the east of us the Tanzanian tree-lined shore, mile after endless mile of vegetation with scattered coastal villages. Small wooden fishing boats anchored on shore and racks held hundreds of drying fish while women washed their laundry and children bathed in the still lake waters.

I felt a level of continued emotional stress in this "hardcore travel." In an unfamiliar environment, unable to speak the local language, the only two Westerners on board in a far-removed part of western Tanzania on a lake that borders the DRC; I realized if something were to go wrong (and lots of things could), there were limited options for assistance. It was the vastness of unfamiliarity on all levels that was so confronting and challenging. Also that everything ahead of us was unknown, so there was no clear end to the unfamiliarity. Over time, mental exhaustion set in while at the same time a slow resilience was developing to the strangeness of travel.

I remember feeling like we'd *achieved* something when we boarded the *Liemba* in the port of Kasanga, having traveled all those buses across southern Tanzania to arrive there. When we disembarked finally in the port of Kigoma, I felt somehow like we'd *survived* something, yet this was the life the locals lived every day, every month, for a lifetime.

Border Towns

After thoroughly cleaning ourselves and some much-needed rest in Kigoma, we traveled overland by bus toward the Rwanda border. *Noooo, please God, no, not another bus!* This bus ride might have been the worst yet. Eight hours on bumpy dirt roads with loud Swahili music blaring through the scratchy speakers. All the previous bus journeys played the Swahili beats too, so we were used to them by now, but this particular bus ride, they played the same four songs over and over again. It was maddening! At first I liked their funky happy Swahili beats, but at this stage, I could barely tolerate another minute of it. Tiny roaches housed themselves in the window curtains, and they always seemed to find my shoulder. As we bumpidy-bump-bump-bumped down the road, my window bounced open in rhythm, and the heat blasted my face. I held it shut for a while but eventually gave up. It rained on this bus journey too, splashing water from the window channel onto my entire right side. In a crammed bus with people sitting in the aisles, there were no options to move. I put on the Englishman's rain jacket, and we laughed. What else could I do?

We finally arrived to a nowhere-town named Nyakanazi. Based on our maps and info we could find, this seemed like the best stopover point before taking the next bus into Rwanda. We exited the bus, and everyone was laughing and pointing at me. *Yeah, yeah, mzungu, I know, I know.* I didn't understand why they were laughing until I caught my reflection in a mirror. The dust from the roads had blown through my cracked window, leaving a crusty layer of clay caked on every inch of exposed skin from my neck up into my hair. I was no longer a white Westerner in northwest Tanzania; I was now of sweet potato decent and root vegetable ancestry.

How can being seated for eight hours on a bus be so exhausting? Maybe the cumulative effect of long-term travel was finally catching up with me, or maybe I had parasites; anything was possible. We had little energy, motivation, or desire to search out decent accommodations, so the Englishman and his sweet potato stumbled with our backpacks into the nearest guesthouse. We arrived around five o'clock in the evening, so we figured we'd drop our bags, grab some beans and rice, take a shower, and sleep before catching the bus the next morning.

We chose our guesthouse poorly. Water came from a barrel in the corner of our bathroom, which wasn't surprising, but this water … this water, contaminated with dead mosquitoes and larvae… no— just, no. I couldn't bear the thought of pouring that water over my body. We used every last one of our Handi Wipes. I washed away my sweet potato ancestry, and we slept in our dirty clothes, not wanting our clean clothes to even touch the bed. Neither of us really cared, and I didn't have the energy to move guesthouses; we resigned ourselves to the fact that this was it for the night.

I'd come to learn it was easiest to accept situations *however* they came when traveling. It was an every day, every hour lesson on nonattachment, acceptance, and tolerance. Anything other than acceptance would've led to childish tantrums at best or demented madness at worst. I regularly returned to the thought I had on my first flight: *as long as I'm safe, I can handle anything.* This led me to wonder, could our first world expectations in our have-it-your-way society be the very thing causing us undue mental stress?

Krishnamurti, the revered spiritual teacher of India, said in his 1977 lecture in California (long before I'd taken to contemplative thought), "Do you want to know what my secret is?" It's said everyone leaned forward in anticipation, eager to hear his wise words. He continued, "You see, I don't mind what happens."[4] *Hmmm, I don't mind what happens. Interesting.*

This doesn't mean we should turn our heads on human rights or important issues of equality, but these humanitarian issues aren't the ones that bring about the majority of suffering we experience in our everyday lives; they're usually much more personal. If we can shift our perception, learning not to resist the world around us, we can exist in it in a more natural and accepting way. I've come to see it's in the *resistance* to life where we find the most personal suffering. What would happen if we learned to embrace rather than resist?

The Man in the Window

The sun was going down, and the end of the day was finally upon us. Soon we could sleep, catch the earliest bus outta there, and be gone. We lay in bed chatting about the bus journeys and the *Liemba* and everything we'd seen along the way. The majesty of the elephants, giraffes, and zebras we'd seen in Ruaha National Park. How beautiful it was to see the animals roaming the grasslands in their natural habitat.

As we lay together reminiscing our journey, anticipating what might be waiting for us in Rwanda, we heard terrible screams nearby. The Englishman and I turned our heads to one another, both having dread in our eyes. I peeked out from behind the moth-pod-infested curtains through our barred windows, looking left and right down the dirt alley and to the mud brick house across the way. Then again, the agonizing screams.

I saw something move in the window of the house. All I could see were hands tied at the wrist, one hand in front of the other, palms facing out the window. In my mind's eye, he was tied to a bed frame, but I saw only brown palms. What *was* clear though was that a man was being beaten, and it was happening twenty feet from our screened window.

We didn't know what to do. Repetitive screams continued. No one we'd interacted with spoke English, and we felt as far removed from society as we had on the *Liemba*. We wanted to help, but what to do? We didn't know the laws or the language. We were in a far-off remote border town closer to Burundi than anywhere else, and no one knew we were there. It seemed to me if we interfered, we could've been swallowed up inside that house, never seen again. It didn't seem logical, sensible, or effectual.

Maybe we should've taken action. Instead we did nothing. We lay in bed horrified at the ceaseless screams. *What could warrant such an act? How can this be a useful form of justice? What is going on over there? Is it one man beating another? Is there a group taking turns? Why, God, why? For the love of humanity!*

Eventually the screaming stopped—in live action anyway. It haunted me the whole night and in my dreams. Etchings of torture left imprints on my mind, for the next week, the next month ... for all of eternity.

We woke early, hoisted our bags on our backs, and stepped from our guesthouse, both of us eager to see the house of pain in daylight. Armed men stood outside the door. It was a police station. Seemingly "justifiable violence" of Tanzanian law? What does that term mean anyway, justifiable violence? Can violence ever really be justified? Perhaps it's one of those things our minds can rationalize in the name of upholding the law, national security, or war, but the heart ... I don't think the heart could ever really understand it.

The Happiness Survey

Rwanda was calling us, and we couldn't wait to get the hell out of Nyakanazi. We happily boarded a bus and rode six hours to the Rwandan border where we crossed on foot.

Rwanda has a completely different feel than Tanzania. It was evident that money and assistance had been funneled into this tiny country after the 1994 genocide.[5] The roads and embankments were clean and planted, the buses were newer and cleaner, and they were playing Phil Collins's "One More Night" of all things, instead of the Swahili beats to which we'd become accustomed. I was never so happy to hear Phil Collins circa 1984. Strangely enough, we were searched at the border for plastic bags of all things, as they're prohibited[6] in Rwanda. That's a forward-thinking concept in any part of the world. Plastic bags outlawed. Brilliant!

I was seventeen and a teenager in love when Rwanda was experiencing the horrific atrocities that would forever make their country memorable. I was appalled at my own ignorance of the country's historic events in *my* lifetime. It's an embarrassing admission, but it seemed until traveling, I'd been largely unaware, uninformed and unaffected by what was happening beyond my borders.

Through the social enterprise Azizi Life,[7] I had the opportunity to spend a day with four Rwandan women, learning to weave in their village. The women showed me how they chopped the four-foot long sisal stem that resembled an oversized aloe plant. They used a machete to strip the stringy fibers, which would then be dried and dyed before the sisal would be used to weave baskets, decorative trays, picture frames, bracelets, and earrings.

The women and I sat together in their living room, hand weaving sisal bracelets while the translator sat with us to facilitate conversation. The floor was hard-packed dirt, the walls were mud brick, and the room was small with only natural light from the window. The women were kind and beautiful and gracious. I felt a connection with them instantly, all close to my age. They were curious about me and my life, and I was curious about theirs.

Since leaving the United States, I'd been talking to people of different cultural backgrounds about happiness in what I dubbed The Happiness Survey (included at the end of this chapter). It turned out to be a great way to learn about other cultures, to open up into honest conversations about life, and to understand the struggles of those outside my world. On my first flight leaving the United States, I came up with nine questions that I'd ask again and again as I roamed the globe. I was desperately seeking happiness and could not, for the life of me, determine how to find it, have it, keep it, harness it, insert it, extract it, or wrap it around me as a protective shield. I wanted to know what the rest of the world had to say about happiness. The happiness survey on this day led us into topics of conversation surrounding depression, education, divorce, clean water supply, domestic abuse, birth control, and of course happiness.

I'd conducted the happiness survey a hundred times before in various countries and locations—cafés and taxis, buses and grass lawns. I'd become good at putting people on the spot, asking them challenging, some might say, intrusive questions with a near journalistic approach, but this time it felt different.

These women I knew lost family in the madness of the genocide and likely themselves narrowly escaped death. All while I'd been crying teenage angst over long-distance love in my bedroom. It seemed to me miraculous to survive such a witch hunt during which nearly 20 percent of Rwanda's population was brutally murdered across one hundred days. Sitting amongst these women in the shadow of what they'd endured, well, suddenly my happiness survey—and even my own search for happiness—seemed inconsequential.

The women wondered why I wasn't married, and I explained briefly that I had been but was now divorced. They said, "Oh, your husband beat you?" *Gulp.* "Uh, no. No, he didn't abuse me. We uh … We weren't happy together. We couldn't be together anymore. Uhhh …" As the words left my mouth, I felt their insignificance as I sat in the living room of a mud house, on a small banana farm amongst a thousand hills of bloodshed. My mind searched itself, looking for something I could say truthfully that would be perceived as a matter of significance warranting divorce in their culture … nothing.

The translator thankfully filled the silence as I whirled in the cross-cultural dichotomy unfolding before me. "They only leave their husbands if they're being abused," the translator said solemnly. One of the women, very timid and withdrawn, had been studying me quietly. I held her gaze for a few moments, seeing the pain and hurt and an indescribable wounding in her eyes, and I knew ... I knew she was divorced.

I asked them about their water supply and if fresh water was an issue. The translator explained to me that the women walk with jugs to collect water from a nearby village. I wondered how they ensured it was safe to drink. He said they were supposed to boil all drinking water before consumption but shook his head. "No one does it."

My mind ran off, consumed by their challenges, their hardships, their mud houses, and their questionable drinking water; their bloodshed, their outhouses, and lives as subsistence farmers.

They pulled me from my thoughts and swept me up and into their afternoon routine of dancing and singing. This is how they end every workday. Tribal chants in their Kinyarwanda language filled the air as we clapped and danced around one another in united fellowship. They'd endured so much, and their lives were challenging, yet they sang and danced in solidarity. Now that's the way to end a workday.

I find the scales of gratitude are rarely measured in our minds against the disparities of humanity. If they were, well, I think the world would look a lot different than it does today. I'd always known I was lucky. Intellectually I could easily calculate that I'd been on the positive end of an irrational equation ... but to see it here. Knowing all the women had been through and the challenges of their lives—the man in the window, the barefoot beauty, and those living on the shores of Lake Tanganyika. All I'd seen. I could barely stand the weight of it! Intellectualized gratitude had left me long ago in India. What settled in me as I traveled, now over twelve months on the road, was something deeper, something lasting, and finally, I *knew* gratitude.

Ocean Dwellers and Land Lovers

The Englishman and I were nearing the end of our three months traveling, and the time was coming for a decision to be made. Would we book flights leaving Africa together or separate, flying off to different countries?

I searched myself, dropping into the heart space, remembering the prayer I'd made in the tiny church in England before we left, requesting clarity. It seemed I'd lived a thousand lives since leaving London, yet here we stood, only three months after our initial departure, contemplating futures. I loved the Englishman; I really did … but something was missing. And although I felt deeply that he wanted me to join him in Germany, he never actually invited me. We talked little about it until a week before our visa expiration, making it necessary to book flights. It was a conversation neither of us wanted to have. That lack of open discussion in itself was an indication of incompatibility.

I've come to realize I need to deeply understand the inner workings of my partner. I need to be able to discuss our respective emotions, feelings, hopes, dreams, and insecurities, freely swimming in the emotional, spiritual, and philosophical oceans between our shores. Here in the depths, I am comfortable. It seems I can't quite find my breath when I've been beached for too long in the intellectual realm. Finally I've learned there are ocean dwellers and there are land lovers, and not everyone wants to explore the depths of themselves or their partner like I do; they simply prefer land. I can't drag land lovers into the depths of the ocean; they have to swim there freely.

As much as it pained me to feel it and to admit the truth to myself, and to the Englishman, I felt the answer deep in my core. I wanted him to be the one. I wanted the search to be over. I wanted our African love affair to blossom into a beautiful lifelong partnership one hopes to find. I wanted the fantasy of running off to Germany with him, starting a new life where I could rest my weary heart forever in the capable hands of another. But I couldn't. We were misaligned in certain key areas, and I couldn't put us through the routine I'd lived so many times before.

With heavy hearts and my streaming tears, we reluctantly parted in the Kigali airport, the Englishman off to Germany where he'd start a new job, and me to Southeast Asia. I'd have to regroup and dive into that creative project—the one I would've started before the Englishman and the African detour brought me to love and humility.

Expansion Exercises

Eryn's Happiness Survey

1. What is happiness to you?
2. What do you value most in life?
3. How do you feel depression or other mental health issues affect someone's happiness?
4. What role, if any, does religion or spirituality play in your life?
5. What does the world need more of?
6. What does the world need less of?
7. On a scale of one to ten, how happy are you in your daily life?
8. If you could change one thing in your life to bring about greater happiness, what would it be?
9. How does one obtain happiness?

Journal Entry
'Goodbyes'

The Traveler's Creed

~ For Siggy and all the others traveling the road of re-becoming ~

We've abandoned the knowns,
The securities, the sureties.
Said long-due farewells to past lives,
Set out into the world
Seeking self, seeking truth,
Casting doubts and all fears aside.
We trust only ourselves
And a small precious few,
Intuition and Spirit, our guides,
Sharing moments, hours, days
With beautiful strangers we meet.
Knowing soon we'll say tearful goodbyes,
We march on across continents
Buddhist temples, Portuguese deserts.
New truths within us arise.
We see glimpses, small eclipses
Of our destinies calling,
Carving futures that light up our eyes.
We tease out newfound wisdom
From our collected experiences;
New versions begin to give rise.
We're going nowhere we've known
But somewhere we must go
Till greater consciousness is fully realized.

PART III

Living Love

Months Thirteen to Twenty-Eight

CHAPTER 12

Month Fourteen–Thailand

Monastery in the Forest

Prayer is you speaking to God. Meditation is
allowing the Spirit to speak to you.
—Deepak Chopra

After Africa, it would've been reasonable to conclude my trip and return to the United States. I was weary and a bit heartbroken, but I had this insistent feeling that I wasn't yet meant to return. I hadn't found my new creative path, and that was just as critical as the healing journey of re-becoming. I couldn't go home yet. I just couldn't.

I chose Chiang Rai, Thailand, because I'd heard it mentioned amongst other travelers as a popular city to visit. A five-minute Google search in a Rwandan café confirmed it met my two requirements; it was a low-cost city so I could extend my budget, and it had a good yoga scene. Chiang Rai seemed like a decent place to settle for a while to see if I could harness my creative energy and turn it into something. And just like that, I was alone in the world again in a new city, knowing no one.

It hit me a lot harder than I expected, the separation from the Englishman. It felt so unnatural; we'd been inextricably linked, nearly twenty-four hours a day over three months in Africa. I didn't stop loving him just because he wasn't right for me. Thrust into detox, recovering from love's drug, I aimlessly roamed the Chiang Rai city streets in solitude. I visited temples and grieved the separation, waiting for inspiration to strike me. I felt lost and without direction.

I knew I had two options. I could distract myself as I would've done in my old life, filling the empty space in my heart with a new man, or I could dive into the grief and face it head-on. I let the grief swallow me, feeling I'd move through it faster if I didn't resist it.

After two months of wallowing, all inspiration lost in the whirlwind of dust behind a Tanzanian bus, I decided, enough was enough. I believed I was meant to write a book, but what did I want to say? How did I want to say it? I wasn't *feeling it*. I wanted to know my purpose, my path, my calling. I wanted a signal or some definitive direction from the heavens above. *Yes, my child;* this *is what you're meant to be doing.* I needed something powerful to kick out all the, *coulda, woulda, shoulda beens* so I could move on with my life.

Arriving at Vipassana

I decided it was time for Vipassana,[1] a Buddhist term meaning *insight* achievable in a silent, meditative retreat. Who doesn't want a good dose of insight? *Me, me, me.* I'd met many people while traveling who'd participated in Vipassana, and although I'd been intrigued by it, there was a high attrition rate, and the all-day-meditating intensity of it frankly scared the be-geez-es out of me.

I first heard the word Vipassana from my German friend Fritz as we talked on the shores of the Ganges in month one of my travels. He raved about it, "Oh, you must do Vipassana one day; it will change your life. You'll know when it's time."

Because Vipassana includes no teachings or philosophy to accompany the meditations, the experience is exponentially more difficult than the first silent retreat I'd participated in at month two of my travels in India. Vipassana isn't the sort of practice you haphazardly decide to do, like booking a weekend getaway or taking up jogging. One has to *arrive* at Vipassana, if that makes sense. The forces of my internal and external world spun me like a tornado around this potential immersive growth experience. I considered it, resisted it, heard stories from others, contemplated it, and pushed back from the idea again and again. For a long time, I didn't really think I could handle it.

One day though, in and amongst my grief, I came to feel it was time. My purpose was buried inside me somewhere, masked by sorrow, waiting to be uncovered. I owed it to myself to dig in and find it. Suddenly, the winds of my tornado ceased, dropping me off at a monastery in the forest of North Thailand.

There are different variations of Vipassana, but as far as I know, they all include sensory-deprived environments (i.e. no speaking [except to your teacher as needed], no television, computer, phone, music, writing, reading, or napping). The monastery I resided in provided two meals per day, and solid food was not permitted after noon. We were asked to limit sleep to six hours a night in the beginning and were required to wear white to minimize the polarity between sexes.

Day 1 to 10
4:00 – 7:00 a.m. Wake, shower, hand-wash laundry, meditation routine
7:00 – 8:00 a.m. Breakfast
8:00 – 11:00 a.m. Meditation routine
11:00 – 12:00 p.m. Lunch
12:00 – 10:00 p.m. Meditation routine
10:00 – 4:00 a.m. Sleep

Test One—Endurance and Will

The intensely regimented schedule of meditations from morning until night were mentally, emotionally, and physically challenging.

In addition, the extreme deprivation of all things comforting made this *the* most difficult thing I've voluntarily undertaken.

One woman with whom I shared a house stormed out, referring to Vipassana brashly as, "One big fucking human experiment." I couldn't deny it felt like that at times. For the first several days, I felt I'd been placed in an off-book CIA facility and this was my pre-interrogation treatment meant to break me down, which it did. Restricted to a far-removed compound in a foreign country, deprived of all things pleasurable, the layers of self began peeling away. By day two, I realized just how mentally and physically challenging it would be to endure this routine for twelve more days in silence.

To begin, the meditations are short and increase each day as far as the student can handle. Ten minutes walking, ten minutes sitting, and fifteen-minute break—repeat. Gradually it increases, 15/15/15, then 20/20/15 and so on up to 60/60/15, for sixteen hours a day!

I felt extreme resistance, agitation, and even anger by the evening of day two. I wanted to quit, my mind revolting against this ridiculous, repetitive routine. The seated meditations were physically painful, my knees and back screaming, and I didn't understand the purpose of the slow, mindful, walking meditations. They were driving me mad; they seemed so pointless and arbitrary!

The morning of day three, I had the intention of quitting when I went to meet my teacher for our daily check-in. It just seemed like such a waste of time, and I was constantly agitated. *This is fuckin' ridiculous! Why am I here? I can't do this anymore. I can't. I can't!*

I've come to see we're hardwired for comfort with a determined navigation system directing us to experiences we find pleasurable, or at worst, neutral, like going to the post office. Rarely do we allow ourselves to remain in situations we find unpleasant (if we have an option). I was also finding it difficult to be at peace with the idea that I wasn't accomplishing anything. The art of *being*, a concept of the East, didn't seem to naturally fit in my Western mind, so hell-bent on *doing*. The physical and mental pains of this experience were telling me to leave the monastery. *Why again did I come here? Good God man, why?*

My teacher encouraged me to stay. I don't know how she did it, and I don't recall her soft words, but she was surprisingly convincing in her hushed tones. After our brief meeting, I went back to my room to brood over my intense internal resistance. I hated it there! Everything about it I hated. The hundred-degree heat of the summer with no AC that meant a near constant stream of sweat that dripped down my back, the bizarre, distinctly Thai flavor of the boiled eggs served in the vegetarian food trays, the gargantuan roaches that patrolled the floors of my room, the mosquitos that feasted on me, and the never-ending routine of walking and sitting meditations that gnawed me. It was dementing.

I had two choices. I needed to mentally get on board with the program to see what positive insights might arise or leave the monastery. If I stayed only for ego's sake to say I completed fourteen days silent, the whole thing would be pointless. I thought of those I'd known who'd entered Vipassana and quit—Siggy and Mr. Handsome. Siggy hadn't explained her reasons for leaving, just, "Dude, I had to get the fuck outta there."

I thought of Siggy's experience, now fully understanding her reaction. I walked to the convenience store outside the monastery to consider this fucking ridiculous form of torture—I mean growth experience. I thought chocolate and coffee might bring answers. *Dammit, Eryn, you gotta go. This isn't working. You gotta get the fuck outta here.* Coffee. More coffee.

I reflected on my resistance. I realized that my meditation practice hadn't been strong enough to support the Vipassana experience. I'd not been regularly meditating in the thirteen months since the first Buddhist silent retreat. Secondly, although Siggy and I had both successfully made it through that first retreat, this was exponentially more difficult because there were no teachings; this was all meditation, all day long. Thirdly, in the previous retreat, we had the support of the group and a classroom environment. We were able to lean on each other in a way, so even in silence, I drew strength from the group in that shared experience. Not so here. In

Vipassana, everyone began independently the day they arrived, so there was no sense of group camaraderie. Here, I'd been instructed on the meditation routine, given a set of clean sheets, shown my room and the few meditation halls, and then dismissed to begin meditations. Sixteen hours a day aaaand go. These factors made the practice more solitary and nearly unbearable.

In dissecting these details and my speculation of Siggy's experience, I realized my anger, my resistance, and my desire to escape this fourteen-day marathon of the mind stemmed from my lack of discipline and strength of will. I wasn't, however, prepared to let myself off the hook so quickly as I would've done in my old life. *Not* being strong enough wasn't an acceptable reason to leave. I asked myself three questions:

1. Are they asking me to do anything I'm not physically able to do? *No.*
2. Are they asking me to do anything I'm not mentally able to do? *No.*
3. Do I feel completing this mental marathon will benefit me in some way? I remembered the words of my German friend Fritz as we walked the shores of the Ganges, "Oh, you must do Vipassana; it will change your life."

I took my last swig of coffee just before noon on day three, resigned myself to this strange, ascetic life, and returned to the temple grounds. I kept going.

Test Two—Patterns

Patterns began to reveal themselves immediately. I noticed a handsome man in silence sitting near me; so peacefully he sat with his perfectly imperfect, beautiful, corrupt self. I could tell he'd been in retreat for a while already—his meditation sessions were much longer than mine. He was so much stronger than I was; I could see it in the dedication to his practice. He inspired me.

We moved independently with our slow, purposeful steps, sharing cosmic space in this small monastic universe. I studied the carpet as I looked down at my feet during walking meditations; a tight-weave burgundy color seamed together haphazardly with black strings unraveling from the edges like the complexities of our minds. Hands linked behind my back, one step, two step, three step, four. I rarely made eye contact with the silent stranger, but his presence motivated and encouraged me. I knew nothing about him, but I was grateful he was there and promised myself I'd continue.

My mind strayed between meditation sessions, wondering where the silent stranger was from and what his name was. I imagined what his accent would sound like whispering in my ear, Israeli, maybe Brazilian. I thought of what his hand would feel like holding mine; the home I'd never known.

Lifetimes passed—sitting, walking, repeat. I began to see my obsession. Even with no words and no contact, I was drawn to the silent stranger as if by magnetism. How would I meet him? What *is* the proper etiquette for picking up a guy in a silent retreat? Is there a Vipassana Dating 101 manual? Should I slip him my number? *No, Eryn, no! You will not allow your selfishness to intervene with his path or progress.*

I decided I'd spend only mornings in the small meditation hall with the silent stranger and instead would spend afternoon and evening meditations at the far end of the monastery where the monks lived. I had to do something to purge him from my thoughts.

On day five, I passed him at the water cooler. Our eyes locked in a butterfly-inducing extended gaze. I felt the warmth radiating from him, and I longed to curl up inside him, my cocoon. On day six, I moved his flip-flops from the sun as they sat perched on the steps of the meditation hall. I didn't want him to burn his feet.

By day seven, my meditation sessions were up to sixty minutes; walking, sitting, break, repeat. During breaks, I'd peer out through the windows, gleaning life from the beautiful garden outside. Bright green leaves hung from the branches, and birds chirped happily in their outdoor fountain (they were allowed to talk!). Nature carried on in its daily routine, paying no attention to the silent humans living amongst them.

On day eight, early in the morning, I found myself waiting outside with the silent stranger for the meditation hall to be unlocked. I wanted to nuzzle in close next to him, yet knowing I had to maintain respectful distance. Stripped of all comforts and in silence, I wanted to hug someone desperately—man, woman, child, or the temple dogs—anyone or anything I might extract connection from. But it wasn't allowed. The silent stranger was there, so close. I wanted to hurl myself into his arms and take a nap. Yet I resisted, an extreme act of will.

The fantasy of a beautiful love story began to unfold in my mind. *Look how the universe so perfectly designed our collision. Two strong, passionate souls, thrust into this monastic village, destined to meet, fated to love.* At first, I decided not to worry about our meeting, so sure the universe would bring us together again in the future when I could freely say, "Hey, I know this is crazy, but I sort of fell in love with you a little bit in the silence." Then again, the universe already put us here together once in a tiny forest monastery in North Thailand. How much can I expect it to do?

There was the most beautiful flowering plant on the dirt road where the silent stranger retired each night. It smelled of honey and spring with a brilliant pink and white bloom. I stopped every day on my way to lunch to fully immerse my face in its magnificence. Finally a permissible sense pleasure! I wonder if he ever stopped to smell it.

On day nine, my teacher said I should reduce my sleep from six to five hours. *Say what?* I pushed aside the thought of sleeping one less hour and wrote a note to my silent stranger. I placed it in a tiny envelope folded perfectly in origami fashion. *Open after you leave Vipassana,* I wrote on the front. I knew this was breaking one of the Buddhist precepts[2] to which I'd committed, and I wasn't sure if I'd give him the note, but I wanted to have it with me just in case the opportunity presented itself. At thirty-eight years old, it felt sophomoric to write a note, but what else could I do?

By midmorning, I realized the silent stranger wasn't coming to the meditation hall. He'd begun his final days of isolation and wouldn't be joining me in silence anymore. At first I was distraught, thinking I'd missed my chance at our fated encounter, but as I settled into my own meditation, I felt an unexpected sense of relief. I realized how my mind had run off with the silent stranger on an imaginary white horse into the romantic sunset that never existed. Only now did I see how out of control my thoughts were in relation to this man. I'd been so concerned about not disrupting *his* practice I hadn't realized the extent to which I'd been distracted from mine. In truth, I noticed it days before, but I'd been powerless to stop it.

In the depths of my distraction, a new truth began to emerge; the time and energy I'd spent consumed by thoughts of this man, a stranger. Look at the wildly beautiful yet fictitious story I'd created. Look at the minor mental anguish to which I'd subjected myself at the thought of missing or meeting this man. I'd attached myself to a story.

Test Three—Days of Determination

On day eleven, I went into the final three days of isolation in my room; solitary meditations. I fetched my meals from the dining hall and ate them alone. I was also asked not to sleep and to continue meditations through the night. *Ummm, excuse me, what? Reduced to four hours last night and no sleep tonight? Are you kidding me? No way!*

I thought of the silent stranger, wondering if he'd just gone through these same sleepless nights. I guessed that today would be his last day and he'd be leaving the monastery. Previously I would've been obsessed with the thought of missing the man that had supported and encouraged me from afar and would've certainly wanted to love me up close(?). Amazingly, my obsession had dissolved. All that remained was the simple acknowledgment of his departure. My mind magically released the love story—it fluttered away like a butterfly in the Thai forest.

In my night twelve, the second night attempting not to sleep, strange things began happening.

In the wee hours of the morning, having been awake for forty-two hours, a storm blew through the monastery. I moved like honey through the meditation routines; my mind, my movements, and my vision all drastically slowed.

Drunk on sleeplessness, I braced the wall during walking meditations, barely able to keep myself vertical. I took slow, mindful steps on a folded blanket to quiet my screaming back. *No more wood floors! I can't do it anymore! Agggggh!* As the storm grew more intense, hundreds of winged bugs swarmed my room through cracks in the screened windows, a strange combination of dragonfly and moth.

Focusing intently on each painful step, the dragon-moths tormented me endlessly, flying into my hair, my arms, and my long, flowy white skirt. They landed on my blanket walkway, their little legs held by the fibers. I halted my steps, watching the winged bandits with my half-shut, contemplative eyes. Blink. Blink. I stood motionless, staring at them in my footpath.

I thought of the Buddhist precepts I'd taken upon arriving to the monastery. I vowed, among other things, to not kill any living being. Ants, roaches, mosquitos, and dragon-moths were off limits. I became angry with them for invading my space, penetrating my sleepless mind, and plaguing my night. They darted around my room like laser lights in a Berlin nightclub, and I couldn't escape them. I could not escape them! *Get away from me! You're keeping me from my walking! Agggggh!* Madness came over me. A sleepy, docile madness urging me to kill them, to kill them all! I wanted to end their little dragon-moth lives. But I couldn't.

Finally my alarm sounded. The brutal hour walking with dragon-moths ended. I happily took my position for the seated meditation. I shielded myself with a sheet, wrapped around me and over my head like a tent, leaving only my face exposed. The dragon-moths kamikazied my sheet barrier, fell to the ground, shook themselves off, and flew away again, swarming my Vipassana skies. I closed my eyes, trying to make peace with them in my mind, remembering the Buddhist philosophy; *the dragon-moths are living beings just like me, only trying to survive.*

Breathe in … Breathe out … Breathe in … Breathe out as I slipped into the meditative cocoon of quietude, finally becoming unaware of the dragon-moths. Deeper and deeper I sank into myself, traversing the hypnagogic zones of consciousness. My body began a series of involuntarily jolts, regularly twitching as I sat in silence across the hour. I was aware of nothing except my body's repetitive movements and my inner state of tranquility. *What do these jolts mean? What is happening to me?*

My alarm beeped, waking me from my altered state, and I opened my eyes to see the dragon-moths once more. They'd multiplied! I lifted myself up and stepped onto my folded blanket to begin walking once more. My back screamed at me to stop. I prayed the hour would pass quickly and the sun would soon rise so the night would release me. *I can't take this anymore. I need sleep! This is madness! My body! My mind! These dragon-moths! These fucking dragon-moths!*

They lifted one by one like harriers from my blanket aircraft carrier. I continued my slow, mindful steps, and then I noticed a gecko on the wall. He looked at me, smiling, silently communicating. I watched him curiously, trying to decipher his cryptic message, but he seemed in a hurry. I couldn't be bothered with his swiftness, so I brought my attention back to my footsteps. *Maybe the dragon-moths aren't real. Have I imagined them? Fuck, Eryn. Fuck! This is mad!* In my sleepless stupor, I began questioning reality. My body was breaking down, my mind fragile—on the verge of something. Transformation? Mental fracture?

The hour alarm chirped, and I sat again cross-legged, eager to leave the dragon-moths and close my eyes. Whatever was happening, nature show or hallucination, I didn't want to be a part of it anymore. I couldn't be a part of it anymore! *Just close your eyes, Eryn. The sun will be rising soon. It'll be better in daylight.* I set my alarm, pulled my sheet protection over my head, and noticed the gecko sitting directly in front of me. He stared at me intently, watching and studying me. *What? What do you want?* I stuck my tongue out at him in a childlike pout, closed my eyes, and fell into the depths.

Almost immediately my body began shuddering again with uncontrolled twitches. *Why is my body doing this? What does it mean?* I was scared. I wanted to understand. I needed to understand. I intuitively felt something was happening; my mind was kicking something out—parts of my psyche that needed expulsion. Purging, releasing, and eradicating. Ousting, cleansing, and expelling. *Get out of me!*

My fears of mental fracture swelled and then subsided. A calm came over me. I felt safe, connected to God and to myself in a way I'd never experienced, like He was orchestrating a critical reconstruction of my psyche except it didn't feel like the paternal God I'd always associated with, rather a genderless Absolute. I was grateful, feeling it, sensing it, knowing something miraculous was happening, yet unable to define it. Time stopped. Nothing mattered. I surrendered to a brief ultimate *knowing.* Then, having no context to understand what I was experiencing, I became frightened again, fearing it could all be a hallucination. I thought of my father, wondering if this was what he'd experienced in his psychotic break—clarity of truth, uncertain—cracking from reality, imminent.

The hour passed quickly and I opened my eyes to see the gecko sitting again in front of me. We stared at each other in an unspoken moment of understanding only two living beings can share. Tears fell across my cheeks, questioning his existence, each droplet containing the possibility of psychosis. A dragon-moth flew between us, and I watched with my sleep-deprived eyes as the gecko opened his mouth, extended his tongue, and intercepted the dragon moth. He swallowed it whole in a slow-motion instant.

A subtle, sleepy, contented smile came to my face. I held my hands in prayer pose and bowed slightly, thanking the gecko. I broke eye contact with him, letting my gaze drift slowly around the room. There were no more dragon-moths, only a dozen fat geckos running around. They smiled at me, proud of the post-storm feast they'd hunted. I smiled back, thanking them for eating my madness.

The barrier of night broke, and the sun finally rose, its yellow arms reaching through the windows to embrace me. The fear melted away, and I wasn't scared anymore. Things seemed more real now that the sun had joined me. Nights can be deceiving that way in their darkness. In the corner of the room, I noticed hundreds of discarded wings whirling like small tornados in the breeze of the fans, the wings of the dragon-moths that were no more. Maybe I hadn't cracked myself open in madness after all.

My teacher came to check on me in my room like she did each morning during the days of solitude. Seeing her brought up the angst and questions that plagued me in the night. First she confirmed there were, in fact, wings floating in the corners of the room. The dragon-moths, the geckos, the nature show had been real. I wasn't delusional. Then I begged to know what had been happening as my body twitched and convulsed in the sleepless meditations. I intuitively knew what it was. I'd released the programming that had been so deeply embedded from childhood when we left my father, searching for completion and wholeness of myself through men. That splintered girl was no more. I felt this, I knew this, I was certain this had shifted, but I was in disbelief. I didn't know this was possible.

My teacher confirmed my impressions that I'd likely released what Buddhists refer to as a karmic imprint.[3] I wept in relief, feeling a part of me had vanished—a part of me that I hadn't liked so much—a part of me that, even once I acknowledged and understood in my twenties, I'd not been able to control. I'd been released from the patterns that had shaped the first half of my life so significantly and would've continued to influence the second half had I not released them. I would no longer be held by the grips of codependency or the attachment disorder I'd clung to in addictive dysfunction.

I paid homage to the lessons my old life had taught me and buried their imprints in the Thai forest, never to be seen again.

Vipassana Afterthoughts

As for the overall experience of Vipassana, it took me to a place of inner peace I hadn't known was possible. By the end of my fourteen days, I found myself a little conflicted about leaving the monastery. On one hand, I was ready to catch the first *songthaew* (Thai local transport) out of the forest into the city to order a gluttonous meal and sleep for three days. On the other hand, I realized how content and still I'd become, finding a near unshakeable peace. But I knew it couldn't last. I knew the world outside the monastery would disturb that state. Part of me wondered what it would be like to live long-term at the monastery and I considered it briefly.

I remembered the Tibetan nun in India who'd lived in a cave for twelve years. Although I couldn't comprehend it all when I heard her speak, now I did. I finally understood the benefit of her time in isolation.

During Vipassana, I was tested regularly. There were mini tests all throughout, like waking up every morning at 4:00 a.m., *grrrrr,* or enduring the physical pain that comes with prolonged meditations, but the significant ones for me were what I labeled:

Test One—Endurance and Will

Test Two—Patterns

Test Three—Days of Determination

These key moments were where my forward momentum was necessary to shift my consciousness. If I'd allowed myself to quit, failing test one, I wouldn't have been exposed so intensely to my patterns via the silent stranger, test two. Even if I'd been able to give the man the note I'd written, I feel it would've changed the energy of the entire retreat for both of us, no matter the outcome. Had I not passed those two tests, I wouldn't have made it to test three, where patterns from childhood and karmic imprints dissolved.

Had I not passed these tests or dropped out of Vipassana, it would've been okay. It just would've meant I wasn't ready for the lesson yet. This is how it works; we're tested with our unconscious patterns again and again in our lives until we're ready for the lesson. I hadn't realized it, but I'd been tested all along with all my relationships in *The Past*. Once I took the initiative to halt the patterned behavior (relationships) and held to my intentions, boarding my one-way flight to India, I began passing tests, integrating the lessons, and hiking the upward trek toward my highest self.

What a beautiful thing it was that I'd not expected the specific transformation related to my happiness being derived from men. Had I gone into Vipassana with an expectation of a certain outcome, I likely wouldn't have had the same success. I may have tripped myself up, hindering the natural process with expectations. Even the unexpected obsession with the silent stranger, I now realize, led me to the night-twelve awakening that I so desperately needed.

I think if we give our minds the opportunity, they will naturally reorder themselves, kicking out what they deem appropriate when the time is right. But we have to pay attention, and we have to start young, allowing space for introspection and expansion. We must learn to listen to the cries of the soul long before our state of desperation propels us onto a one-way flight to never-never land.

On reflection, I see the first fourteen months of my trip were preparing me all along for this marathon of the mind called Vipassana. I believe I experienced two occasions where I released deeply ingrained subconscious programming. One was this Vipassana experience, and the other was the Facing Freedom practice I write about in an upcoming chapter. It's a practice I conceived initially for myself in hopes of overcoming issues of low self-worth and body dysmorphia. Upon completing it though, I saw how it changed me profoundly, bringing me to a place of radical self-acceptance, and I knew I had to share it with you. It's a practice you can do in your own home, and I'll guide you through it.

As my trip unfolded, each experience and every person opened me to something new. In those fourteen days in the Thai forest monastery, I called back the spirit of my seven-year-old self and reintegrated her into my psyche. I was a sponge, amazed by the awakenings I'd been led to and eager now to immerse myself in my creative project and whatever Thailand would offer me next. I surrendered myself to this wild ride around the world, trusting that I was being guided. Breath by breath, I was returning more and more to my true self.

Expansions Exercises

1) Spend fifteen minutes each day in a quiet space journaling your thoughts. Take note of repeating thought topics. Relationships? Work? Children?

2) Throughout your day, bring awareness to the stories you tell yourself about each topic. Does your mind create different variations of the story and then repeat them? Are the stories we tell ourselves true? Choose one topic and note the different variations of the stories you've told yourself.

3) Could these stories be creating unnecessary mental agitation or emotional stress in your relationships or your work?

4) Bring awareness to emotional stress throughout your day. Can you recognize that the *thoughts* repeating your stories *are the cause* of emotional stress?

5) How would you benefit from catching your thoughts in action before they brought on emotional stress?

6) If you're open to other deeper insights I had during Vipassana, turn to part IV, "Eclectic Teachings," on page 306 and read further.

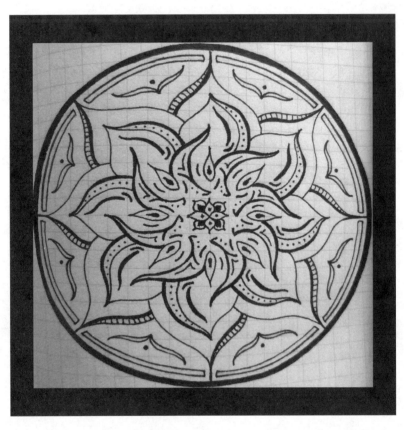

Journal Entry
'Silence'

CHAPTER 13

Month Fifteen–Thailand

Raising Resonance

> The day science begins to study the non-physical
> phenomena, it will make more progress in one decade
> than in all the previous centuries of its existence.
> —Nikola Tesla

After Vipassana, I faced one final hurdle before I could relax fully into my new Chiang Rai surroundings where I'd settle for the unforeseeable future and give rise to my creative project. I had to secure my long-stay Thai visa, which required what's known as a "visa run"[1] to Laos, a necessary aggravation for most expats in Thailand. This was what led me to my first friend in Chiang Rai and my next set of transformations.

To Vientiane and Back

The sun was falling over the Mekong River as we crossed the Friendship Bridge[2] on foot. I stood in the middle of the concrete handshake connecting Laos and Thailand, looking out over the mocha-colored waters flowing far beneath me. Fierce wind blew me like a dandelion, and a multitude of emotions flooded me. Tears of gratitude collected in the corners of my eyes. *C'mon, Eryn, pull it together. You can't cry now.*

Flashes of the last fourteen months played like a movie in my mind. The sheer vastness of all I'd seen and experienced was overwhelming. I'd seen so much, stretched and challenged myself, faced so many fears, and met so many special people from all corners of the globe. Sometimes it felt insignificant, and other times I realized it was a minor miracle that I overcame my initial fears and left the United States. The question came to me, *What would my life be right now if I'd never left?* It made me nauseous to consider that unhealthy version of myself now. I didn't know who *she* was anymore.

I opened my eyes, looking left seeing the Laos flag, then right seeing the flag of Thailand. I was almost home, and my plan of action was playing out perfectly: (1) secure apartment; (2) Vipassana; (3) visa run; (4) start writing project. I'd experienced extreme moments of gratitude like this many times during my trip, but I knew in this moment, something was different. This was the end of something beautiful—the nomadic part of the journey that exposed me to so much of the world and the healing that came with it all. Now it was the beginning of something more beautiful, where I'd begin living life from this new version of myself and would carve out a new future. I brushed the tears away and ran to catch up with my new friend Joshua.

Joshua and I stood in a short line at the Thai immigration checkpoint and waited for Mr. Grumpy immigration official to stamp our passports. He was quick and efficient—stamp, grimaced face looks up at me, stamp—done. We left the small building and rested on a bench waiting for a bus to fetch us.

Joshua is from the Netherlands. A lawyer turned yogi, in his midthirties like me. We had the chance to talk quite a bit at the embassy earlier that day, so I knew we had a lot in common. We talked about our respective Christian upbringings and leaving the hamster wheel of Westernized life in hopes of finding something simpler and more meaningful. We'd also both completed Vipassana retreats in the not-too-distant past, and I was excited to meet someone I could discuss that unique experience with. He shared with me an intense emotional release he had in an airport right after his retreat. It seems these retreats cause such personal seismic shifts they often result in emotional aftershocks. I hadn't had mine yet, but I could feel it coming.

The small, clunky, unmarked brown minivan pulled up from 1979 to retrieve us on the Thai side of the border, making a quick U-turn with a screeching halt in front of us. The expressionless Thai driver called us over with the tilt of his head, *come on*. I assumed he was Thai, but he could've been Laotian or Burmese; it's hard to know. I didn't understand his language, and he didn't understand mine.

Joshua and I looked at each other, *oyyyy*, and jumped in. I went through my standard *this could be a kidnapping* fear scenario. This seems to happen anytime I end up in these one-off transportation situations in a faraway land. At least they're just passing thoughts now rather than the internal freak-outs they used to be. That said, if I was going to be kidnapped and held in a bamboo cage, I hoped my new friend would be nearby so we could talk more about the revelations of Vipassana.

These visa runs are notoriously exhausting. I'd been warned how atrocious the trip would be. It's a twelve-hour overnight journey from Thailand to Laos, then staying overnight to secure visa paperwork and finally hopping the twelve-hour overnight bus returning to Thailand. With the mass exposure to bus rides across Tanzania and Rwanda, you'd think I would've banned myself from long-distance bus travel, but I couldn't avoid the visa run, and my parsimonious nature kept me from flying. I'm a glutton for punishment, I suppose.

We switched buses, picked up twelve other people also on visa runs, and zoomed off into the night. I moved around, fidgety in my seat, trying to find a comfortable position. The seats were uncomfortable and too far from the window to lean against. *Grrrr.* The temperature changed regularly from arctic blast to desert heat wave, carrying frequent unpleasant odors. *Lovely!*

I pulled out my travel pillow and tried unsuccessfully to bridge the gap between my shoulder and the window. I've never been one who can sleep upright in my seat. I'm so envious of people who can do that. I made peace with the idea that it would be a sleepless night. I put in my ear buds and listened to my favorite Siggy playlist.

We sped through the night, up and down hills, like a roller coaster driven by the wind, challenging the universe to see if we were meant to arrive safely to our destination. These cross-country bus journeys always seem dangerous; whether it's India, Indonesia, Tanzania, or Thailand—testing fate. I think drivers must receive bonuses for every minute they shave off of the trip. It always seems we've entered the final heat of the Grand Prix, overtaking cars around hairpin curves in the bottomless night.

I learned long ago these dangers were out of my control and released my fears. If I was meant to die on this lonely road in the middle of nowhere, Thailand, well then that was how it was meant to be. I somehow knew though, this wasn't my night to die; I still had important soul-cultivating things to do on this earth. Plus I now knew with certainty I was meant to write a book. It had all been revealed to me in Vipassana somewhere between I'm starving and I'm exhausted on day seven.

We passed through lush, dark forests and tiny villages unknown, and I settled into my little space in the van. I could feel a mighty heaviness shedding off of me. Remember *Shawshank Redemption,*[3] when Andy Dufresne escapes from prison and emerges from a sewer pipe into a small retention pond? He pulled off the layers of wet clothes in a final triumphant display of freedom. Andy's friend Red said, "He swam through a river of shit and came out clean on the other side." That's how I felt, free from the confines of the old Eryn that had held me in my own prison. *Yes, freedom!*

I closed my eyes and let the words of my favorite Ben Howard song drift through my mind, hearing his soft acoustic strings:

> … I'm walkin' back down this mountain
> With the strength of a turnin' tide
> The wind's so soft on my skin,
> The sun so hard upon my side …
> Feelin' blind and I realize,
> All I was searchin' for was me …

I thought of my soul sister, Siggy; Ben Howard was her favorite artist the last time I'd seen her, so I always thought of her when I heard his music. I thought of his lyrics and how I'd been searching for myself this whole time. This song so poignantly spoke to me in this moment. Music has a brilliant ability to bring you back to certain moments in time. I so love that.

I remembered the last time I'd said goodbye to Siggy in a Lisbon train station nine months earlier. Then my mind flashed back to the first week of my trip when I met Siggy on my thirty-seventh birthday, then to my decision to leave the United States, to my divorce, to my father's death, to *The Past*, my challenged relationship with my mother, my parents' divorce and how it changed me, and my father's mental illness that began before I was born.

These memories came fast, one after the other, but without the pain I might've experienced in the past. Instead I was liberated. I knew these events would no longer determine my future. I saw with total clarity how each decision I'd made on my trip, listening to the whispers of my soul, had led me again and again toward the best version of myself. I was free. And I was so incredibly grateful for the grace of God that had safely guided and protected me.

I felt the tears welling up in my eyes; I couldn't contain them any longer. They streamed down my face in an uncontrollable, heaving sort of way as I sat listening to Siggy's playlist. I was helpless to contain the gratitude and emotion pouring out of me, seeing the old dysfunctional version of myself that was no more, feeling the promise and hope of the new me, thinking, *What if I never left America?* I cried and cried.

I reached back behind the seat along the window and held out my hand. Joshua reached back. "Joshua, I think I'm having one of your airport moments," I said, choking back on my salty, uncontrolled tears. He gave me a sweet smile. "Just let it out," he said. "Let it out." We carried on speeding into the night toward Chiang Rai, and I held onto my new friend's hand until my tears ran out.

My friendship with Joshua is what led me to Tantra yoga, which proved to be a pivotal introduction. Having just maxed myself out on Vipassana, I thought I was done with major transformation for a while and would focus only on writing, but, as I discovered, it doesn't work that way. Once I jumped on the spiritual path, intentionally running toward my highest self, opportunities and growth leapt out at me from around every corner.

Yoga of the East

Yoga of the West can be very different from yoga of the East. In my observation and experience, Western yoga is primarily fitness based, aimed at increasing strength, flexibility and toning the body. Yoga of the East, specifically the Tantra tradition, places high emphasis on toning the mind or elevating consciousness with physical sculpting as a side effect. The same postures are used but with different intention, which, to my surprise, changed the entire yoga experience.

In considering the ancient yogis and what their intent might have been, it made sense; were they striving for a tight ass or abs of steel? No, they were working toward attaining enlightenment. In *The Yoga-Sutra of Patañjali: A New Translation and Commentary,* [4] Georg Feuerstein writes, "All too often, Western students want to bypass the philosophical aspects of Yoga and get on with its practice. But it is impossible to practice Yoga authentically without first having grasped the metaphysics. Conversely, Yoga metaphysics will not reveal its full depth to someone who stays aloof from the practical disciplines" (Feuerstein 1979, Preface). Tantra yoga thoroughly combines the physical, mental, emotional, sexual and spiritual aspects of a person, bringing about a more integrated, high-frequency[5] yogi.

My Tantra Family

In Tantra yoga, I was first struck by the group of special people who offered a sense of community I'd never before experienced—a place that felt more like "home" than any home I'd known. Arriving at Tantra yoga, I was greeted by the teacher with sincere warmth and enthusiasm and most often with a hug. Not just any hug. Tantrics believe in thirty-second hugs, no quick hug and release here; these hugs were full of acceptance and belonging. Still missing the Englishman and new to the city, I'd finally found comfort and community.

The word Tantra[6, 7] holds such mystery, no? Most who've heard of Tantra know there are aspects of sexuality that are explored in the teachings and practices. This was intriguing, but it also made me extremely skeptical. *What's it all about? What's really going on here?* I wanted to make sure I wasn't entering a strange sex cult. The origins of the teachings are also mysterious, as they seem to be an amalgamation of several Eastern philosophies, including Hinduism, Buddhism, and Kashmirian Shaivism. Concepts and theory are also included from Christianity, Judaism, and the secular world with the ultimate goal to enrich each person and help raise them to their highest self. I'd landed in the right place.

I soon came to understand the Tantric view on "sacred sexuality,"[8] and my cultish fears subsided. Tantra is a spiritual path that embraces *all* aspects of life. Whereas Buddhists and Catholics have celibate monks, priests, and nuns, Tantrics believe we should not resist our sexual nature; rather, it should be *incorporated* into our spiritual practice. When a couple comes together *in love* to experience sex, they have the opportunity to elevate in sacred union to a state of bliss. The Tantrics bring their spiritual practice to lovemaking—a beautiful idea.

I dismantled my protective shield and dove into Tantra.

Monday night classes included yoga practice and Tantra teachings where I began learning about chakras, or energy centers, in the body. There were other full-time Chiang Rai expats who attended class too, so now that I was settled in my apartment and found this special group of people, I was no longer a lonely nomad. I'd found my tribe, my people, my family, my home.

Saturday workshops were interesting, each week a new topic; forgiveness, devotion, attachment and detachment, saying yes, and the aspects of love. I felt fortunate to have found this school, and I saw it as the perfect sustaining practice to immerse myself in while working on my book. It was soul growth and maintenance wrapped in a community hug. By day, I wrote in Thai cafés, working diligently on my passion project. In the evenings, I spent time with my Tantra family. Before long I was seeing them five times a week in workshop, Tantra class, yoga class, movie night, karma yoga volunteering, and shared meals.

Personal Power

Five weeks of study were dedicated to each chakra (there are seven). I offer a brief introduction to the chakra system along with other Tantra principles on page 293 in the "Eclectic Teachings" section in the back of the book.

I found significant growth when we studied the third chakra, responsible for personal power and confidence. I'd come a long way since my first flight, but part of me felt incomplete, and I'd not been able to pinpoint its origin. Even after Vipassana where I'd shed the pattern to *need* a man in my life—a major milestone—there was still a little part of me that continued to believe life wasn't complete without one. How could I shed that aspect of myself?

With the Tantrics, I studied willpower and transcending the ego, devotion and attachment. I'd not realized how I'd attached myself to stories of *what should've been,* and this held me in an unhealthy cycle of thought. I wasn't grieving the relationship I'd *had* with the Englishman. I was grieving the relationship I *wanted* it to be. I did miss him and the time we spent together, but I came to see the relationship more clearly. I now saw things *as they were,* not how *I wanted them to be.* This was a massive shift. Through meditation and balancing my third chakra, I began transcending my cyclical thoughts and regained confidence in the decision to part ways, whereas I'd previously been checking flights to Germany and wishing he'd come profess his love. I learned to love and appreciate the Englishman from afar, not for the man I wanted him to be but for the man he actually was. I let go of my story about the *us* I wished we'd been.

I began what's known as a *tapas.*[9] Tapas is a word of Hindu origin meaning "to heat" and is associated with spiritual practice and self-discipline, like bringing fire to your practice. When one takes a tapas, it's a commitment not to be broken under any circumstance. I began a morning yoga, internal cleansing, and meditation routine and approached it with tapas fire. My teacher Avi explained, "If you decide to do something and do it, your willpower will grow. If you decide to do something and don't, your willpower will decrease." I'd not considered that willpower could be developed like a muscle. I reflected on the multitude of promises I'd made to myself, and broken, through the years. No wonder I had no willpower. I'd been continuously diminishing my inner strength since my first lapsed diet at age ten.

I committed to my tapas. I honored that commitment to myself. Willpower and inner strength began to grow.

Nearly every month, I joined an intensive retreat in order to deepen and strengthen my spiritual growth. A group of us, many regular students as well as travelers, would stay at an ashram outside the city and immerse ourselves, day and night, in an expansive subject. The immersive retreat environment provided maximum opportunity to maintain forward progression in the quest toward expansion.

One of the main tantric practices, known as transfiguration—a practice to help students see divinity in others—was practiced in nearly every gathering. Either sitting or standing, I'd face someone, and we'd stare into each other's eyes for several minutes. It was awkward and confronting and beautiful. Transfiguration strips away the physical form of each partner, showing his or her true nature and divinity. This, "prolonged open visual gaze induces a state of love and peace" (Hawkins 1995, pg. 113).[10] When labels and judgments and prejudices fall away, what's left is love. Whether they were traveling strangers or familiar students I'd see week after week, there was love. Everyone was different, yet everyone had the same divine essence behind their physical form. It bonded me to humanity.

Tantrics strive to bring their spiritual practice to everyday life with every action having purpose and meaning. What a novel idea to approach each day with conscious intention instead of chaotic, haphazard, overbooked, and manic unconscious days. I began approaching life with purpose. *I am eating this Burmese tea-leaf salad to nourish my body so that I can continue my writing project that will inspire others. I am practicing yoga daily so that my body and mind will continue to support my purpose. I am nourishing my soul with meaningful friendships so I am happy and content and can be a light in the world.* Before long, each day, each week, each month became a spiritual practice supported by a group of likeminded individuals.

We explored our lives at length, delving into all aspects of self. I observed my sadness and fears. I immersed myself in forgiveness, acceptance, and patience. As I faced myself honestly, the nature of my insecurities became clear. As clarity came to my weaknesses, the less they seemed to affect me. Through introspection and self-awareness, insecurities and dysfunctional habits lost their power over me.

The Law of Resonance

The Tantrics give much credence to the *Law of Resonance*,[11] which states that we are all operating at a certain vibrational frequency, compared often times to a radio frequency. Some people think, feel, and act from low frequencies of fear, guilt, anger, shame, greed, discontent, or negativity. Whether in relation to others *or ourselves(!)*, this holds us in low resonance. Some are tuning into happiness, joy, love, bliss, gratitude, positivity, and abundance, and these resonate at a higher vibrational frequency.

I recognized that I'd spent the first part of my life primarily in low resonance. Even though my primary wish had been to love, which is high resonance, because the unconscious intention behind giving love was to receive love, this held me in low resonance.

I remembered reading about the law of attraction, which, with the publication of the book *The Secret* became an everyday concept. The law of resonance is closely related to the law of attraction, but as I see it, the law of resonance is the backbone of the law of attraction and should've been given fundamental attention.

The law of attraction tells us to ask the universe for what we want and to hope and expect a tangible return. *The Secret* and its spin on the law of attraction encourages us to wish for things to be brought into our lives, but it doesn't address the underlying force that determines what's brought to us; that's resonance—or the quality of our consciousness.

Wayne Dyer was part of the original force behind *The Secret* but withdrew his involvement, saying, "I would've liked to have seen a little different emphasis, myself. I think too much of it is on getting, rather than giving. And if you have this incredible power to align yourself with a Universal Divine mind that is always giving and always offering, then it seems to me that that's where we ought to be putting our attention." When he was asked why he, the "father" of *The Secret*, wasn't on *The Secret* movie, he said, "I didn't want to be a part of that emphasis any longer."[12]

Related to resonance, John Kehoe writes in *Quantum Warrior: The Future of the Mind*, "Our mind has many habits, and many of them we discover are not beneficial for us. For example, the mind talks to itself almost constantly … We can be happy, miserable, bored, upset, frightened, sad, disappointed and then happy again, all within a couple of hours, depending on the inner conversations we're having with ourselves. Living like this offers no inner stability, no place to find peace or rest in the confidence of who we are, no trust in the rhythms of life, no security in the laws of the universe, just endless thinking … We also maintain our limitations with our internal talk, renewing them constantly with the energy of our chatter" (Kehoe 2011, pgs. 126–128).[13]

Remembering times past when my negative inner dialogue ruled me and held me in lower resonance, I attracted experiences I found challenging and often painful. Conversely, as I've come to raise my resonance, finding peace within myself, I'm attracting situations that are more pleasant. This doesn't mean life is free from challenges; I'm still tested regularly, but I'm now better equipped to handle adversity. If something doesn't work out, I see it as a lesson, not a failure. Answers come more quickly, emotional pains are less severe, and the best path reveals itself with minimal effort. I don't force my way through life anymore; instead, I trust the path to unfold while I make the *conscious choice* to live in high resonance. I invest my energy in developing this practice every single day.

That said, it would be remiss of me not to recognize that each person is dealt different life circumstances. Some are presented with advantageous situations, and others extreme hardship. It's an unending cycle of questions as to why this is; call it karma, God's will, or random coincidence. Whatever the case, I've come to think it's part of the spiritual journey to find peace with our individual circumstances and the courage to raise ourselves from any victimhood. Perhaps each of us is presented with the specific life lessons we're meant to overcome in this lifetime.

Living Love

My favorite tantric concept is that we should strive to live *in love* in all areas of our lives. I find that choosing love and not fear creates positive life experiences, whether I'm in line, agitated with the slow cashier at the grocery store, or interacting with my mother, or in love relationships. When there's anger, discontent, or disagreement, I add love, and amazingly, negativity and friction dissipate. Choosing love means seeing every person and situation through a lens of compassion. When it comes down to it, every living being is striving for the same thing in life—to experience maximum pleasure and minimum pain. This is a central concept in Buddhism as well. Once I opened myself to the idea that we're all seeking the same thing, I found it easier to view others with a compassionate heart.

I remembered times when I experienced jealousy in relationships. I see now that originated from a deep-seated lack of self-love, which translated into fear of abandonment and that I wasn't truly loved by my partner. I was full of insecurities and held myself in a cycle of *not enough*. Had I been able to approach my relationships from a place of self-love instead of fear, there'd be trust, integrity, and honesty, leaving no room for jealousy. Until I was able to overcome my insecurities, I lacked the internal power to live from love. I unconsciously reverted time and time again to fear-based emotions and behavior, which ironically kept me from *receiving* love from men who truly valued me.

Under the positive influences of yoga, meditation, developing personal power and inner knowing, my insecurities began to dissolve and allowed space for love. Now I live in love nearly all the time. Not in a relationship necessarily but in my everyday life. Someday I'll find a relationship that resonates with me, but I'm in no hurry. For now, I'm finding true contentment in the love of life, love for my Tantra family, and for the future I can't even imagine.

Expansion Exercises

1) Note times when you made a commitment to yourself but didn't follow through with it. Is this a repetitive pattern?

2) Can you acknowledge that breaking commitments to yourself is reducing willpower over time? Does this diminish your sense of self? Self-worth?

3) Would you be willing to start a tapas and dedicate yourself to it in order to build willpower and personal power? Choose something that you'll do every single day for a specific amount of time, a week or a month. It doesn't have to be diet or exercise related. To start, choose something simple like, at noon every single day I'll fold a piece of paper, or write a postcard, or drink a glass of water. The important thing is to *make and hold the commitment*; it doesn't matter how menial the task.

4) Give thought to the law of resonance and consider whether you are living in low or high resonance. If you knew your thoughts and feelings, as well as your actions, were causing certain experiences to be brought to your life, would you be willing to change your thoughts? Begin by bringing awareness to your thoughts.

5) Which of your thoughts and feelings are based in fear and which are in love? Notice the different feeling in your body with each.

6) What would it look like for you to *live love* in your day-to-day life? Can you bring compassion to the situations of others, understanding we are all seeking the same thing? In a stressful situation, can you make an attempt to add love and notice how it diffuses the situation?

7) Are you open to reviewing more concepts from Tantra? If so, turn to part IV, "Eclectic Teachings," on page 293 and read further.

CHAPTER 14

Month Sixteen–Thailand

Mirrors

If beating yourself up worked, you'd be rich, thin and happy.
Try loving yourself instead.
—Cheryl Richardson

I was settling into my Chiang Rai apartment and elated to have my own space again. After Vipassana, the visa run, and finding my Tantra family, I could finally focus on the important things in life—like shopping.

The excitement of unpacking my backpack and putting my belongings into drawers and in a closet was incredible. Drawers! A closet! Imagine the joy that came with the knowledge that, after carrying all I owned on my back for over a year, I could now put my clothes in a drawer. This is when I realized just how ragged my clothes were. I'd been wearing the same clothes for fifteen months. *Sigh*. If I'd bought clothes along the way, I would've had to carry them. I couldn't be bothered. Now I had drawers. It was time to go shopping!

It'd been a long time since I'd given any thought to my body image or needed to present myself in any fashionable way. Strangely enough, at month sixteen, I rarely considered my appearance or compared myself to others. This was one of the most freeing and unexpected aspects of travel. See, traveling is much different from vacation. On vacation, the tendency was to splurge on nice things, fancy dinners and expensive experiences like shows or cruises. That was my one or two weeks to let loose, relax, and enjoy myself. Traveling is the total opposite. My goal was to extend my budget so I could stay on the road longer. I stayed in cheap ashrams, hostels, or guesthouses, and my primary expenses were food and shelter with little desire for new clothes, souvenirs or extravagant experiences. Even my morning routine no longer included a hair dryer, hair products, skin moisturizers, and eye makeup. I'd given those up the first month in India. I figured as long as I was clean and didn't smell, I was all right. Okay, full disclosure; sometimes I did smell a little. Ever since I read about the possible link to deodorant and breast cancer,[1] I've been trying all those chemical-free natural deodorants. Some were more effective than others. Anyhow, if I'd worn mascara, jewelry, fancy shoes, and fashionable clothes, not only would it have been insensitive in developing countries but also it would've drawn attention to me as a "wealthy Westerner." This is best avoided, I've found.

There was such freedom in escaping the made-up life I'd been used to. Traveling was the great equalizer. In a shabby café in North India or Thailand, I could've been sitting next to a traveler with $300 in his bank account or a millionaire; I could never tell. Everyone appeared the same, and this released me from constant comparisons. I'd not even known this was possible; mental freedom from the bars of our consumerist society and the prison cell of expectation so cunningly constructed around the female form. *You're free little bird, you're free. Fly away now. Fly away.*

If I'd only been able to travel for a few weeks, I think this realization would've passed me by, but because I lived in this new mental freedom for such a substantial period of time, it made a huge impact on me. Comparisons and self-loathing simply drifted away like flowers on the Ganges, disappearing so effortlessly. I'd forgotten that most of my life, my internal dialogue had scorned me constantly of my body's inferiority. Better than forgetting though, I'd forgotten that I'd forgotten, like that part of me never existed. It was freeing but in an uneventful way. All because in traveling I was removed from television and media influence, parties and social circles, business events, networking, and commercials slowly conditioning me to consider plastic surgery and Botox to extend youth and artificially insert beauty to fit into our airbrushed society. Interestingly, even though I was dressed down as I traveled and wearing only a wee bit of foundation, handsome men were attracted to me. I think it must've been the release of stress over time. Maybe my bitchy resting face had finally left me. Siggy would be happy about that.

Now, sixteen months after leaving America, it all came rushing back to me. I stood with my head cocked sideways, looking at my reflection in a full-length mirror at a boutique. My heart rate increased, and my mind began obsessive "not good enough" slogans. My nose crinkled, and my eyebrows showed dejection. A wave of disgust and self-loathing rose from within.

You're too fat.
You could never look good in this dress.
Your arms are flabby
Your tummy is too roly.
You're not pretty enough.
Not thin enough.
Not good enough.
Not—enough—period—exclamation point!

I tore off the sundress to try on another and then another. The more dresses I tried on, the more agitated I became. I threw the dresses on a nearby rack. *Fuck this, I'm outta here!* I forced a fake smile to my friend who owned the pop-up boutique and left in a quiet rage, apologizing. I jumped on my scooter and sped home through the rush-hour Chiang Rai traffic to brood.

To drive a scooter in the city is to enter into a collective, unspoken agreement of organized chaos. Like hurried, impatient ants, we all moved, scrambling in different directions; stopping, engaging, pausing, swerving to avoid dogs and monks, jumping sidewalks, scooters filling any open spaces at the corner of supreme craziness and Pad Thai junction. I tried to focus on the road instead of the family of four on their underpowered scooter. *How do they do that?* I thought briefly about a stop for my laundry and a massage at Supaporn's house. Yes, that's her real name, Supaporn, and she does have magic hands. No, not *those* kind of magic hands. She's a legitimate Thai masseuse and runs a laundry service. I thought a massage might calm me down, but I didn't want my favorite laundry lady to see me this way. I was just so ... so angry. *Eryn, where has your inner Zen goddess gone?*

I made it home safely and gorged on chocolate while trying to reclaim my calm, chill, live-love attitude. I hadn't experienced any feelings like this since leaving the United States, and it was, frankly, shocking and disturbing to feel them again.

Extracting Fibers of Pain

Early in my trip, after the Buddhism course, I began the habit of self-reflection, and I found it extremely helpful with negative emotions. I'd feel something painful—anything—and I'd stop my thoughts, observe the emotion, and then tease out the little fibers of pain to determine the root cause. In doing this, after my bombshell boutique experience, I extracted two major insights:

1) This incident was striking because it had been sixteen months since I'd last experienced these self-loathing negative emotions. I'd hardly seen myself in a full-length mirror over that time and I'd forgotten how I used to berate myself hourly, daily, and with each glance in the mirror for two-plus decades. I was taken aback by the sudden resurrection of old, familiar emotions; frustration, agitation,

anger, disgust, and the negative inner dialogue related to my body.

2) My frame of mind had changed in ceasing my nomadic life, now settled in one town. On my first flight, I decided to take on a new approach to life. I realized that if I wanted to integrate into foreign cultures, especially those of extreme poverty, I had to drop my, some would say, spoiled standards that I'd been accustomed. Questionable food, safe water supply, squat toilets in dirty places, hard, thin mattresses in dingy rooms would be drastically different from the American life I'd left.

I saw it as a necessity to be at peace with whatever my surroundings would be. Actually, I wouldn't say I knew I needed to be at peace. I wasn't so Zen about it then. I just knew I was stepping out of the comfortable life I'd known and entering a world I couldn't possibly fathom—just little ole me from the South going out into the world.

The unknown was so incredibly frightening, with endless possibilities for disaster; the only way I could calm myself, even a tiny bit, was to believe that it didn't matter what happened as long as I was safe. To be blunt, I decided I would consider the trip a complete success if I could avoid being raped, kidnapped, or murdered.

I had a little talk with myself on the plane to calm my nerves.

Eryn, does it matter where you sleep? Nope, not if you're safe. Does it matter what strange foods you eat? Nope, as long as you're safe. What if your bag gets stolen? Or your passport? What if you're attacked? Pen defense skills, Eryn. You got this—jab!

It was a very long forty-six hours of traveling from Atlanta, Georgia, to Rishikesh, India, with a lot of time to anticipate all that could go wrong in my decision to solo travel—starting in India! I finally concluded that nothing mattered—nothing, *nothing*—as long as I was safe. It was the global scale survival edition of *Don't Sweat the Small Stuff*.

In that small intentional shift, my entire perception changed. I viewed the world through a different lens, safety my only concern. It served me well those sixteen months, but now things were different. In settling and having my own apartment, learning the streets, having a scooter, making friends who lived there, frequenting my favorite restaurants, I wasn't worried about my safety anymore. I was feeling at home in Chiang Rai. Now that life safety was of less concern, my mind was freed to obsess on other nuances of life. The critical voices of my old self were quick to fill the space, and just like that, I was my own worst enemy again.

It had taken me many months to notice how different I felt *not* making these habitual critical jabs. They'd magically dissolved with each border I crossed, yet it only took an instant to recognize their return when I went shopping. Suddenly, I reverted to my "less than" self.

Then I got angry.

Eryn, you're telling me after ten days of Buddha boot camp in India, psychic surgeries in Brazil, humility rising in Africa, fourteen days of silent epiphanies in a Thai forest monastery, a thousand other jumped hurdles, and overcoming The Past, you still hate yourself? After all the climbing you've done, arduously ascending the emotional, psychological, and spiritual Kilimanjaro, you still hate your body? I still hate my body. I still hate my body! Are you freaking kidding me? Aggggghhhh!

I'd been thrown back into the prison I'd escaped once before—my *less than* mind. That's when I realized I had a choice. I may have been sucked into the vortex of self-judgments spanning from adolescence into my thirties not realizing another way of life existed. But now I knew better. I'd lived in freedom for over a year. I could not—I would not go back to that prison of self-hatred.

There I stood with the reflective revelation I could no longer avoid, *I still hate my body.*

This event sparked the intention to heal this aspect of myself and ultimately to write this book with a healing theme knowing so many women struggled with similar *not enough* feelings. I didn't know it then, but this was a pivotal moment that would take me from self-loathing and *I hate my body* to inner contentment and *radical self-acceptance* in less than thirty days.

Expansion Exercises

1) What negative inner dialogue repeats in your mind? *I'm not enough, I'm too fat, I can't do* _____, *I'll never find love.* Anything repetitive or negative, make note in your journal.

2) Think of a time recently you were upset about something. Were you actually upset about what you thought you were upset about or was there an underlying pain coming out? *I'm not being heard. I'm not being accepted. I'm not being understood.* Next time you feel emotional pain rising, make efforts to slow down the emotion and extract the root cause of the pain. It's rarely about the surface issue that has upset us and is most often deeply rooted.

3) If you could live with the mind-set *all that matters is my safety,* how would that allow you to live a happier existence with fewer preferences and expectations?

4) How often do you compare yourself to others? Does this create a state of unworthiness within? If so, note your thoughts.

5) What would it feel like to release comparisons and the negative inner dialogue?

Journal Entry
'Possibilities'

CHAPTER 15

Month Sixteen—Thailand

Facing My Freedom

When we sit with ourselves in total truth,
we change the world; it starts with changing ourselves.
—Eryn Donnalley

After the boutique, it struck me: we *must* love our bodies; anything else is unacceptable. I decided I couldn't go *one more day* disliking myself! I was done. Over it! I was angry that I'd gone so long not realizing I still hated my body, but there ya go. I guess we wake up to these things when we're meant to.

I said to myself, determined:

I've overcome all sorts of emotional and psychological hurdles since I've been traveling. How have I done that? Through various types of meditation and facing myself in truth, not hiding from anything. Okay, then how can I translate that into a practice that will heal this distorted view of my physical self?

This is where the practice was born that I would later name Facing Freedom. I decided to sit in front of a full-length mirror, naked, for thirty minutes each morning, forcing myself to *just be with my body,* allowing no distractions. I would commit to this practice with *tapas fire* for thirty days.

In this chapter, I share the personal journal entries from my thirty days Facing Freedom. In the next chapter, I'll lead you to take this journey on your own. When I first began this exercise, the primary goal was to overcome body image issues. Upon reflection though, having completed the practice over two years ago, I realize it created a shift that extended *far beyond* the love/hate relationship with my body. It instilled a deeper sense of self-worth and self-respect I didn't even know I could develop. I no longer have thoughts like, *I'm not good enough* or *I don't deserve* _____. Insecurities and lack of confidence have vanished. I had no idea this practice would propel me to an existence where I eat healthily and exercise regularly, doing it because I truly *want* to nourish and support my body, not because my inner bully told me I should. I don't have an inner bully anymore.

The truth is the first day I sat in front of the mirror, I changed in some way. The day after that, I changed in a different way, and the next and so on, compounding with cumulative effect. Once I set the intention and committed to the practice, the shift began. We are never the same person as we were yesterday or will be tomorrow; whether we realize it or not, we are constantly evolving. It seems to me it's just a matter of what new experiences we expose ourselves to, whether we will evolve slowly or at an accelerated pace. This is an integrated fast-track exercise that can bring transformation at any stage of your journey, but no two people will experience it the same.

It's not a fun exercise. I won't lie to you. And I'm all too aware of the comic opportunities surrounding this practice. I fought many battles with my ego the night I came up with the idea that tried to tell me how ridiculous it was. I overcame those sabotaging voices for lasting change, and I hope you will too.

Facing Freedom—Thirty Days

Day 1   July 19, 2015

It took me awhile to get over myself—a long while. I sat with a variety of obsessive critical thoughts: Oh, look at how my breasts sag too much. Sigh. Ugggh, there are veins I can see under my skin on my breasts; that's not very attractive. Geez, I wish my nipples were a darker brown; I always thought women's breasts looked so much more beautiful if the aureole were dark brown and not light brown like mine. Look at my belly button how it's barely visible, only a slit because, well, I'm a tad roly-poly in that area. I'm glad I can't see the cellulitis and dimples that are surely on my butt and thighs.

Hmmm, look at my pubic area with brown hair, trimmed and short yet unacceptable now by American standards. I wonder, are all women really waxing, shaving, and spending hours, not to mention countless dollars, on such beautifications? I'm a grown woman, not a nine-year-old girl. I am meant to have hair down there! When did it become unacceptable to be natural?

I'm disgusted looking at my body. I feel like I'm auditioning for a movie I'm not pretty enough to be in; Genevieve the casting director sits in the corner of my mind, disapprovingly, and dismisses me with the roll of her eyes and the wave of her hand. *Who let fatso in here?*

I'm annoyed with Genevieve for showing up uninvited and already bored with my thoughts, not to mention it's so freakin' painful to sit here with my own negativity.

How long can I really sit here, just me and the saggy sisters? Saggy breasts, saggy breasts, *saggy breasts*! Aggggghhhh! This is some bizarre form of mental and emotional torture. Maybe this whole mirror meditation is a terrible idea!

Must switch gears, my mind is swirling out of control.

How would it feel to visualize another person sitting naked across from me? I wonder.

I'm going to start with a man. How do I feel if Avi, my Tantra yoga teacher, is sitting in front of me right now? He sees only beauty in me. I trust him, and he's someone I'm comfortable with. He's a good, safe, supportive male figure I can try this out with in my mind. As I imagine Avi sitting in front of me, I'm surprisingly calm and comfortable with it. Would he see me as a sexual being and look beyond my imperfections? I feel a certain feminine power and could seduce him if I wanted to—in my mind anyway—he has a girlfriend.

Men from my past come to mind. I'm struck that my past relationships were with men that were both older than me and at least a little overweight. I realize I'd unconsciously chosen these partners so they wouldn't criticize my unhealthy eating habits and we could perpetuate the cycle of unhealthy living together.

I'm remembering my first love, a very good-looking, age-appropriate boyfriend who I spent several years with—my world at the time. He regularly criticized my weight and encouraged me to exercise. Sitting in front of the mirror, I realize that this regular criticism when I was young was quite damaging. After that relationship ended, I almost exclusively became involved with men who were overweight and older. Pattern awareness—check.

Perhaps I felt more comfortable with older men having been an only child and so close to my father. The father/daughter relationship is delicate, and these early interactions have much influence on the women young girls will become. Or perhaps I'm just an old soul. I don't believe the soul has an age, and there's nothing wrong with relationships with older men, but the pattern is worth examining.

Since traveling and overcoming insecurities, I'm naturally drawn to more age-appropriate men who were also physically healthy. Yay!

Okay, enough about men. Now I imagine Mila, a yoga instructor from the Tantra school, was sitting in front of me. She's a goddess!

Changing from a man to a woman changes my emotional state drastically!

With Mila sitting in front of me, I feel my body tense up immediately. I sit straighter, I suck in my tummy, and negative feelings and insecurities flood me. I'm angry and feel like crying, mostly out of embarrassment. I feel awkward, judged, and compared. I scan the differences of our bodies, nitpicking every single detail of how she is more beautiful than me. Her hair, her skin, her eyebrows, her long legs, her perky breasts. Self-disgust overwhelms me.

Reality check: I'm participating in self-hatred and comparison because of women. Not men! It's related to women! It's the women! Aggggh! I see instantly how I create my own cycle of body dysmorphia and low self-esteem, obsessively comparing myself to others. When I compare and obsess, this diminishes my self-worth, which leads me to emotional overeating and weight gain. Pattern awareness—check.

We're doing it for the women. We must stop this!

Post-Meditation

I notice an increased feeling of confidence, happiness, and energy. I also feel *enough*—content with myself. Is this first-time meditation excitement, thinking this could really help? It feels good. I wonder if this could help other women too.

Day 2   July 20, 2015

Today doesn't feel as powerful as yesterday. *Waah, waah, waah disappointing.*

No major realizations. I don't feel like crying or have severe emotional pain, yet I'm still uncomfortable. Seems more matter of fact today. I'm sitting here looking at myself, trying to get used to the idea of doing this every day.

Saggy breasts, stretch marks on my thighs, frizzy hair, sigh.

Genevieve gives me her dirty looks from afar, though it's not quite the contemptuous glare she gave me yesterday. Progress?

I feel less than adequate looking at my breasts asking them why they don't stand up in a salute-the-world sort of way. They look back at me sadly and say, *"We're doing the best we can."* I notice tiny stretch marks on my inner thighs as I sit cross-legged. I remembered sitting next to other students in adolescence, how uncomfortable I felt with my stretch marks visible. I'd intentionally adjust my sitting posture, stretching my legs out straight so they wouldn't be visible. Ridiculous! We all have stretch marks when we sit like that!

I notice my faint tan lines and wish I had perfect brown skin like the Asian women here. I notice my red rosacea cheeks, something I've dealt with for decades with much embarrassment, wishing they could be different.

On the plus side, I'm not quite as critical of myself as I was yesterday, and that *is* profound, isn't it? If yesterday it took me fifteen minutes to stop berating myself, and today it only takes me ten minutes, that's a huge improvement!

If we're all facing our insecurities and our true selves in the mirror, wouldn't that take away the power of comparing ourselves to one another? Isn't it in the hiding from ourselves, masking reality, where much damage is done? But we're all flawed—all imperfect. If we simply acknowledged the imperfections, choosing to see beauty instead of defect, wouldn't we be happier? Isn't anything else denying what is—what's real?

I also see glimpses of beauty. This is surprising. Simple, as nature intended beauty. Then a striking vision—other women doing this same meditation and how painful it would be. I see dozens, hundreds, thousands of women unknown to me, all caught up in the same pandemic of low self-worth and similar body-image issues, all sitting simultaneously across the world, facing themselves in front of their mirrors.

I cry for the collective suffering that we've experienced and continue to experience as women.

Day 3   July 21, 2015

I'm bored today. Wish my boobs were perkier. Wish my tummy tighter so my belly button looks round. Genevieve is pointing her finger and shaking her head. *Fatso, what are you doing here?* Two things come to mind.

1) We're all the same, all imperfect. This realization takes away the power of comparison. Yesterday it was a question; today it's an answer. Comparison is the seed of envy that sprouts jealousy and unearths the tree of low self-worth.

2) It would benefit me if I got real with myself. To be realistic and to accept things as they are. This is a big one. Now that I've been out of the United States for a while, I see that people in our developed world have come to expect instant gratification—text, e-mail, phone, Facebook messages, food, Amazon shipment—everything is fast. Is this good—the expectation of instant everything, including weight loss? When I don't lose weight quickly enough, this causes me mental anguish. This anxiety and frustration decreases my desire to exercise and makes me turn to food for comfort. Then I feel guilty, which drives me back to food for comfort. The cycle repeats. I cannot expect Ramen Noodle healing or weight loss in this microwave society!

In front of the mirror today, I realize I'm in control. It's empowering. I realize I want to eat healthily and to stop eating before I feel full. Not because I want to lose weight, because I want a healthy body. My body *is* a temple!

I'm feeling a shift.

Day 4   July 22, 2015

I'm still judging and belittling the saggy sisters and wishing I had a better haircut. It's so hard to get a good haircut in Thailand. I hold up my breasts and feel much happier. At my thinnest weight, I'm a D cup, and my heaviest, a DDD, and at thirty-eight, gravity is taking its toll. I think traveling has even been hard on my breasts for some reason; maybe they've suffered from travel fatigue too. I hold my breasts higher again, and that makes me happier. That's not being real, Eryn! I let my breasts rest naturally. If I hold them, I'm hiding from *what is*. Why would I do that? This is who I am. This is reality. The saggy sisters sit nicely in their natural resting position.

Leaning back, I sit cross-legged, resting on my hands. Ohhh look how it stretches my tummy to look flat. Much better. Yes, almost seductive. No, Eryn, that's trying too hard. Back to my saggy sisters and tummy rolls. Sigh.

I'm bored with this frontal view, so I sit sideways.

Oh, please God no, not the side view! I see a whole new perspective of grossness! Like starting all over again on day one. Genevieve rolls her eyes.

My little pooch looks fatter and more roly from the side. I notice the flab on my upper arms. If only I could eliminate that little fat pooch between my armpit and breast. Grrrr. My breasts look even lower than they did when I faced forward. Shall I have a breast lift? Wait, surgery is hiding in a way too—not accepting what is. I am so tired of not accepting myself as I am. I've read enough Eckhart Tolle to know this is my ego fucking with me. Get real! Defeat your ego, Eryn! *Yarrrrrr!* I see myself standing *Braveheart* style declaring victory—except I'm holding a bouquet of Gerbera daisies to the sky instead of a warrior weapon. *Yarrrrrr!*

I don't want to hide from myself anymore. I want to accept the natural progression of life—to be strong enough in myself and in my character to know that I am enough no matter how my body changes. What if a man won't love me with my little belly roll? Well if he doesn't, then he's not the man for me and I don't want him.

My yoga teacher Avi said in class today, "Happiness is accepting the necessary." Yes, that makes a lot of sense. It's my resistance that causes anxiety and anguish. Hmmm. Must give this more thought.

Day 5   July 23, 2015

Definitely don't feel like doing this mirror meditation today. Had beer and chocolate last night, and I wasn't looking forward to seeing the results in the mirror. Genevieve scorns me, *You'll pay for that!*

Happily I see there are no larger bulges or noticeably negative results from the chocolate and beer. Yay! I didn't grow two more fat rolls overnight!

I don't feel guilty about eating sweets like I used to. I eat when I'm truly hungry, and mostly I eat healthy foods, so it's okay to treat myself once in a while. I am filling the emotional emptiness inside with self-love instead of sugary, fatty foods. *Gerbera daisy warrior salute. Yarrrr!*

I see that as I've traveled and gained more emotional stability, I don't participate in emotional eating nearly as much until there's a man around. I noticed this in Africa with the Englishman. I eat more food even at standard meal times when a man is around, whereas when I'm alone, I eat smaller meals only when I'm hungry. Eating habits are different when single versus in relationship. I've identified another pattern!

Today I'm alone, and I notice that I'm more balanced. Does this mean I should remain single to maintain a healthy equilibrium? Perhaps. Hahaha. Why do I get pulled off my center when there's a man in the picture? The good news is the happier and more emotionally balanced I am, the less I need to have a man in my life. I am finding balance on my own. Go me.

Observation: I've been choosing partners with the wrong intention. I wasn't so much asking if the men were good for me. Instead I was making sure I was good for them. *Love me, love me.* Embarrassing but true admission. Next time I'm going to slow down and ask more questions of potential romantic interests.

I think I will do some push-ups. Yes, that would feel good right now! That's new. I *want* to do push-ups. What the hell? Big day.

Day 6 July 24, 2015

I am so tired this morning. I don't want to do the meditation. I do it anyway. Still think my boobs are hanging like the African village women. Genevieve stands in the corner of my mind with her hands beneath her perky breasts. *Look how perfect mine are! Na-na-na-na-na-nah.* Grrrrr.

Maybe this meditation isn't working. I hate this. I hate this!

What if I took away my arms and my legs and my breasts. Wouldn't I still be Eryn? Wouldn't the true essence of who I am exist beyond my physical form? Why have we conditioned ourselves to see beauty on the outside before looking inside? Is it our overly stimulated sensory world that causes us to make judgments? Perhaps another trick of the ego constantly looking to say we're better than someone else? I'm so annoyed with us as humans in this moment. I really am.

What if we followed the Tantra transfiguration concept with ourselves and only saw love?

Hmmm, I think I'll do planks today.

Day 7   July 25, 2015

I watch my body move with each breath. There is a little area on the side of my neck that expands and contracts with the flow of blood through my veins. My breasts move up and down slightly as I breathe. I stare into my own eyes, getting lost in the layers of color. As I watch myself move, I think, *What a beautiful miracle of creation.*

I've never, before this *Facing Freedom* practice, looked at myself in the mirror for this long. I realize how quickly I used to turn away from my image, especially when naked. It struck me that when I hated and judged myself harshly, it was because I only stayed in front of the mirror long enough to give myself the *not good enough* jabs. If I force myself to sit and observe the subtle movements of my body, being fully present and aware of myself, then I move beyond the judgment. This is important. If I look at myself long enough, I cannot hate myself! I feel a major shift right now. Big realization for today. Whoa!

Now looking at the saggy sisters—the last six days, I've been saying, "Oh damn"; now I'm saying, "So what." My skin isn't perfect, *so what.* Stretch marks on my thighs, *so what.* Veins showing beneath my pale skin, *so what.* Not only so what, but I'm thankful because that means my body is working and functioning as it's intended.

I remember the village women in Rwanda and wonder if they hate their bodies. I somehow feel the view they have of themselves is less critical than a typical woman from the West. I wish I could ask them now.

Today I realize I've been manipulated and molded by a billion-dollar marketing industry. *Buy this high-end label handbag; you'll feel so much happier carrying it. Wear this brand-name clothing line; you'll be more beautiful. Apply this free radical micro bubble foundation, and your skin will be flawless.* I see the advertising industry relies on making me feel inadequate, and I've colluded with it, believed it, and bought into it! If I feel enough, I'm not receptive to their propaganda.

Perhaps the conversation we should be having is why we have become an overweight nation. It's not about the food we're eating; it's about *why* we're eating it. Perhaps it would be helpful if we started a conversation about the underlying intention of overeating and optimal emotional health instead of fad diets. I was caught in the cycle of acceptable overconsumption for decades now with no understanding or control over it.

I'm thinking about how long I hated my body. When did it start? I can't really say, but it was around eight I think. It began with sitting hours in front of the television soothing myself with cheese. I refuse to spend another day of life hating myself. Thirty years is long enough.

Day 8   July 26, 2015

Again. The mirror. Again! This is getting really monotonous day after day. Geez, the boredom. The minutes seem to stretch into hours.

The sun peers in through the window, and I notice hundreds of tiny hairs on my skin, and I wonder why they're there. They must have a purpose. I am perfectly created, and everyone else is too.

It seems so against nature for a species to think lowly of itself. Does a tree judge its bark? How can we find a deep inner acceptance of self?

Keep doing this exercise. Something good is happening. I hate this process, but it's good. See where this goes.

Day 9   July 27, 2015

Wasn't able to meditate this morning, so I'm doing the meditation at night after dinner. Not a good idea. My belly is fatter, and I feel worse about myself. I ate a big salad and bread for dinner, but I am telling myself that I shouldn't have had the bread. I'm not one of those people that will eat a salad because I'm *supposed* to—not anymore anyway. I wanted the salad, and I wanted the bread. But now it's me and my mirror and Genevieve flipping through her carb-counting book.

As I sit tonight with my full belly, I realize I am sucking in my tummy. No one is here, no one is watching me, and I'm sucking in my tummy? I've been doing this for the last nine days of meditation and probably every single day of my life and have not realized it until this moment! That's disturbing.

I release the tension in my tummy and sit completely naturally, except it doesn't feel natural. Sucking in my tummy feels more natural. Apparently it became habit without my even knowing it. I've been walking around my whole life sucking in my tummy! Pattern awareness—check.

Tummy in. Tummy out. Tummy in. Tummy out. I want to feel the difference. This brings up painful emotions. How could I have been doing this my whole life not realizing it?

Fuck this meditation. I hate myself! I want someone to tell me they love me. To need me. To want me. I realize in this moment I want some external validation or support. Is there cheese in my refrigerator? Or chocolate? Or wine? I slow the emotion down and feel the feeling fully, the feeling that directs me to believe something *out there* will make it better *in here*. This is a false idea. Something inside tells me I need something or someone to fill this void. Why aren't I enough within myself? Why is this so painful? Why? I'm going to bed.

Day 10   July 28, 2015

I want to accept imperfection. This is the key.

I want to embrace imperfection.

I have a habit of filling the emotional void with external sources, and in the past I've found acceptance and validation in that. I want, I wish, I intend, I choose to overcome this habit. This is the key, I think. The key that unlocks true happiness.

Do I exist outside of my physical traits? Yes. I am a soul. I am everything, and I am nothing. I am love. That sounds like some spiritual bullshit, Eryn. No, it's not. I am love. I am love.

Day 11   July 29, 2015

Hiccups! So bizarre to see my body convulse involuntarily with each hiccup. My stomach moves, my breasts move. What is the reason for hiccups? Our bodies must be perfectly designed, and they serve some purpose.

Thinking about my visit yesterday to the mall and an American Eagle store. Been a long time since I've had exposure to Westernized shops or television. Over the last sixteen months, that's played a huge part in my altered perception of self. Just being removed from these external influences has allowed certain comparisons to fall away. But yesterday, I watched the store's television ad, beautiful women running seductively on a beach in their short shorts. No wonder I don't miss television! Immediately I took up my old habit of comparing myself to these "perfect" women. *Ohhh I could never wear those shorts. Look at her perfect skin, her hair and her body.* Negative inner dialogue resumed. Pattern awareness—check.

Day 12   July 30, 2015

Deviation from mirror meditation.

I missed my morning routine today and planned to do it in the evening but instead took part in another powerful experience with my Tantra family, so I've included it here.

Several yogis and I from Tantra began what's known as the Oshawa diet.[1] It's named after the Japanese man who founded the macrobiotic philosophy and is said to balance the body and eliminate diseases. Some of the serious Tantra yogis participate in this restricted eating plan once a month. Only four foods are allowed for ten days: brown rice, wheat, millet or buckwheat, and salt. Brown rice + ten days = good times. *Not!*

We met regularly during Oshawa for dinner at the yoga studio/ashram where Avi my teacher and some of the serious yogis lived. If we couldn't have yummy normal food, at least we could have good friends to share the oh-so-exciting brown rice with. At dinner, I finally mentioned to my friends that I'd begun this mirror meditation and how I felt it was already bringing a deep shift only at eleven days. I was curious to hear what Avi had to say about my special project with his vast meditation experience and psychology degree. I really valued his input. "Yes, that could be a really powerful tool, Eryn," he said. That's when Avi suggested we do an adoration meditation. *Say whaaaaat?* I didn't know what it was, and I didn't like the sound of it, but I played along.

In the studio, each with a cushion, we sat in formation like a small baseball diamond with me at home plate, Avi at second base directly across from me, and Sasha and Mila at first and third. They all sat facing me, and Avi said, "Just receive us adoring you. We're honoring the divine feminine in you." *Say whaaaaaaat?*

I closed my eyes and immediately started laughing, feeling so uncomfortable with their eyes focused only on me. I wanted to get up and run away. I felt exposed, seen, unworthy of their attentions. I laugh when I'm uncomfortable, and I couldn't stop laughing.

Awkward, embarrassing, and uncomfortable. *Run away, run away!* I stayed.

I suggested we switch our gaze to someone else until I could stop laughing.

Mila, one of my teachers was the next focus. She sat tall and confident in herself, a true goddess. We all looked on admiring her beauty, her radiance. She closed her eyes to pause between making eye contact with each of us individually. I was still getting used to these transfiguration exercises, and it was awkward for someone like me who'd become adept at avoiding prolonged eye contact with other people, except for romantic loves.

Avi next. He's a beautiful soul, full of love and grace, masculine yet so full of emotion, charisma, and warmth. We sat staring, me adoring him, he receiving it. Sometimes I wondered if I was in love with this man. Sometimes I saw him only as my teacher. Other times our special connection confused me and I wanted more. There were blurry lines filled with question marks, knowing his connection to me wasn't unique, while mine to him was.

Finally we focused on Sasha. She and I are both from America, whereas Avi is from Israel, and Mila from Bosnia. Sasha and I were new friends, but there was something familiar about her. As I looked into her eyes, adoring the strong, beautiful woman she is, I saw her internal power and her soft femininity. I wished I could somehow achieve that combination.

As I gazed at Sasha, her eyes locked with mine. I saw her. I saw me. I was Sasha, and she was me. I sent her adoration. She received it. I began asking myself why I had such a hard time with this exercise. Why is this so hard? Tears fell across my cheeks as I continued to hold her gaze, knowing soon they'd be looking at me. *Why can't I be seen?*

All attention turned back to me. I closed my eyes, grounding myself in this moment. I opened my eyes, beginning transfiguration with Sasha, still seeing myself in her. I smiled at my beautiful friend, tears rolling down my face. I felt love and adoration from her. Such an intense expression of platonic love, yet I felt uncomfortable receiving it. *Why can't I receive this? Why? They're trying to give me an incredible gift, and I can't receive it.*

Closing my eyes, I centered myself, then looked at Avi. He adores me, I know. He looks on me with nothing but love and admiration for, as Avi calls it, "the divine female form." I couldn't use those words, but he does. Avi and I connected in our intense gazing, and I received his adoration without laughter for the first time.

Then I turned to Mila. I'd already noticed I was comparing myself less to her now than I was eleven days before, when I started the mirror exercise. Still I recognize she's thinner than me with perfect skin, beautiful mermaid-like hair, and perky breasts. She's a sweet and vibrant spirit. In the past, I would've retreated from friendship with Mila, disliking her because of her goddess-like features and angry that I didn't have her beauty. I think this is the first time I am recognizing a woman's beauty without secretly hating her for it. It wasn't supposed to be about her. *Right, I forgot.* In this moment, it was meant to be about me. I looked at Mila and tried to receive the love she radiated outward toward me.

Tonight I learned to receive. It was confronting and awkward and painful but necessary. I received and accepted their love and adoration. Truly transformational.

Day 13   July 31, 2015

I'm back at my mirror, thinking of the day I had hiccups when I realized my body was made to perfection. I carry on with this line of thought.

Yes, because of my age, my body is changing in ways I don't like. This is a reality I must face, and this resisting nature is what brings me emotional suffering. The Buddhists might say that it is my own desire to look a certain way and my grasping at that youthful image that causes my suffering.

Why am I so hell-bent on resisting nature? Where does this begin? I consider the beauty and cosmetic surgery industries banking on my "not enough" fears so I will buy more things. What a well-crafted and perfectly executed business plan I've colluded with all these years.

I wonder. Our evolution has taken us from primitive to modern, from nature to shopping malls, further from reality and closer to delusion. Should we consider this progression or regression?

Day 14 August 1, 2015

I am so bored with this freakin' meditation! I hate it, I hate it! I'm tired of looking at myself. Maybe I should say "I love you" out loud as my friend Joshua suggested when I told him about the mirror meditations. That sounds stupid, Eryn.

Hmmmm. "I love you."

I cringe as I say the words.

"I love you." My nose wrinkles up, and I am averse to this declaration of self-love. I say it again. "I love you." And then I say it again and again.

Cringe.

Will I ever believe this?

Day 15 August 2, 2015

"I love you, I love you, I love you, I love you, I love you, I love you, I love you," I repeat to myself in the mirror over and over again, each time wincing and cringing a bit less. Since I'm learning Thai and because I'm so damn bored with this routine, I say, "I love you," in Thai. "Chan rak khun, chan rak khun, chan rak khun." It didn't hold the same power as it did in English.

Am I genuinely connecting with myself in saying this, or am I brainwashing myself? I suppose if there ever was a healthy brainwashing, this is it. Carry on.

"I love you I love you I love you …"

Hmmm, I wonder if I were stranded on a desert island, would I still think my body imperfect? No is the simple answer. I'd be too concerned with finding food and shelter, and there'd be no one else for comparison. I am perfect as I am, and so is the next woman.

Does low self-esteem correlate with being overweight? Not necessarily. There are plenty of thin women with low self-esteem. This is a dysfunction of the mind, independent of the body. We must explore and heal from whatever pains of life have caused us to consciously or unconsciously devalue ourselves.

Pattern awareness: My emotional imbalances of times past caused me to turn to coping strategies like emotional eating, binge television watching, drinking, and shopping. If I cure the imbalance, I stop the need for the coping strategies that plagued me for decades and possibly what would have been my whole lifetime.

I am perfect, just the way I am. "I love you." Cringe.

I'm tired of brown rice.

Day 16   August 3, 2015

"I love you, I love you, I love you, I love you."

"Chan rak khun, chan rak khun, chan rak khun."

This is ridiculous, Eryn! Keep going.

Day 17   August 4, 2015

Who am I? Avi says if we ask ourselves this simple question, contemplating it at length, we will eventually come to a place of unshakable confidence. Unshakable confidence? Foreign concept.

Who am I?[2] Am I the arms and legs of this body or am I my memories or my mind? Am I my lips or my hair or my hands? What if I lose my arms? Am I still Eryn? Yes. What if I lose my memory? Am I still Eryn? Yes. There is a deeper Eryn inside me that exists even if my body and mind don't. How can I not love her? She is perfectly designed to exist and to be.

"I love you, I love you, I love you, I love you, I love you."

"Chan rak khun, chan rak khun, chan rak khun, chan rak khun."

P.S. I am thankful for my arms and legs and the rest of my functioning body.

Day 18   August 5, 2015

"A flower doesn't compare itself to the flower next to it. It just blooms" (unknown).

What is this not enough feeling? Where does it come from? It comes when I compare myself to others. Why do I compare? Because my egoic mind tells me I should be the prettiest, the smartest, the most talented, and, and, and … I know, intellectually I can never be the best at everything. Why would I hold myself to an unreasonable standard I cannot live up to? This is crazy.

I used to think ego was related to arrogance. Eckhart Tolle,[3] in *A New Earth*, is helping me see it differently:

> A shy person who is afraid of the attention of others is not free of ego, but has an ambivalent ego that both wants and fears attention from others. The fear is that the attention may take the form of disapproval or criticism, that is to say, something that diminishes the sense of self rather than enhances it. So the shy person's fear of attention is greater than his or her need of attention. Shyness often goes with a self-concept that is predominately negative, the belief of being inadequate. Any conceptual sense of self—seeing myself as this or that—is ego, whether predominately positive (I am the greatest)

or negative (I am no good). Behind every positive self-concept is the hidden fear of not being good enough. Behind every negative self-concept is the hidden desire of being the greatest or better than others. Behind the confident ego's feeling of and continuing need for superiority is the unconscious fear of inferiority. Conversely, the shy, inadequate ego that feels inferior has a strong hidden desire for superiority. Many people fluctuate between feelings of inferiority and superiority, depending on situations or the people they come into contact with. All you need to know and observe in yourself is this: Whenever you feel superior or inferior to anyone, that's the ego in you.

I'm not better than anyone else. I'm not less than anyone else. I am simply me.

Day 19   August 6, 2015

I continued with the "I love yous," sometimes looking at my body, sometimes looking into my eyes. As I stare into my right eye, I drift into a trancelike state. I go into and out of it. When in trance, my body loses its form and appears as a hologram, shifting and changing ever so slightly yet in a noticeable way. I appear black and white, once thinking I can see through myself, as though my body isn't really there.

What the hell is this?

I don't know, but in this moment I feel like nothing and everything at once. Sitting right here in front of myself, I don't exist, yet I'm aware of my existence beyond physical form. *Whoa.*

Must ponder this further …

Day 20   August 7, 2015

Today I'm sad and lonely. I cry while I watch myself in the mirror. I'm questioning so many things in life now. Why am I here in Thailand? Why am I here on Earth? Have I truly found my purpose? Why is my writing not flowing well? I've been gone from the United States seventeen months now. Will I ever want to return? Maybe I will stay here with my Tantra family, but how will I make money? Will I find a life partner? What does my future hold?

I'm lonely. I'm sad. That's all. This will pass. Today is the last day of brown rice. Real food resumes tomorrow.

"I love you." Cringe.

Day 21   August 8, 2015

I think I'm coming to accept "I am." I am human. I am a being. I exist. I am spiritual. I am love. I am light. I am. This is enough. This is everything.

Day 22   August 9, 2015

Here I am sitting in front of this stupid mirror again! I'm so over this morning "self-love" routine. *Grrrr.* I carry on … Dammit, carry on!

Today I notice that I'm still holding in my tummy. This involuntary habit really makes me sad. Some visceral reflex to decades of internal judgment? Are other women spending their whole lives holding in their tummies too? Could this constant tension cause internal damage to my organs? I release the tension from my tummy and let it fully relax. I play with this motion— tensed, relax, tensed, relax. Genevieve appears disapproving of my extended tummy.

"I love you." Hmm, I didn't flinch. That's a good sign.

"I love you, I love you, I love you, I love you." I think I almost believe it. Almost.

Day 23   August 10, 2015

Today I make sure my tummy isn't tensed. *Be yourself, Eryn! Relax in yourself!*

Seeking this unshakable confidence Avi speaks of, I ask with interest, "Who am I?" Eventually I will come to the simple answer we supposedly all know deep inside, "I am." Not, I am my name, not I am a writer, not I am a woman, not I am creative or I am fat. I strip away all labels. When I reach "I am," unshakable confidence will come. Yes, confidence, you will be mine. Muaahahahahahaaaa! Unshakable? Let's be realistic, Eryn. Might be asking a bit much …

I understand this "I am" concept, but I don't. I don't know it deeply, that's for sure.

Who am I? I am.

I'm thinking about the third chakra we've been studying in Tantra, responsible for our self-esteem, self-worth, and personal power. I can feel myself changing, and although I don't understand how, simply acknowledging a low sense of self and making a commitment to address the issue has begun a snowball motion toward radical self-acceptance. Good stuff is happening.

Radical self-acceptance, you will be mine! I'm feeling the *Braveheart* Gerbera daisy warrior salute again. *Yarrrrr!*

Day 24   August 11, 2015

Again today, "I love you." Today is different. No cringing, no wrinkly nose. My mind answers back, "I know." *Whoa.*

I look around to find Genevieve, knowing she'll have something to say about this profession of self-love. She is nowhere to be found.

"I love you." *I know.*

Today is a big day!

Day 25   August 12, 2015

I sit down today, and get this, I realize I've actually missed myself since the last time I sat in front of the mirror. What the?

"I love you." *I know.* Whoa.

Day 26   August 13, 2015

"I love you." *I know.* Yay!

Day 27   August 14, 2015

"I love you." *I know.* It hasn't left me yet.

Day 28   August 15, 2015

"I love you." *Of course I do.* Yay! This is not temporary.

Day 29   August 16, 2015

"I love you." *Hell yes. I mean, why wouldn't I?* This is a big deal.

Day 30   August 17, 2015

"I love you." *I know. You've conquered the enemy within. You are now free from this pattern.*

Holy wow, it worked! *Yarrrrrr!*

Radical self-acceptance: check. I think I'll take a nap now.

Expansion Exercises

1) Do you have an inner Genevieve that criticizes you? What does she say? How often does she appear?

2) Identify the topics of those criticisms. *Body image. Not good enough. I'm not doing enough. Not smart enough. Not pretty enough. Not deserving of* _____.

3) Where does that inner criticism come from? Is it the voice of another person? Is it another version of you?

4) What would it feel like to be free from your inner Genevieve?

5) How would it feel to move toward a place within of radical self-acceptance?

6) How would it feel to stop critical comparisons and live in the freedom of that mental space?

7) Can you envision prioritizing yourself and dedicating thirty minutes per day for thirty days? Envision life ten years from now continuing as you are. Now envision life ten years from now living from a place of self-worth and self-acceptance. Can you afford *not* to prioritize yourself and carry on as you have been?

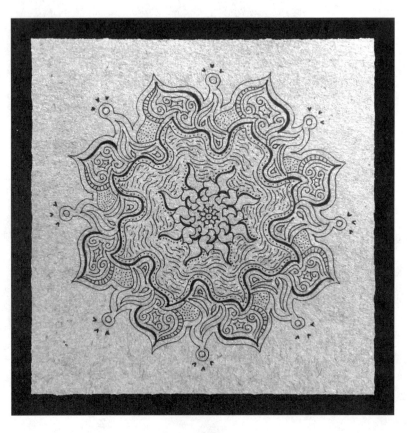

Journal Entry
'Freedom'

Chapter 16

Inward Traveling

Facing Your Freedom

Perhaps, we should love ourselves so fiercely,
that when others see us they know exactly how it should be done.
—Rudy Francisco

The time has come for you to face your freedom. This book, this practice, this healing experience is for you. Yes, you! It started for me, and I'm grateful for it, but I see now it was always meant to be shared with you.

See, when I first began my writing project, it was another book entirely. I was over one-third into the content of that book when I came to sit in the Facing Freedom practice you read about in the last chapter. By the end of my thirty days, seeing how it changed me so profoundly, I felt a compelling urgency to halt progression of my original project and begin a different book with a healing theme that would allow me to bring this practice to you.

I knew I wasn't alone in this *not enough* feeling that had plagued me, and although I resisted changing projects at first, it quickly became clear; sharing this story was part of my life purpose, and it needed to be told ... now. In that resolve to change course, the underlying intention of the project immediately shifted from entertainment to healing, and in that alone, I knew I made the right decision. I switched projects and began again; there was no other option.

The Power of the Mind

Our minds are powerful. More powerful than most of us realize. We can have our minds work *for* us or *against* us, and this one choice will shape our lives. John Kehoe writes in *Quantum Warrior*, "The ability to choose what we think and so direct our thoughts is a creative act of volition of enormous significance" (Kehoe 2011, pg. 16). Our tendency is to allow our minds to wander off, working against us with deep-seated patterns and negative inner dialogue. Like anything, sports, musical instrument, career, the more energy we dedicate to a practice, the greater the result. We can consciously choose to have our minds work *for* us, and I humbly invite you to join me in this journey to face your freedom.

Tapas

As I mentioned in a previous chapter, the Sanskrit word tapas traditionally translates "to heat" while also being associated with "austerity." Combined, we bring fire to discipline, a concept of classical yoga philosophy.

When we take a tapas, we make a firm commitment to ourselves. It is not a wish. It is not a desire. It's not *we will try to do this or that*. It is an unbreakable commitment, so it's important we are truly ready before we commit to a tapas. When you decide to start your Facing Freedom practice, be strict with yourself.

Breaking a commitment to ourselves I now realize is a deeper layer of not loving ourselves, and it's damaging on a soul level. If we don't have honor to ourselves, what do we really have? When we break our own commitments, this leads to decreased confidence and disappointment in ourselves and perpetuates the cycle of *not enough*.

I'll ask you some questions at the end of this chapter so you can gauge your level of commitment. When you're really ready to take control, ready to rise above your perceived *not enough* self, you'll know.

In *Anatomy of the Spirit*, Caroline Myss writes, "Self-understanding and acceptance, the bond we form with ourselves, is in many ways the most crucial spiritual challenge we face. In truth, if we do not like ourselves, we will be incapable of making healthy decisions" (Myss 1996, pg. 169).

This is a practice that will lead you not only to like yourself but to love yourself, and in that, you'll find it easier to make healthy decisions in all areas of life.

Myss goes further to say, "Belief in oneself is required for healing. Before I realized the significance of self-esteem for developing intuitive skills, I would have stated that faith is the most important factor in healing. I now equate faith with self-esteem and personal power, because low self-esteem reflects one's lack of faith in oneself ..." (Myss 1996, pg. 182).

It's possible and even likely to believe in ourselves in certain areas of our lives while simultaneously feeling inadequate in others. Perhaps we are confident in a thriving career but struggle with emotional eating and weight issues. This Facing Freedom practice aims to realign the mind, body, and spirit to work in harmony. In that place of harmony, we'll choose healthy lives. Not because our inner bully told us to but because we truly *want* the best for ourselves. I never even knew I had the ability to kick my inner bully out of the playground of my mind. It can be done.

Every single day you honor a commitment to yourself, you build personal power—one step closer to unshakable confidence. Making a firm commitment to ourselves requires first, choice, that we are willing to prioritize our well-being, and second, taking action.

Choice + Action = Results

Intentions and Expectations

It's important to set an intention. Setting an intention reminds us of why we dedicate ourselves. It may be something like, *I am setting the intention to remain open and committed to trying something new in order to bring about emotional healing.*

Be careful not to set expectations. This can be tricky; we're so adept at anticipating outcomes before we've even begun an exercise. Simply proceed with openness.

As we all come from different backgrounds and life experiences, we will progress differently. No two people will experience this the same. When the time comes for you to begin your thirty days, please don't measure yourself in any way against my journal entries from the previous chapter. Have faith that you'll experience this in the way that's right for you at this stage in your journey.

Had I gone into the Intro to Buddhism course or the Vipassana retreat with an expectation to grow or heal in a certain way, having an outcome in mind, I would've disrupted my own healing process. I feel we have within us a set of equalizing forces that will activate healing in whatever way is most advantageous to our individual soul if we put the effort toward growth. If we try to force a specific outcome, we may disrupt the process.

Pitfalls of the Facing Freedom Practice

When you decide to begin the practice, be mindful of your thoughts. When I began the journey, I decided I'd let thoughts and emotions flow freely as long as they were related to my emotional, physical, or spiritual self. If a critical old boyfriend or emotional memories came to mind, I explored those. Try not to censor these thoughts and feelings. They've arisen to help you address an old wound on your journey. If, on the other hand, I started thinking about my to-do list, work commitments, or what I'd make for dinner, I consciously stopped those thoughts and brought my mind back to the present—just me and my mirror. If our minds wander off with all the distractions of life, the exercise will not be effective.

In the beginning, I fought my ego regularly—that part of myself that told me this was a ridiculous exercise, laughable even. Luckily, I overcame this aspect of myself and progressed, but it wasn't easy. Some may feel uncomfortable looking at their bodies in such an in-depth way. Depending on your religious background, you may even associate it with shame, guilt, or fear. I would argue we should know our bodies intimately and feel completely comfortable with them. If you feel resistance to that statement, perhaps that's worth exploring. Resistance can be a signal that we want to avoid something. Why would we avoid our own body? That said, place no judgment or guilt on *not* doing the exercise. When you are ready, you will know.

Because of the immersive, confronting nature of this exercise, painful emotions may surface. If you suffer from depression, suicidal tendencies, or other extreme issues that may cause you to harm yourself or others, please seek appropriate professional guidance before undertaking this practice.

The Litmus Test

Before you begin, please take the time to have an honest conversation with yourself about this practice and where you are on your journey. Reflect on these questions, perhaps journaling your answers so you can refer to them later.

1) Do I experience a general feeling of *not enough*? Do I feel negatively about my body? Or my performance at work? Or my parenting skills? Or any aspect of my life?

2) Do I regularly criticize myself? Can I acknowledge that my inner dialogue is critical and repetitive?

3) Do I say yes when asked to do things I really don't want to do? Do I agree to do things because I want to gain approval or acceptance from others?

4) Do I have chameleon tendencies where I change behavior to accommodate others? Am I a people pleaser? Do I overextend myself and sacrifice my own needs for others?

5) Do I return to relationships that I've previously determined were not healthy for me? Could this be an indicator of my unwillingness to be alone? Might there be an emotional dependency there?

6) Do I feel painful emotions when I look in the mirror? Do I avoid mirrors altogether? Do I look in the mirror, stay just long enough to give myself the *mental jab*, then leave my reflection quickly?

7) Can I relate to some of the revelations Eryn had on her journey, and do I trust this process will benefit me?

8) Do I feel ready to forge forward with a deep commitment to become more authentic? Am I prepared to commit thirty minutes *each day* for my own development?

9) Would it be helpful to make a promise to myself before beginning the Facing Freedom practice that I will review before allowing myself to quit? (I discuss this further in the Reinforcement section below.)

10) Am I ready to reclaim my personal power and move toward radical self-acceptance even if the process seems difficult?

Expansion Exercise—Facing Freedom Practice

1) Set an intention. I suggest writing it on a single page in your journal.

2) Commit yourself with tapas fire. You may want to record your commitment in your journal, perhaps a contract with yourself.

3) Sit naked in front of a full-length mirror thirty minutes per day. This gives enough time to overcome the initial mental tantrums and move into growth.

4) Sit for thirty consecutive days. This provides maximum cumulative effect and initiation of personal power.

5) Sit in truth with yourself. Let emotions surface, whatever they are. Try not to judge your internal processes. Just observe. If task-oriented thoughts or to-do lists surface, dismiss those and return to yourself.

6) I suggest journaling directly after your time in front of the mirror so you have a record of your feelings and progress.

Remember to be mindful of your thoughts, allowing only those that are related to your mind, body, and spirit.

Reinforcements

You will likely feel the strong urge to quit at various intervals throughout this exercise. If you trust my story, if you resonate with this journey, if you hope to overcome these *not enough* feelings, then ask yourself these three questions before you allow yourself to leave the practice. These are the questions that propelled me onward when I wanted so badly to quit the fourteen-day Vipassana retreat.

1) Am I being asked to do anything that I'm physically unable to do?

2) Am I being asked to do anything that I'm mentally unable to do?

3) Do I feel there will be some value that will come from this process?

Choice + Action = Results
Are you with me?
Yowza, people, let's do this!

CHAPTER 17

Messages from Beyond

When I look inside and see that I am nothing, that is wisdom.
When I look outside and see that I am everything, that is love.
And between these two, my life turns.
—Sri Maharaj

I walked along a lonely cobblestone street one Friday afternoon, streets nearly empty as women prepared their festive meals for Shabbat.[1] The sun hung high above me, resting on fat marshmallow clouds in a clear blue sky.

A woman across the road swept her driveway, and we exchanged pleasant smiles. She held my gaze as I walked past her. She was sizing me up. I gave her a reassuring nod and waved hello. She reminded me of my grandmother, although it's fair to say nearly all old ladies with sweet, wrinkly faces remind me of her. Grandma motioned for me to visit her side of the street, and like any good granddaughter would do, I joined her.

She began speaking to me in Hebrew, and I interrupted. "Sorry, I don't speak Hebrew. Do you speak English?" She shook her head, *no, no* and continued with hand gestures and animated facial expressions, quite happy to converse with me in this way. I'd become good at these charade-type discussions as I traveled, meeting so many speaking different languages, but I found it exhausting at times, two people wanting so desperately to understand one another, left only with hand gestures and pidgin English.

Her excitable signals and nods told me she wanted me to deliver a package to someone in need. She pointed at her knee and cane. *See, I couldn't possibly go. I'm old and feeble and can't walk very far. See, see ...* "Okay, okay, how far is it?" Habit I suppose, but I still tried to speak in English as if she'd magically picked up the language since my first attempt. Pulling out a scrap of paper and a pen, Grandma sketched me a map.

I watched her as she drew, wondering what kind of life she'd led and what she'd seen in her long life here in Israel. I saw every conflict, every war, every altered landscape, and every death in this war-torn country, each etched in the creases of her face. She'd led a life with a lot of love, it was obvious, but like most in the region, she'd endured much pain.

She held up one finger, then her hand, the universal signal for *wait one minute, I'll be right back,* and left me there on the sidewalk.

Moments later, she returned with an overloaded grocery cart motioning that this was my delivery. "What? Are you kidding me? A grocery cart?" I quickly assessed the items in the cart to see if I could carry them—a blender, mixing bowls, two bags of groceries and a box of baby clothes. It was too much to carry. I rolled my eyes, annoyed by Grandma's unreasonable request of a stranger, but she was emphatic. I couldn't deny her. I nodded, "Okay, okay, I'll do it."

She smiled a grateful smile and pinched my cheeks like grandmothers do. She reached into the cart to pull out a bright blue ball cap with white *New York* letters and placed it on my head as her gift to me for this favor. "Okay, okay, thank you. *Toda, toda*" (thank you in Hebrew). *New York* didn't match my outfit, so I put it back in the basket. She shook her head at me, *no, no,* and picked it up again, gesturing for me to wear it. *Go on now, put it on,* she insisted. *Geez, Grandma, you're a little pushy, aren't ya? All right, calm down, I'll wear it.*

She shooed me away with my sketched map, and I began my trek up the hill. The sidewalks were cracked and disjointed, and the road was cobblestone—neither ideal for pushing a cart on wheels. *Grrrr.* I arduously carried onward shouting expletives every ten feet when the wheels caught in the deep cracks. The Israeli summer sun was relentless, and I found myself happy with New York shading me despite its tragic fashion statement.

The hill was steep, and I knew not what lay ahead. All I could see was the bright blue-sky horizon, houses, olive trees on either side of the road, and cracked, oil-stained sidewalks. Over the hill, on the downslope, I came to a fork in the road. The map showed either road met my destination street, so I chose the easier path to the left. *Ahhh yes, smooth asphalt. That's better.*

I noticed the houses looked different. Everything was different actually; architecture, fences, landscaping, and paint colors. *Hmmm, that's odd. Like I've entered another city.* I carried on down the road pushing my cart when I noticed another grandma sweeping her driveway. She had a sweet, wrinkly face too, but she wore a Muslim hijab[2] covering her head. I realized I'd left the Jewish village and was now in an Arabic area. *Hmmm ... Am I safe here?*

As a traveling foreigner, it's difficult to fully understand the nuances of cultural conflict in this region between the Christians, Jews, and Muslims, but I knew enough to feel it may not be safe for me. I exchanged pleasant smiles with Grandma, and she held my gaze as I walked past her. She was sizing me up. I gave her a reassuring nod and waved hello, realizing I looked like a homeless person with my bright blue New York hat and my creaking grocery cart. I guess in a way I *was* homeless with my nomadic existence. Grandma motioned for me to visit her side of the street, but I waved my hand and shook my head, *No, no, I'm going this direction.*

Grandma crossed the street, grabbed my cart, and pulled us both toward her driveway. "No, no, I need to carry on this way," I said politely. She spoke in Arabic, but I didn't understand her. She possessively rummaged through my cart, seemingly annoyed as if late for an appointment. "No, these are for someone else. I need to deliver these things. Me—go—this—way." I pointed down the street.

Grandma became more and more flustered. She tugged on my cart and resisted my attempts to leave. She pointed her finger at me, pursed her lips, and furrowed her brow in an accusatory way. *What, Grandma? What are you trying to say? Oh geez, does she think I've stolen these things?* I plead my case to her and pulled the map from my pocket to show her, but her Arabic ears didn't understand my English tongue. I pointed to the phone number scribbled on top from Jewish grandma, hoping Muslim grandma would call to verify my story. *Hmmm, do the Israeli Jews and Muslims, as such close neighbors in this tiny country, even speak a common language?* I'd never given it much thought until now. Before I had time to contemplate the answer; me, my cart, and New York had been pulled into Grandma's house.

The living room was suspended in time, straight out of 1972 with burnt-orange shag dreadlocked carpet and plastic couch covers. She motioned strongly, finger pointing to the floor, for me to sit, which I did, like any good granddaughter would do. She looked at me intently for a few moments, holding out her hand, taking the scrap of paper from me. I watched her as she watched me. I wondered what kind of life she'd led and what she'd seen in her long life here in Israel. I saw every conflict, every war, every altered landscape, and every death in this war-torn country, each etched in the creases of her face. She'd led a life with a lot of love, it was obvious, but like most in the region, she'd endured much pain. Grandma stormed from the room.

Like a child, I sat dejected on the floor, wondering what I was doing here. At the dining room table, I saw Grandpa and their adult daughter, but oddly enough, they seemed unaware of my presence as they sang cheerfully "We Are Family" by Sister Sledge. It was all so bizarre—Jewish grandma, Muslim grandma, my shopping cart, New York, orange shag, and "We Are Family." I started wondering if I was dreaming. *What in the world am I doing here?*

My mind searched itself with a thousand questions but found no answers. The daughter smiled sweetly at me while singing, and that brought me comfort. She was somehow familiar to me but not. I started to feel uneasy about the whole situation, and the longer I sat, the more frightened I became, wondering if I might be in danger. I felt tears welling up in the angst of unknown, but I pushed them back.

Recent news flashed to mind: the bodies of three Jewish boys from the West Bank[3] had been found the day before, and the country was in the crucible of grief. Emotional fires were blazing in every heart as conflict brewed between these clashing cultures. Although I'd not been able to understand their language, I felt the heat in every syllable and every word. I felt it in the newscasters; I felt it in my Israeli friends and inside me here on 1972's orange shag.

I asked the daughter with my eyes, *Am I okay? Am I safe here? What's happening? Am I in the process of being kidnapped?* She carried on singing with a smile, bobbing her head, "We are family. I got all my sisters with me ..." I checked my pocket, no cell phone. Who would help me anyway—911 Israel? I'd have to assert myself with Grandma, reclaim my grocery cart, and hand signal my way outta there. How does one maintain her southern charm and cultural etiquette in a situation like this?

In timeless terror, I sat... waiting, wondering, frightened, and desperate to flee. I found my body uncooperative, and my legs refused to lift themselves from 1972's shagginess. I sat immobile, waiting—for what I didn't know. Grandma returned to the living room, scurrying about the house with great agitation. "We Are Family" carried on in an endless loop. I didn't know what was happening. I felt in danger. Grandma was irritated. *Is Grandma calling the police to report me for stealing these things? Why am I here? I don't understand!*

Yes, I'm being kidnapped. Now I'm sure of it. Grandma will return soon with another man ... and a rope ... and they'll tie me up. I'll be smuggled off to a desert bunker, then taken by tunnel into the Gaza Strip and sold to the highest bidder. I'll end up in Egypt or Morocco or who knows where! Will I be ransomed or just beheaded for CNN?

Slow-motion Sister Sledge tunes kicked in again. I sung along faintly as I fought back fearful tears, my bottom lip beginning to quiver. *We are family. I got all my sisters with me. We are family. Get up everybody and sing. Oh God, I'm gonna die. I'm gonna die, right here on 1972's best orange shag.*

Grandma returned carrying a large box, and I curtly pled with her, "I must go *right now*! I need to deliver these things! I'm doing someone a favor! I have to go!" She looked at me blankly, standing above me with the box, her eyes blinking widely, not understanding my words. I still couldn't move from the floor. *What is wrong with your legs, Eryn? Why aren't you moving?*

I didn't know what she'd pull from that box. Whatever it was, I knew my fate was in there. *Rope, handcuffs, a weapon, zip ties, or a burlap sack?* She reached into the box in slow-motion madness, my heart pounding outside my chest, waiting in impatient agony—for life, for death, I didn't know what. *Stay strong, Eryn. Stay strong.*

I closed my eyes, prolonging one last moment when I was free and safe and all was right and good in the world. I opened one eye and then the other to see my fate. Grandma began taking household goods from the box. *Household goods. Huh?* One by one, she placed them into the cart, now smiling at me. Two loaves of bread, folded towels, a book, baking trays, and a collapsed baby stroller. *Kitchen stuff. Baby stuff. Oh my God, I'm not being kidnapped. I'm—not—being— kidnapped! She's adding items to the cart!*

My fears had led me astray again. This woman was doing something good. *She's doing something good.* Then a deeper realization: *Look at these two women from conflicting cultures uniting to help someone in need! Coming together despite their differences for the common good. Good God man, if these two women can rise above, why can't the rest of us do the same?* Emotion flooded me in this monumental display of cross-cultural compassion. I was beside myself. Speechless. No words, all emotion.

I turned my hands, palms facing upward resting in my lap, and asked myself, "Am I dreaming?" I'd been a part of a lucid dreaming retreat with my Tantra yoga school, and this was how I'd determine if I was awake inside my dream. I'd been training for days now to ask the question, "Am I dreaming?"

I looked at my palms, orange shag in the background, and before I could ask if I was dreaming, I saw the world in my hands. Continents and oceans were clearly tattooed on my palms. Time stopped. I sat in Grandma's living room in Israel, the center of the ancient world, peering into our collective futures, the world stage before me, the big curtain of life pulled back revealing secrets of the universe. I saw the whole world, my palms full of color; the West etched in my left hand, the East in my right, connected only by the tiny bridge of my converging pinky fingers.

In that moment, I knew everything. All egos fell away. Classes and races dissolved into the ether. We were all one—beings of light just floating on this earth, separate but not. All the labels we apply to one another—man, woman, doctor, prostitute, white, black, intellectual, uneducated, religious, atheist, Muslim, Jew—all labels separating us and keeping us from our true nature: love, bliss, human connection, and pure consciousness.

It was a simple yet profound truth that we were nothing and everything all at once, connected by love and compassion, separated by judgments and fear. Fear had overtaken us and was destroying our minds; ruled by fear and judgments and labels of division and in our actions with guns and war and acts of hatred and violence. Each progressive year, spurred by media and fearful conditioning, we're giving away little bits of our soul, and this is what's preventing us from inner contentment and peaceful coexistence. Individually and collectively, we have the power to change the world. Each has a power so vast we can't speak it. This intense *knowing* swallowed me.

I stared into my palms as the world spilled her secrets. Quiet tears fell from my cheeks, dripping into the oceans of my palms, flooding them. The world slowly faded to nothingness. That's when I woke up crying. I shot up in bed in a Thai ashram remembering I was on the fourth day of the lucid dreaming retreat. I turned on the light, checked my palms again, looking desperately for the world, now seeing only flesh and lifelines. The world was gone, but the awakening was permanently imprinted inside me.

Lucid Dreaming

Lucid dreaming[4] is the practice of being awake when dreaming and is known to some as *dream yoga*. Mastering the ability to be conscious during dreams enables adepts to do all sorts of things—fly or to visit faraway lands and loved ones who've died. The possibilities are endless because the laws of time, place, space, gravity, and society don't bind us in our dreams.

This all sounds like new age fantasy, yet certain lineages of the East, including Tibetan Buddhism, use lucid dreaming to raise consciousness.

Serious scientific study is being dedicated to measuring different states of consciousness, showing how lucid dreaming affects physiology. Amongst the foremost researchers for twenty-five years is Stephen LaBerge, PhD,[5] psychophysiologist. Dr. LaBerge gave a lecture, (www.scienceandnonduality.com published November 17, 2015) during which he was asked if the vastness (intense meaning and awakening) happened in the dream or in the waking state. Dr. LaBerge replied:

> They happen together. One of the things, when you have this kind of realization; it's a realization that isn't dependent on the dream. The dream was an occasion for having an experience and then also for a reflection upon the experience … What we perceive is our interpretation of reality, so the interpretive process is important here … In the dream world you have a freedom where you can try out anything … By choosing to make what you

decide to do in the dream, changing your frame on the circumstance, the way you experience and respond to the circumstances as opposed to magically altering it, you then get something you can use in other states. You see the immediate effect of what's in your heart in terms of other dream figures, they change instantly, unlike *this* world where it takes more time and maybe not in a lifetime you experience this, but in the dream state there's this perfect instantaneous response it's like the place where Christianity works, love your enemies and they become your friends the moment you love them. And this is something that I really wish everybody could experience for themselves, the power to be able to transform the experience of a dream just by the genuine authenticity of love, for example. If you're in touch with love and you apply it, it creates a direct result. So that for me is the most powerful aspect of how one can learn from the lucid dreaming and what can happen in the rest of your life with more work.

Dr. LaBerge states that our dream experiences can provide the same level of profound change within an individual as if we'd experienced it in *real life*. I can say with certainty I feel this to be true based on the dream experience I had about peace in the Middle East and worldwide compassion. It somehow altered me massively.

Introspections and Reflections

Why did this dream have such a profound effect on me? Was it the intense experience in the dream alone or perhaps the collective awakenings of my trip that culminated in this dream? Maybe it was related to the visualization I'd imagined before going to bed that evening. I'd watched a documentary in the weeks before about near-death experiences where a woman gave an account of the white light, saying she "was standing in the breath of God."[6] That really struck me when I saw it, and I connected again to that feeling. When I lay down that night and closed my eyes in pre-sleep meditation, I envisioned myself floating in the breath of God. And this was the dream that came and changed me. I was now, unequivocally, a different version of myself.

Perhaps witnessing the breadth of life beyond our US borders shook me to my core; each person, village, town, and country touched me. I pondered the challenges others faced and the opportunities with which I was blessed. The girl on the Ganges, my homeless friend in Dublin, those seeking miracles in Brazil, the barefoot beauty in Tanzania, the survivors in Rwanda, and now my two new compassionate grandmothers. They all resided in me now, deep in a place that no one could touch, where ultimate understanding rests.

---

*I spent three weeks in Israel between month three and four of my trip when the tragic kidnapping of the three Jewish boys took place. I revisited that time and place through my dream from Thailand in this chapter.

Expansion Exercises

1) What belief system stands in the way of accepting that all human beings are related, part of the same human family, and of equal value?

2) What would it look like to investigate this limiting belief system?

3) How could you bring compassion to all people and their suffering?

4) Can you consider that fear is the underlying emotion behind the limiting belief system that creates inequality in the quiet spaces of our minds?

5) What would it look like to remove fear from the equation? What would it look like to add love?

Journal Entry
'Infinite'

CHAPTER 18

Month Twenty-Three—Thailand

Living on in Love

In the end these things matter most. How well did you love?
How fully did you live? How deeply did you learn to let go?"
—Buddha

In the middle of month twenty-three, about halfway through my
book project, an opportunity arose with the Tantra school that
I couldn't pass up. Their ashram was expanding to accommodate
serious students who wanted to immerse themselves more fully
into the spiritual path and Tantra life. I'd spent time in an Indian
ashram early on in my trip and found it to be a haven where I could
dedicate myself to personal development, so I was excited to have
this option with my Tantra family.

My days were full, consisting of two-hour morning tapas of
yoga and meditation at home, followed by six hours of writing at
one of my favorite cafés, and then joining in at the Tantra school
for frequent activities. At this stage in my journey, I had no doubt
moving into the ashram was the next step for me. Focusing on
inner transformation would not only benefit me personally, but it
would help me produce a better book, I felt. Those were my two
goals when I left, after all: to find my highest self and a purposeful
creative project. *Let's take this to the next level, people. I'm in!*

Five other Tantra students and I decided we'd commit to ashram life.

That's when things began to unravel.

Those of us interested in the Tantra ashram were told the head teacher of the school in Europe needed to approve us, and photos were required before moving in. Fair enough. A smiley headshot? *Hi, I'm Eryn. I'm moving into your ashram.* Nope. We were told we'd have pictures taken individually in our lingerie. *Say whaaaaaat? Screech, halt, stop, what?*

Nothing about this felt right to me. Nothing.

There was uproar amongst the women. All four of us had issue with this requirement. Not surprisingly, the two men were less concerned. Meetings were quickly organized to discuss and calm the group. What credible explanation could bring reason and logic to this unthinkable prerequisite? Answers escaped me, and the request was disturbing, but I had trust and admiration for my teachers, so I wanted to hear them out. *What am I missing? Lingerie pictures required to further my spiritual development? Really?*

We were told that the teacher in Europe needed to "read our auras"[1] to determine if we were vital enough to handle the intensity of ashram living. We were also told this could be seen as spiritual test. *A spiritual test, uh huh, I see.* I was familiar with spiritual tests. I'd been tested many times along the way—from overcoming my initial fears and leaving a new love to board my first flight, to the determination I pulled from the depths of self to continue Vipassana and a thousand tests in between. I'd been tested.

Traveling was a constant source of new experiences leading me time and time again to question the limiting beliefs I held to so tightly when I stepped out into the world nearly two years before. From the first time I opened myself to the Buddhist retreat in India that was so beneficial, I vowed to explore new things with an open mind. It was a spiritual practice in itself to examine boundaries and beliefs as I was exposed to new things, instead of *reacting* from those limitations. I regularly asked myself the question: do I feel resistance to _____ because it's unfamiliar and outside my mind-generated limitations, or does it make me feel truly uncomfortable or put me in harm's way? Exploring and unraveling the tapestry of my beliefs was tricky at times—like right now—and this lingerie request, from people I deeply trusted, was fraying me.

I remembered my initial hesitations about Tantra because of the sexual nature of the practice then unknown to me. The intensity of study on emotional, psychological, spiritual, and sexual levels was such that I maintained a few red flags of caution as I progressed, but nothing strange had been asked of me so far. However, when once I considered it a major benefit that my teachers were formally trained in psychology, I now wondered if we were being psychologically groomed. I didn't want to think this way. I loved my teachers! But now ... now I was left with lingerie pictures and question marks.

I paused at this fork in the Tantric road, considering the intention, meaning, and symbolism of their request. Lingerie would've been no different than a bathing suit, right? Would I care if they'd asked me to wear a bathing suit? Surely far more seductive images could be found online. *This still feels wrong.*

I struggled with the decision. I battled it with swords in my mind. *Look at the wisdom these people have shared with you! Look at how their teachings have elevated you. You'll be going home in another six months when you finish the book. Why not live in the ashram where you'll further develop and write a better book? You can always leave if anything else questionable comes up. You trust your teachers. They are family to you.*

I spent the weekend detangling the web of thoughts and feelings that had become so intertwined with my Tantra family. Where do my thoughts end and theirs begin? How could I *not* live in the ashram to further my practice? I never knew one could experience such concentrated growth as I'd found on the "fast path" of Tantra. I had to keep going! Perhaps this *was* a test. How could I halt my progression?

That's when I realized I was bargaining with myself.

A troubling statement from months past returned to the forefront of my mind. During a girly chat about open relationships with my female teacher—a concept I'm personally not keen on—she said her teacher once told her, "A good woman dedicates herself to one man, a great woman dedicates herself to two men, and a divine woman dedicates herself to three men." *Screech, halt, stop, whaaaaat?*

When I put it all together, it symbolized something far deeper. *Lingerie pictures today—what tomorrow? A statement about dedication to multiple men today—what tomorrow? A question? Then linking that to a spiritual test?* My mind ran off with questions of what might be in this immersive family I'd become so involved with. *Eryn, you'd never be forced to do anything; you know that.* Was I part of a slow, manipulation effort now engrossed in a school offering progressive study for upward of sixteen years? *No, my teachers wouldn't intentionally collude with anything harmful. They're bringing light and healing to the world!* Confusion, inner angst, betrayal, and fear met at the crossroad of trust, progression, growth, and love.

I reflected on how I was affected by Avi, the male teacher. He had a certain soft influence over me, and I allowed it. Perhaps I cared for him beyond the teacher/student bond. Of course I did. I loved him. Tantra taught us to feel love in our hearts and see the divine in *all living beings*. It was easy to see love in him, and it's a beautiful sentiment, but for me it brought confusion to boundaries between platonic, romantic, sexual, and spiritual love. Love and, love for all, it seemed could be a subjective ideology loosely used when in conjunction with sexual attraction. We were never sexually intimate, Avi and I. Sometimes I wish we had been, but because of my own past and because Avi was in a relationship, I felt it essential to hold a clear boundary, but the line between platonic and romantic love blurred in my mind regularly, and I loved him deeply on multiple levels.

I stood back from my family and considered my options. Move into the ashram or leave the Tantric community. It wasn't all-or-nothing from the perspective of the school, but it was for me. If I lost faith in what the school asked of its students, then how could I continue? I questioned my structure of beliefs. Do I gain personally by living in the ashram? Do I lose anything by living in the ashram? Is the lingerie photo bringing light to fundamental aspects of the school worth questioning—sincerity or exploitation? Perhaps this is just another organization created by a man for the benefit of men? Am I holding myself in a strange human experiment of will to see how long I can maintain perspective if I move into the ashram? Have I already lost objectivity to even consider taking these lingerie pictures? Perhaps the simplest, purest, highest answer *is* to love everyone. Or maybe this is a convenient teaching so we're more receptive to the idea of multiple partners. It crushed me to be standing at this crossroad questioning my beloved spiritual family.

I knew what I had to do. I had to leave them. How could I respect a spiritual path that asked this of their students? I could no longer support the school with my mind, my money, my time, or my heart. Although I loved the students and my teachers with a full heart, knowing they unequivocally believed in the goodness of their Tantra school and teachings, I knew I had to separate … detach … painfully and forcibly disconnect myself from my Tantra family.

Silver Linings

Devastated by this spiritual and familial divorce, I struggled with feelings of betrayal. I was numb and in shock at this bizarre turn of events. In the wake of my departure, I felt a sense of panic, wanting to maintain everything I'd learned. I'd jumped from the Tantric path and was flying solo again—alone in Chiang Rai, in Thailand, in this big world—a little lost now without the family I'd grown so attached to over nine months and with half of my book yet to complete.

The challenge now was to decide what of their teachings still worked for me and what I needed to dismiss. My instinct was to say *fuck it all* (low resonance) and detach myself completely from the group and everything I'd learned, but I knew that'd be a mistake. I couldn't let my departure from the school tarnish the growth and healing I'd already integrated or my path moving forward. This was another spiritual practice entirely when my feelings of betrayal told me everything was now tainted.

I continued with my yoga and meditation tapas and struggled to find my equilibrium, filling the empty spaces with texts by Yogananda, Caroline Myss, PhD, Bruce Lipton, PhD, Sogyal Rinpoche, and David R. Hawkins, PhD, to name a few. I was determined to maintain forward momentum, so I sought trusted theory from Eastern and Western sources that might bring supporting information and clarity to some of what I'd learned in Tantra. None of this personal expansion required lingerie pictures.

Like most challenges in life, the struggle of leaving Tantra made me stronger in the end. I realized I'd leaned on my Tantra family too much, similar to the support I would've found in a romantic relationship or a best girlfriend—still dependent on an external source for emotional equanimity. In leaving them, I found another level of self-sufficiency and resilience that I wouldn't have found otherwise, and for that, I'm grateful.

Sometimes I wonder … Did I make the decision to leave based on fear—that I didn't trust myself enough to maintain objectivity in this close-knit family environment isolated from the life I'd left behind so long ago in America? Or did I make it out of love— that I fully investigated my intuitive reasoning that reminded me a spiritual organization asking this of its students didn't resonate with my authentic self?

I could've wallowed in the sadness of it all, and I did for a time, but to remain in that space would've been very un-Tantric of me. I came to accept things *as they are* and made peace with it all, knowing that everything was playing out exactly as it should. I remain extremely grateful for the teachings, support, and many special moments I shared with my teachers and fellow students. I'm certain my exposure to Tantra greatly contributed to the solid emotional grounding I live in today. I will always have the Tantric teachings and the individuals of the school in my heart. I live on in love.

Expansion Exercises

1) How does your intuition speak to you? In your body? Thoughts? Emotions? Dreams?

2) Do you trust your intuition to guide you? Do you listen to your gut feelings and act on them?

3) Have you ever gone against your intuition or participated in something that didn't feel authentic to who you were? Can you identify why you participated? Was it to be accepted? What were the positive and negative consequences of that decision?

4) What does it feel like when you follow your intuition? What does it feel like when you don't follow it?

CHAPTER 19

Month Twenty-Four—Australia

The Siggy Effect

The sign of a beautiful person is that they
always see beauty in others.
—Omar Suleiman

It was burning season[1] in Chiang Rai, the expats were leaving in droves, my thirty-ninth birthday was approaching, my third on the road, and I'd just made the devastating split from my Tantra family. I was just a hop, skip, and a jump away from Australia—sort of, not really. I could think of no better reasons to visit my dear friend Siggy who'd been home for a year now, living a "normal life." I hopped a plane, and before ya know it, I'm hugging my long-lost soul sister on a downtown street corner in Sydney.

Different Perspectives

Siggy was always teaching me things in her own way. She's fourteen years younger than me, it's true, but she's been one of my best teachers. We come from different backgrounds, and we have wildly different personalities. She's never lived away from her parental home, yet she feels completely at ease solo-traveling Southeast Asia.

251

I, on the other hand, had my first mortgage at age twenty and lived with skepticism and fear in leaving my home country.

It's been interesting to observe how traveling has changed us both but in drastically different ways; I suppose because of our age difference and varied life experiences. I feel a profound sense of gratitude that I pulled together the courage and will to extract myself from the stultifying, life-sucking qualities of a nine-to-five career, mortgages, credit scores, relationship dramas, car payments, insurances, coupons, and the monotony of climbing corporate ladders. Siggy works full-time but hasn't yet been beaten up by the ceaseless societal commitments and the cumulative dementing effect of enduring life's adulthood obligations.

I understand that in traveling I escaped something, whereas Siggy has not yet grasped that there is anything from which to escape, although it would be remiss of me not to mention that she left law school in year five to choose another path for herself. I admire her for realizing, before running a decade-plus on the hamster wheel, that she wanted off the track of modern society. I also think she should've finished school. We've debated this at length. But it takes courage to go against mainstream pressures at that stage of life, and she followed her heart.

When Siggy went out into the world, she left with youthful curiosity. She possesses the playfulness, fearlessness, femininity, and innocence that I lost long ago. These traits vanish so unexpectedly and without warning as we age, navigating this thing we call life. Whatever it was that led us to experience the world differently—age, innocence, or culture—she viewed it with love, whereas I viewed it with fear. It took me over a year to shed the layers of life that jaded me before I was able to see the world through Siggy's lens of love.

The Beauty of Interdependence

I met Siggy two years ago in the first week of my trip in India, then again for brief stints in France, Spain, Portugal, later Thailand, and now Australia. We'd grown up together in a way, out there in the world. Now we were here together with her family in her home country; it was a completely different experience to engage with her in this family environment.

It was odd to me that at twenty-five Siggy was still living at home with her mother doing her laundry. This is common in Australia, and the cultural difference really struck me. Unlike in the USA, young Aussie adults don't feel the need to make a quick getaway from their parents' house the moment they turn eighteen. I wonder what it is that makes Americans want to flee from home in a display of independence at the first opportunity.

Siggy and her mom were happy to have me stay for three weeks, and I could tell I wasn't a burden to them. I was like the sister she never had and welcomed into their home. I can think of few people in the States who'd happily welcome friends for that length of time. It seems our cultures have a different threshold of acceptance for houseguests. Odd.

That got me thinking about independence versus interdependence. I've noticed this deeply rooted trait in many Americans *not* to impose on others. It makes sense on one hand, a country of determined people so intently progressing themselves forward; but I've also come to think this fierce independence limits our opportunity for real connection with people, and in a world of such *disconnection*, I wonder if this increased isolation may be a factor in our mental health decline.

Our independence—or our ego's desire to appear that we don't need anyone—is that healthy or not? I wonder if, in our financial progression, we've lost the aspect of community and interdependence that's so vital for emotional well-being. We've become a society of acquaintances and work associates, networking opportunities, dinner parties, and big, lifeless houses. We're more connected than ever in the way of e-mail, text, phone, and Skype capabilities, yet we have fewer meaningful and soul-cultivating connections. Is this progression or regression?

Shedding My Tin Armor

Siggy and her mom had a beautiful way of interacting, and it made me think of my relationship with my mother. Siggy and her mom were playful, and they bickered about silly and important things alike. My mom and I hadn't disagreed about anything for years because my mom was afraid I'd not speak to her—occasionally months on end—as I'd done in my younger years. I'd been angry and hurt and not known how to deal with my feelings or conflict between us.

I liked seeing Siggy and her mom fight and then hug it out in the middle of the kitchen floor; then it was over. It all seemed so … mother-daughter. I had a hard time relating to it honestly. I'd not lived with my mother since age twelve, but I'd be lying if I said I didn't long for that in some *let's rewind the past and try again* sort of way.

My mom and I seemed to share an awkward hug, both wearing our tin armor suits of protection. Our hugs were clanky with loud clashes and hard-riveted angled metal that bounced off one another—completely unnatural considering I spent the first nine months of my life, the most miraculous transformation a human makes, inside her belly. Life between us had just been too big. Distance and time and hardened hearts had their way with us. We didn't know any other way to hug.

As I watched my soul sister and her mother in their natural embrace in a kitchen on the outskirts of Sydney, my relationship with my mother came into focus. I reflected on the decisions my mother had to make for us. When, at age thirty-two, I'd read my father's medical records, finally understanding the scope of life they'd endured, I could do nothing but forgive her. I realized then what heartbreaking trials she'd endured under the chaotic and confusing symptoms of my father's psychosis. But not until now, seeing a healthy example of how mother and daughter could be, did I fully realize our distance.

I never held the same animosity for my father that I had my mother. Psychosis struck him like lightning before I was even born. Never again would he be quite the same person; he'd be on antipsychotic medications for the next thirty-plus years, the entire duration of our relationship from my birth to his death. I always felt Mom and I had abandoned him when he needed us most. But that wasn't the whole story, and when we left my father, I didn't know any of this. I couldn't have. I was a child, and they hid it well to protect me.

Something about seeing how Siggy's mom loved her, I understood how my mom had made decisions to protect me and to save her own sanity, which I now respected. In that moment, I forgave my mother everything. I understood my mother's decision to take me away from my father. It was the only decision she could make at the time. As I stood there watching Siggy and her mom, I fell in love again with the woman who gave me life. I finally understood, and understanding changes everything. I dismantled my tin armor and joined Siggy and her mom in their family hug.

Girl Power

Siggy taught me how to love women again. Not in a lesbian sort of way, although many assumed we were lovers—no, in a soul sister, female bond sort of way that I'd squandered in my younger years. It struck me in India on that first bus ride we took how special that female bond was, and it carries on between us still today. She made me softer with her big heart, more trusting with her young soul, helped me to see how pointless it was to live in fear, and pried me from the comfort zones I clung to so fiercely. She taught me how to live and how to love again. Everyone needs a soul sister like that.

Siggy, Grrrrr!

Limitations. Yes, Siggy taught me about my own limitations. As we traveled together before BAM festival, for example, I found that it's important for me to know where I'll sleep each night. I'd never tested this personal limitation when traveling on my own, always having at least one night booked when I'd arrive to a new city. With Siggy, it was different. She was more carefree, trusting of the world, and happy to wing it. In a way, I wished I could be more like her, so I played along … for a short period.

Siggy and I decided we'd walk the coast of Spain in the general direction of Portugal and treat this as a pilgrimage inspired by the forty-day El Camino. This is a *serious* trek. Pilgrims plan for El Camino years in advance, and the route has frequent cheap accommodation and food stops, so only a small bag with a few changes of clothes and water is necessary.

We'd given little time to planning our pilgrimage walk. We shed as much as we could from our bags, made our way to the Atlantic Ocean, and followed a sidewalk down the beach heading south. Quickly we realized that we were carrying too much.

"Siggy, this isn't working for me!"

"I know, babe; we got this. Just keep going."

"Nope, I'm done."

We only made it a few miles.

As dusk approached, we needed to start figuring out where we'd pitch our tent for the night. We stopped at a grassy lawn near the shore, laid a sheet out, and sat for a while, exhausted, munching on crackers and peanut butter. Tides and policemen were likely to take us if we slept on the beach. Now what? We surveyed our options.

The lawn where we rested was a good location near the public beach bathrooms and a restaurant for safety, but it was too exposed. There was an area of tall reeds, twice my height a few hundred feet away. They looked like they'd conceal us. I was formulating a plan. We'd wait for dusk so we could inconspicuously pitch our tent behind the reeds and blend into the night.

Next thing ya know, a tall, skinny, handsome guy walks down the edge of the lawn carrying a pool lounge chair and disappears into our reed bed.

"Dammit, Sig, that guy is moving in on our bush! Look!"

"He's kinda cute," Siggy says.

The dude exits the bush, minus the chair, and starts walking in our direction. He passes us, smiling and saying hi as he makes his way to the bathroom. He doesn't know we've just seen him steal *our* bush.

He passes us again returning from the bathroom.

"So, watcha doin' with that lounge chair?" I asked.

"Oh. You saw me with that? Uh … well, I'm going to sleep on it tonight."

"Dude, we were scoping out that bush. We were gonna sleep there tonight."

"That's my bush," he said. "I've been sleeping in there for a while now. I got lucky and found that lounge chair today. But hey, you can stay in there with me; there's room for all of us. We can even pitch your tent."

Siggy was sending out her goo-goo eyes, the ones she wears when she likes a guy. I was worrying about the minor detail of where we'd sleep and if we'd be safe.

On one hand, it seemed like a decent idea—that is, if you trust an anonymous male stranger you've determined has good character based on ten minutes of conversation. On the other hand, if you were skeptical like me and judged man by what I'd seen on American television, it seemed risky at best.

We gathered our belongings and slipped out of sight into the reeds. I realized in that moment how *homeless* this felt, shuffling around with everything we own on our backs, looking for a place to sleep in a bush near public bathrooms. *Who have I become?*

The three of us slept in our two-person tent, he and Siggy lying close to one another, cuddled up in some newly formed love connection. I lay there, increasingly annoyed and worrying all night. I decided this was the last night I could handle the uncertainty of not knowing where we'd sleep. It was just too much! Siggy could be wild and carefree and trusting, but I'd watched too much crime drama television for that.

Traveler or Tourist?

Siggy taught me to follow my heart while traveling, which presented me with all sorts of unplanned experiences; it changed my entire trip actually.

The first week I met Siggy in India, I'd already begun planning weeks ahead to make my way to Nepal. I'd met a Japanese girl that was going to Nepal as well, so although she spoke little English, we decided we'd coordinate our schedules and go together for safety. Siggy asked me, "Do you want to go to Nepal with her?"

"Well I want to go to Nepal, and she's going around the time I was thinking of going. It makes sense."

"Yeah, but you don't *feel* to go with her? If I were you, I'd wait until you *feel* to go somewhere or with someone. What's the rush to leave India anyway?"

"Well I don't know, I figured a month would be enough. I guess I want to see a lot of places."

"Babe, just relax and go with the flow. Why don't we go to Dharamsala together and see what happens there?"

The Japanese girl needed to change her plans anyway, so I was free. Siggy and I went to Dharamsala, and I ended up in the Buddhist retreat. That profound experience solidified for me that I needed to trust the path more and stop forcing my way in this or that direction. Much of my life, I'd done things that made sense in my head but not in my heart. Siggy taught me how to drop down from the analytical mind and into the heart space, and this changed everything.

When I left America, I suppose I still had a very American mind-set where I hoped to see a lot in a short amount of time and check countries off like a to-do list. But what good would it have done for me to see the world if I was just going to zoom by it, counting countries? I'd never questioned this *zooming by* mentality we've become so accustomed to in the West. It's what we Americans do. What immersive healing experiences would I have incorporated speedily moving through countries and snapping Facebook selfies in cool locations?

I wonder where I'd be now if I hadn't been gifted a soul sister on my thirty-seventh birthday, the first week of my trip.

> "Faith is taking the first step, even when
> you don't see the whole staircase."
> —Martin Luther King Jr.

Time with my soul sister in Sydney came to an end, and I reluctantly returned to Chiang Rai. Everything felt different there now, having left my Tantra family. I considered relocating to Bali or Vietnam or a Thai island to finish the book, but in the end, I decided to finish my trip out in Chiang Rai. I'd focus all efforts on completing this book so I could finally plan my return to the United States. I was starting, for the first time at month twenty-four, to feel like I really wanted to return home, and that was a good feeling.

Expansion Exercises

1) Unresolved relationships cause us to harden ourselves over time. What quarrelsome familial or personal relationships need resolution?

2) What would it look like to choose love and connection over fear and estrangement and reach out to that person? Even if they were not in a place in their journey where they can accept your good intentions, would it be worth making the effort for your own peace of mind?

3) Can you envision the release it would have for you to make the attempt at reconciliation? Can you approach the situation with no expectation of a certain outcome? This is important. Not everyone will be at the same place in their journey as you are.

4) If no resolution is possible, can you bring compassion to the circumstances, knowing that each person was doing the best they could do in any situation and find understanding, acceptance, and forgiveness in that?

Journal Entry
'Simplicity'

CHAPTER 20

Month Twenty-Eight—Thailand

Individuation

We shall not cease from exploration, and the end of
all our exploring will be to arrive where we started ...
and know the place for the first time."
—T. S. Eliot

L ooking back over twenty-eight months of travel, from the
moment I stepped onto my first one-way flight to now, nearing
my return to the United States, I see what a metamorphosis has taken
place, a process of *re-becoming* spurred on by purposeful intentions
and unlikely serendipitous encounters. Even in my last month, as
I diligently plowed through the final chapters of this book, I was
led to one last special person who opened me to new perspectives.

My journey unfolded, surprisingly, as a spiritual quest through
Buddhism, meditation, yoga, spiritual healers, Tantra, and questions
of belief and spirituality, although I'd not intended to explore
spirituality at all. When I left the United States, I kept saying, mostly
to myself, *Why am I going? I'm searching for my highest self.* I didn't realize
then like I do now that the search for our highest self and the
spiritual path are really *one in the same.*

As this book was coming together, I was thinking how nice
it would've been to be introduced to someone or something with

a pure psychology base, if for no other reason than to reinforce the strides I'd made on the spiritual path but with mainstream credibility and understanding. I'd noticed the links were there between spirituality and psychology, with both Buddhism and Tantra presenting heavy undercurrents of psychological study and investigation; in fact, Buddha is widely considered to be the first psychologist. Especially with my break from Tantra, I was thirsty to explore the distinguished greats like Freud, Jung, or Maslow, but with my goal to finish this book and my impending return to the United States, I'd not made it a priority.

One day, as I sat writing in my favorite co-working café, I struck up conversation with the gentleman sitting next to me. Would you believe it, he was a retired psychiatrist from Scotland. Immediately we were drawn into daily in-depth coffee talks, he fascinated by my two-year spiritual journey and I by his extensive psychology background.

We compared notes, swapped stories, and explored the correlations between spiritual and psychological ascension; the cross-theoretical dots connected in the sky of my mind, lighting up stars like magical constellations. I could think of no other introduction that would've been more meaningful for me at this stage of my trip, and this is where I first learned of Swiss psychologist Carl Jung's[1] theory on individuation[2]. My new friend said, "It seems like you've successfully navigated the Carl Jung individuation process."

"The Carl Jung individu- what?" I asked.

The Return to Self

As I came to learn, this spiraling inward journey I'd taken back to myself is one we're *all* meant to undergo—not like I did it necessarily, in the full-immersion, globetrotting sort of way, but Jung attests that it's an essential process in healthy psychological development as we cross the midlife threshold. Jung felt it *so* critical to achieve this selfhood he dedicated much of his career to this subject—the monumental process of midlife re-becoming he called individuation. Jung states, "Individuation is only experienced by those who have gone through the wearisome but indispensable business of coming to terms with the unconscious components of the personality" (C. G. Jung, *The Collected Works*, 1953, Volume VIII, pg. 3179).

Anthony Storr shares in *The Essential Jung*, "The goal toward which the individuation process is tending is 'Wholeness' or 'Integration': a condition in which all the different elements of the psyche, both conscious and unconscious, are welded together. The person who achieves this goal possesses "... an attitude that is beyond the reach of emotional entanglements and violent shocks—a consciousness detached from the world. Individuation, in Jung's view, is a spiritual journey; and the person embarking upon it, although he might not subscribe to any recognized creed, was nonetheless pursuing a religious quest" (Storr 1983, pg. 228).

Just like that, the credible link between spirituality and psychology revealed itself with my new Scottish friend in a Thai café.

I saw it now clearly. I'd been on the path to individuation since day one, taking to an all-encompassing internal exploration, including childhood issues, spiritual investigation, belief systems, making the unconscious conscious, and overcoming The Past. In that I was able to find understanding, forgiveness, and acceptance, all compulsory to reintegrating the splintered aspects of myself and to my re-becoming. Ultimately the journey to find my highest self was really about the *return to self*. The self I'd always been but had heavily obscured with layers of dysfunction and veils of emotional angst that began long ago.

Hmm yes, the return to self. So simple yet so profound.

My Scottish coffee-talk guru explained that Jung felt the individuation process was most often spurred on by crisis, and it's in the way we choose to answer the call of the soul that dictates the path we follow into the second half of life, either through midlife transition or, more commonly, midlife crisis.

I imagine many back home thought I may have been experiencing a midlife crisis when I chose to leave the United States. Perhaps they secretly wondered quietly to themselves or aloud at their dinner tables, "What is she searching for? Why has she been gone so long?" Or my favorite question of those who travel, "What is she running from?" I didn't have the terminology for it at the time, but I knew when I left I wasn't running *from* myself, rather *to* myself, and that was a good thing. I now know I was circumnavigating the world and myself on the path of individuation.

Jung came to his own individuation process when his intense collaboration with Freud began to unravel. Jung and Freud had conflicting views on the subject of God and religion, and Jung's reluctance to embrace Freud's atheistic approach would eventually be the undoing of them. Jung's intellectual divorce from Freud left Jung devastated and was the catalyst for his *dark night of the soul*. This would lead Jung to his own individuation and to develop his theories further.

I'm remembering my own period of the *dark night* in the six months before leaving the United States that propelled me to this re-becoming, although I had no awareness, terminology, or conceptual plan for it then. I found a journal entry from that time just before I was swallowed by the dark, grasping at light, long before the idea to travel had even sprouted. I'd written:

> You will be okay. You will figure this out. You will find your way. You will persevere. Don't worry so much if people like you. Stop worrying if you're fat; just live a happy, healthy life, and you'll be beautiful. Stop being a people pleaser and shed your chameleon ways. Don't justify things; you know the truth. Listen to your intuition ...

I *hoped* I could see all those statements come to fruition, and I *wanted* to feel those sentiments, but I had no vision of how to achieve them. I didn't even know it was possible, as it would require a paradigm shift in my personality, and I had no tools, inspiration, or knowledge that I had the ability to accomplish that. I still can't really make sense of it all—that all the right people and experiences came to me at the right time. Perhaps in the determined declarations in my journal of "You will" instead of "I want," I unknowingly collaborated with the universe, and we manifested a new path that would take me to the new me.

Looking back, sometimes I think when I stepped onto that first flight, the universe sort of turned and looked at me, saying, "Hey, this girl is finally serious about the personal quest for betterment. Let's keep her safe and give her some opportunities and see what she does with them." I couldn't have known that I'd be led to the journey that unfolded and that one day I'd be where I am now—to feel the sentiments from my journal entry so deeply that I don't have to ponder the ideas anymore or ask God or the universe how to attain them. They're now intrinsic to who I am, living and breathing inside me. And I'm relieved … so incredibly relieved and grateful to have arrived here.

Although it's difficult to see when we're immersed in periods of intense emotional pain, they can be a catalyst to spark the quest toward our higher selves; but we have to pay attention when the soul cries. I think that's one of the biggest lessons of all, to recognize and give credence to our thoughts, emotions, patterns, intuition, signs, and coincidences. If we're not listening and responding to the whispers of the soul, we may miss our calling for change and our chance at re-becoming.

The Power of Looking Inward

Socrates said, "The unexamined life is not worth living."

Across my journey, I've found such value in simply examining my own life and my behavior, when in the past I'd spent little time reflecting on my actions and the reasoning behind them. David R.

Hawkins, MD, PhD, writes in *Power vs. Force: The Hidden Determinants of Human Behavior,* "If we look within ourselves at the instant-by-instant processes of our minds, we will soon notice that the mind acts much more rapidly than we would acknowledge. It becomes apparent that the notion that our actions are based on thoughtful decisions is a grand illusion."

I couldn't see it in my old life, but I now realize the power of slowing life down and spending time in introspection to dissect my actions and the root emotions behind them. Even when we're in the throes of an emotional experience, if we can create space between the stimulus and our response, we become more able to handle challenging people and situations with compassion and kindness. When we bring awareness to experience, we have the opportunity to elevate ourselves.

Awareness + Experience = Elevated Consciousness

I was one who unconsciously looked outward to repair the cracks and voids of my heart; some were coping mechanisms like emotional eating, love relationships, extreme television watching, or drinking. Others were healthier attempts like prayer or seeking guidance from God. What I've come to see though is that when we look outward and turn our problems over to anything or anyone else, this creates a disempowered state within oneself; looking *out there* to fix what's *in here.* It starts innocently enough with a self-soothing new habit; then before you know it, you've spent half a lifetime filling the voids and mending the cracks with high-carb foods and relationships.

It seems to me we've become quite comfortable with lives of imbalance, constantly agitated, judgmental, irritated, discontent, dissatisfied, unhappy—this is not our natural state of being—yet it's become our default. We don't really question it anymore or the side effects plaguing us. We're more comfortable taking prescription pills and antacids rather than listening to our bodies and minds screaming at us. Interestingly, Carl Jung said, "[Contemporary man] is blind to the fact that, with all his rationality and efficiency, he is possessed by 'powers' that are beyond his control. His gods and demons have not disappeared at all; they have merely got new names. They keep him on the run with restlessness, vague apprehensions, psychological complications, an insatiable need for pills, alcohol, tobacco, food—and, above all, a large array of neuroses" (Jung 1964, pg. 82).

Neuroses is defined as "a variety of psychological problems involving persistent experiences of negative affect including anxiety, sadness or depression, anger, irritability, mental confusion, low sense of self-worth, etc., behavioral symptoms such as phobic avoidance, vigilance, impulsive and compulsive acts, lethargy, etc., cognitive problems such as unpleasant or disturbing thoughts, repetition of thoughts and obsession, habitual fantasizing, negativity and cynicism, etc." (Boeree 2002, para. 1).

I found it interesting that Jung viewed neurosis as a warning sign that one "was straying too far from his own true path" and that it (neurosis) was, "part of a self-regulating mechanism whose aim was the achievement of a better balance within the psyche." He went further to say, "In Western man, because of the achievements of his culture, there was an especial tendency toward intellectual hubris; an overvaluation of thinking which could alienate a man from his emotional roots" (Storr 1983, pg. 17–18). Oh my goodness, Carl Jung was a genius! Why aren't we teaching him in our public schools?

I didn't see it back in my old life, but my dark angel depression and coping strategies should've been warnings that I'd gone off track somewhere. The soul was crying, but I ignored her. I heard her, I watched her cry, I felt her pain deeply, but I misinterpreted the message. I carried onward, the choices of my life taking me further and further from my true self and expanding the cracks and voids within. Who knew the way to repair the cracks was to look at them and dive into them instead of resisting, placating, and running from them.

There's great power in looking inward.

The Mandala Connection

I began drawing mandalas on my first layover in Delhi before I'd even heard of Carl Jung. Only now in month twenty-eight did I find that mandalas were one of Jung's favorite tools to aid in self-realization and individuation. Jung said that mandalas *are* "Formation, Transformation, Eternal Mind's eternal re-creation" (Storr 1983, pg. 230). He proposed that drawing mandalas leads us on the unconscious path toward the self by reducing confusion within the psyche and reinstating natural order.

Of his own mandala drawings, Jung writes, "My mandalas were cryptograms concerning the state of the self which were presented to me anew each day. In them I saw the self—that is, my whole being—actively at work ... This is evidently an attempt at self-healing on the part of Nature, which does not spring from conscious reflections but from instinctive impulse ... It became increasingly plain to me that the mandala is the center. It is the exponent of all paths. It is the path to the center, to individuation ... I knew that in finding the mandala as an expression of the self I had attained what was for me the ultimate" (Storr 1983, pg. 234 and 236).

I was gob-smacked when I read Jung's theories, at this stage of my trip, on mandalas and their benefits. I'd been drawing them all along! Coincidence? Synchronicity? Divine inspiration? I had no idea my artistic pastime was aiding in my return to self. With only my pen and a journal, mandalas were my creative expression as I lived from my trekking backpack. What began as a few creative doodles gradually transformed into a meticulous art form. While I traveled outwardly, mandalas allowed me to travel inwardly. They were my companion when alone, my meditation when confronting myself, and a description of the day when there were no words. They were an extension of my traveling self on the path of re-becoming.

Expansion Exercises

1) Are you now hearing, or have you ever felt, a cry from your inner self, encouraging you to choose another path? What is that calling?

2) Have you denied your inner voice that's tried to tell you you've gone astray somewhere on your path? What would it look like to listen to the inner voice?

3) Is there something significant you want to do in life and are not doing? What is it? Why haven't you acted on it?

4) Do you have any apprehension or inner angst about your life? Can you understand the importance of acknowledging the inner angst? How does it express itself in you? Depression, neurosis, unhealthy habits, or addictions? What can you do to change this aspect of your life?

5) If you haven't already, would you consider journeying inward with the Facing Freedom thirty-day exercise as a means of tuning into your mind, body, and spirit? If not, are you willing to investigate the resistance within?

Journal Entry
'Self'

CHAPTER 21

Last Day—Thailand

Closing Thoughts

Everyone thinks of changing the world, but
no one thinks of changing himself.
—Leo Tolstoy

I'm packing my bags and preparing for my return flight tonight. As I sit at my dining room table writing this final chapter, I'm overwhelmed by the significance of this book. Not necessarily in the way of popularity or how readers might receive it. I couldn't possibly put an expectation like that on the outpouring of my globetrotting thoughts. This may very well be a drop in the ocean of printed content floating the planet. What I've realized though is that it's significant to me. As I return to the States, a little trepidatious to leave the bubble of expat life I've come to love in Southeast Asia, I see that this will be my own guidebook to healthy living—a reminder of all the lessons I've learned, knowledge I've gained, the special people that changed me, and the hurdles I jumped to elevate to a healthier plateau of existence.

I'm told reentry to "normal" life can be quite an adjustment for long-term travelers, and it will be a challenge in itself to maintain the equanimity I've found and to continue growth. Life in the United States is feverishly focused on *doing, doing, doing,* and I now see the necessity and benefit of a slow life and simply *being*. So although I was originally writing this book to inspire you, I see in this moment it's just as much for me. It'll be Eryn's guidebook to soul growth, preservation of happiness, and sustaining emotional contentment.

For a time, I was reluctant to return home. I really was. And if I'd not split from my Tantra family or had I found myself with a Tantric partner, I probably would've been so captivated by the path I may not have returned to the United States to live. I've come to feel though that I'm meant to return to my home country. I was born there for a reason, and perhaps there's a new calling and a purposeful life waiting for me there. Whatever I find, it will all be another set of fears, challenges, and spiritual tests to overcome.

I see that I'll *experience* American life differently now because I'll *view* it differently. As Wayne Dyer famously said, "When you change the way you look at things, the things you look at change." I now view the entirety of life from a different perspective, and that in itself is pretty magical. If I'd remained abroad because I didn't think I could maintain my newfound health and equanimity, then that would've been a choice made out of fear instead of love, and I don't make decisions based on fear anymore. I'm prepared for the next phase of my life, whatever that may be, and I'll embrace it with open arms and a full heart.

In an effort to bring focused awareness to the needs of others, I've decided to add an element of *conscious capitalism*[1] to all new business endeavors, including this book. I'm making a commitment to myself and to all of you that I'll donate significant proceeds from book sales to charitable organizations at home and abroad. When I sell ten thousand copies, I'll donate 20 percent of the profits, when I sell one hundred thousand, I'll donate 25 percent and if a higher power is shining on me and one million are sold, I'll donate 30 percent. I can't have any expectation that it'll reach these sorts of numbers, but I can send my book out into the world with good intention.

The Perfect Ending

There was a time when I felt there'd be a hint of failure to return home without finding a lasting romantic love on my journey. Isn't that how every great story, travel or otherwise, should end? I used to have that false idea deeply embedded in me, I really did.

Fortunately, I've risen out of that form of thought. To be honest though, I'm still surprised the book I was called to write didn't revolve around a man or romantic relationship. All the stories of my life before this included men; in fact, they were the leading characters, even ahead of me. For the first three decades of life, I didn't know how to live any other story. Now I see what a victory it is to return unattached. It means I didn't grasp at the wrong relationship because I was attached to the story of love. It means I gave love a chance when it felt right, but I learned to say goodbye when I needed to. That was one of the main goals when I left, to find that emotional independence away from codependent attachment, and I've achieved it, so I can see that only as success. I found the only love that will ever really sustain me, and that's the love I now have for myself and my connection with God/Spirit/Source.

I'll find the right relationship one day, and we'll ride off in the sunset on a white horse (well, maybe not a white horse), but it'll be when I meet the right person—the person that enhances my life with their own perfectly imperfect combination of mad, quirky traits that will mix and mingle with mine in the depths of the mind's ocean. We'll help each other breathe a little easier when life gets rough, and we'll laugh and sing and make love and cry and work and disagree and make up and travel and love. I don't care anymore about picket fences or big houses; I'd be perfectly content in a small flat in India. I just hope to find someone who understands me and can flow like water through life with me, but it'll happen when it's meant to. If there's anything I've learned on my journey, it's that we're led to the right people in the right time. I don't worry so much about these things anymore. I somehow know the universe is working its magic right now, orchestrating it all with divine intelligence.

Dark Angels and Patchwork Quilts

I feel to share with you that my dark angels of depression don't fly with me anymore. It's been a long time since I've seen them actually, back in the period before leaving America when I was merging with my mattress. They were with me all the time back then and in the decades before. You know, I didn't even know I could live life without them; they'd been my longstanding shadows.

I see now they'd been trying to warn me and teach me all those years, showing me that I'd gone astray, but I didn't understand or pay attention to their messages of my inner angst. I couldn't see it clearly then; I was caught in the web of my patterns that kept me under their wings.

In this dedicated quest to find my highest self, coming to release so much, I intuitively feel I've freed myself from the karmic imprint, as the Buddhists would call it, of my dark angel depression. I can't be sure if they'll try to visit me again, but I'm now in control of this aspect of my personality, and I never felt that before. I have the tools and the *inner knowing* to keep myself from sliding into the darkness, and that's powerful. If I spend time worrying about their return, it will certainly be a call for them to visit. This is how it works, you see; what we give energy to, we manifest. I don't think about them anymore, those dark angels. I hope they're napping and playing bingo in retirement, deservedly resting after the heavy workload I subjected them to the first half of my life.

I've come to feel that in healing the past, I've rewritten my future. In shedding the painful parts of self that once led me to make decisions from ego and fear, I now make them from love and compassion. That one shift changes everything. In finding this sustaining inner peace, which was a culmination of all I experienced on my trip, I also feel that I've put an end to the generational cycle of mental health issues that plagued my family and that I've released my father from his dark angels. I don't know how the afterlife works, and my father is long gone, but I somehow feel that deeply to be true; in healing myself, we've both been released from that cyclical pain. Is it possible that I was able to holistically overcome my depression through introspection, silence, integrating Eastern philosophy, and learning to hear and follow my intuition when my father and his mother were less successful in formally studying psychology and participating in mainstream treatments and pharmaceutical drugs? The answer is clear to me.

As I traversed the globe shedding the old me, I stitched a new patchwork quilt. I gathered up little threads of love and light along the way, swatches of India and Indonesia, Israel, Ireland and Italy, fringes of Tanzania, Rwanda and Thailand; they've all merged now in the fabric of my mind, a blanket of gratitude, compassion, and equanimity that I wrap myself in daily.

I'm overwhelmed in this moment at all I've experienced and how the journey has unfolded so perfectly in a way I couldn't have planned myself. All the people that were so serendipitously sent to me as teachers and unlikely experiences I was led to. And I see I was fully supported along the way—by a higher power, the universe, by good intentions.

I'm grateful for it all, I really am.

The Call for Change

It's a big ask for me to suggest that you begin an inward quest and to consider navigating the Facing Freedom practice as a launching point. People are busy, and our lives are full, I know. What I hope is that, in my story, you'll see that it's worth it. The twists and the turns, the scars and the burns, the crying, the hurting, the silence, the searching, the shedding and pealing of life's painful layers; it's all worth it to reclaim the inner contentment, the happiness, the

peaceful existence that we're all meant to kno⋯
just have to get quiet enough to find the an⋯

I can't know how the women of th⋯
book, but if it can be a catalyst for just one ⋯
and overcome those *not enough* feelings, to find con⋯
herself out of pain, or to have her own personal awa⋯
leads her to take steps toward her highest, authentic self, we⋯
the book and my year plus of writing will have been worth it. If ⋯
only reaches a small few, I'll sleep a little deeper at night, knowing
I contributed something to help another.

You can read this book and put it on a shelf or you can let it
propel a shift in you, giving you the motivation to rise up. The key is
to integrate the experience of what you've just read and to navigate
your own journey, which is why I feel the expansion exercises in each
chapter and the thirty-day Facing Freedom practice are so powerful.
It *will* shift something in those who experience it, bringing you to a
greater sense of self: self-love, self-respect, self-knowing, self-worth,
self-awareness, self-acceptance … radical self-acceptance, yes!

Let's work at building each other up instead of tearing each
other down. Let's work to appreciate our differences instead of
comparing ourselves to one another. This is the key, to elevate each
other. It will require a dedicated revolutionary approach because we
must choose it every day in our thoughts, intentions, and actions.
It's a cause I'm dedicated to, *the revolution of radical self-acceptance and
compassion for all.*

Siggy came to visit me in Thailand a few months before my
return. We met up on an island and were sitting by the pool sipping
beer. What? I had to have some fun every now and then in and
amongst all that growth! So ya know what she said, that crazy girl
that I love so much? You'll never guess. She said, "Babe. I just
noticed something. You don't have bitchy resting face anymore!"

I smiled a big smile, and we laughed. "Well, it only took two
years to undue three decades of internal dysfunction—that's not
so bad, really. Hey Sig, what if I'd never left? What if I'd let my

keep me from taking this trip. I nearly stayed, you know?"
se call, babe ... close call."

It feels good to know that I'm now one less unhealthy person roaming the planet; it feels monumental if you want to know the truth of it. Not only for my own internal state but also knowing I can trust myself to handle others with care. I'm not perfect, and I'll still make mistakes, but I enter my relationships with friends, family, work, and romantic interests from a different perspective now, and that allows me to better handle all personalities and situations.

What I see clearly and feel to intently express is that this journey of mine, it wasn't just to make myself feel better. Initially, I suppose my leaving was a desperate attempt at figuring myself out and finding peace, so that was a selfish motivation, but what's obvious to me now is that *it's in a place of our own pain and inner disorder that we bring pain to others*, whether in morning road rage or in our meaningful relationships. Simply put, hurt people hurt people.

When we make the effort toward individual change, healing and elevating ourselves, it changes how we interact with the world—our colleagues, our partners, parents, friends, and even strangers on the street. Individual change propels collective change, and in this intention to heal, we *can* change the world. I've now fully integrated the sentiment of Lao Tzu when he said, "If you want to awaken all of humanity, then awaken all of yourself. If you want to eliminate the suffering in the world, then eliminate all that is dark and negative within yourself. Truly, the greatest gift you have to give is that of your own self-transformation." Before this journey, I didn't quite grasp this fully. Now I understand.

Find silence for yourself and become comfortable with it. Ask yourself what you gain from spending free time with constant noise, television, and Facebook; do they enhance or detract from your life? Take time for introspection and learn to hear your intuition and the cries of the soul when they speak to you through your body, your dreams, gut feelings, synchronicities, and recurring emotional pains. These are important messages from within trying to catch your attention. When you come to hear your intuition, you'll be able to align yourself with pure intention to your soul's purpose, and life will unfold more smoothly. You don't have to travel outwardly to travel inwardly. You are your own refuge, remember—only you can save yourself. No one else will do it for you.

Well, I'm saying goodbye to Thailand tonight and 28 months of travelling. It feels so strange to be catching my last tuk tuk that'll take me to the airport for my final flight home. I was a different person the last time I saw America, that's for sure. I'm looking forward to seeing my never-forgotten K-9 companion and hugging my mom—one of those warm, fuzzy, extended hugs, free from the tin armor I once wore with my bitchy resting face.

PART IV

Eclectic Teachings

Here I combine concepts from Buddhism, Tantra, and specific relatable insights from Vipassana with text from credible scientists and researchers to consolidate these teachings. Together they've given me greater understanding and relief from many of the mental poisons that plague us in society today. These are my interpretations based on countless lectures, research, workshops, retreats, and encounters across twenty-eight months and are not, by any means, formally presented here. Take only what feels right in your heart and discard the rest.

CHAPTER 22

Petals of the Lotus

Don't try to use what you learn from Buddhism to be a Buddhist;
use it to be a better whatever-you-already-are.
—His Holiness the Dalai Lama XIV

The Cause of Suffering

Buddhist teachings[1] suggest that all happiness and all suffering come from our own minds. Now, I don't know about you, but this had not occurred to me. I thought some people have happy lives and some people struggle more, perhaps with depression or anxiety or financial difficulties, and that's the way it is, largely out of our control.

When I truly understood and came to *know deeply* that the mind is the basis for happiness and suffering—and that I could create a new environment in my mind—I realized how it benefited me to understand and harness the mind. Tenzin Palmo referred to the mind as a "monkey mind" bouncing around, running wild, hopping from one idea to another, and grasping for the next pleasurable experience. My monkey mind was deranged and addicted to the search for love as if at Disney World riding the Space Mountain roller coaster—sometimes fun, sometimes out of control and scary. I came to understand that my mind was creating discontent and that

I could change that through various tools, including meditation, challenging my inner dialogue, limiting obsessive thoughts, and embracing change.

Meditation

Buddhists (along with other traditions) believe meditation is a powerful tool to understand and transform the mind. There are many different forms of meditation; sitting silently and looking within, watching the thoughts, acknowledging thoughts, dismissing thoughts, chanting mantras, singing meditations, walking meditations, dancing meditations, and undertaking meditative activities are just few. What all forms of meditation intend is to increase concentration, clarity, emotional equanimity, and calm; and if you can quiet the mind enough, wisdom *will* arise.

I'd heard about the benefits of meditation and attempted it a few times unsuccessfully in the States in yoga classes and again in the ashram in India. I found it to be the most boring and frustrating exercise! I couldn't stay with it, and I didn't feel it helped me. I was impatient. I couldn't justify it as valuable use of my time. Meditation didn't work fast enough for me at first, so I gave up. If only someone had been able to explain *how* meditation was of such tremendous personal benefit, this would have helped me to stick with it.

Holy wow! Did I see results when I entered the full-throttle immersion of the Introduction to Buddhism course, then in the Vipassana silent retreat, and again in my own Facing Freedom practice and several Tantra retreats! Trust me, I wasn't participating in them because they were fun; I did it because I saw results. Here, I was able to truly integrate and understand on a visceral level what meditation was about. The wisdom didn't exist as a concept outside myself; it became a lived experience that changed me at my core.

Tenzin Palmo was quoted in *Cave in the Snow,* "Meditation is where you begin to calm the storm, to cease the never-ending chattering of the mind. Once that is achieved you can access the deeper levels of consciousness which exist beyond the surface noise. Along with that comes the gradual disidentification with our thoughts and emotions. You see their transparent nature and no longer totally believe in them. This creates inner harmony which you can then bring to your everyday life" (Mackenzie 1998, pg. 30).

This is the essence of Buddhism and any mindfulness practice for that matter, to train the mind just as an athlete trains the body. Imagine the mind like a muscle that can be trained to expand, strengthen, and grow by applying different ways of thinking and meditation. Alternatively, the mind may be left to its average neurotic, obsessive, and degenerative state. Like anything, it takes work, and we have to choose it. It's a practice.

Not only did I see results on a mental and emotional level, but I feel my body was physically healing as well. Intuitively I felt in the emotional release that came with my deep meditation experiences, my body was beginning to repair itself, although I had no formal knowledge to accompany my *internal knowing* until month twenty of my trip when I was introduced to the work of Bruce Lipton, PhD. In his book *The Biology of Belief*, he states, "A recent study revealed that just eight hours of mindful meditation was sufficient to significantly change vital gene function. Compared to controls, meditators exhibited a range of genetic and molecular differences that included reduced levels of pro-inflammatory genes and altered levels of gene-regulating machinery. These observed changes in genetic expression are associated with faster physical recovery from stressful situations and prove that mindfulness practice can lead to health improvement through profound epigenetic alterations of the genome" (Lipton 2015, pg. 144). In studying Lipton, I started to truly believe that my mind had an enormous effect on my physical health and this is when I began the dedicated quest to heal my thyroid holistically.

Over the course of my trip, I went from meditation skeptic to meditation evangelist. I experienced major changes in the way my mind processes information and in my life overall, which you've read about already. And isn't that what we're all looking for really, a happier, healthier, more contented state of reality? So, I'm here to tell you, meditation is powerful! It's worth the effort. In the stillness of meditation, the whispers of the soul will speak.

Attachment—Nonattachment

Understanding attachment/nonattachment and integrating this concept has drastically changed my life. It's one of the most valuable teachings I picked up while abroad.

Attachment is the natural human tendency to give power to external circumstances that we hope will bring happiness. A man? New car? Promotion? Bigger house? A promotion is a good example: You're up for a promotion, and there are several other people in line for the position. You know you've got a good shot at it, and you've worked hard, you deserve it. Your mind rides the obsessive roller coaster of expectation up, up, up, waiting to hear that the promotion is yours. *Ohhh when I get the promotion, we can buy a new house, maybe even a new car. We can afford private schooling for the kids.* A new version of life is imagined, and it hinges on securing the promotion: *Of course I'm going to get this promotion. I've been there the longest, I've worked harder than the others, I'm more dedicated.*

What happens when you don't get the promotion? The roller coaster plummets downward into devastation, anger, discontent, and resentment. You're no longer happy with your current position. You feel resentment toward the coworker who received the promotion that should have been yours, and you're now irritable with your family because you're in a state of mental agitation. You're angry because you'd already decided you'd buy a bigger house once you got the promotion. All your internal suffering and negativity has arisen because you attached your happiness and future planning to something that was beyond your control.

What if you hadn't placed attachment to the outcome? Instead of devastation and resentment that may take days, weeks, or months to shake off, you'd recover from the disappointment much more quickly. You may still be disappointed, yet the emotional angst would be far less. Attachment is about placing too much emphasis on things going right *out there* to maintain equanimity *in here*.

Attachment extends also to objects and people we cherish—heartbreak over losing your favorite necklace, disappointment over the discontinuation of your favorite coffee, and, oh, the suffering over attachments in love relationships! How many times have you thought after only a few dates, *Is he the one I'll spend my life with?*

To stay in the present moment and *detach from the outcome* of an event helps maintain a more realistic existence in the face of disappointment and change. It also helps to enjoy each moment more fully. When attachments are reduced, so is internal suffering, and life becomes more content.

It's a powerful concept to integrate and implement. Like anything, hard work reaps rewards, but we have to choose it. I've lived life on both sides of the monkey mind fence, and I no longer choose mental chaos. It's a simple concept but not an easy one to master. I *practice* nonattachment every day.

Self-Cherishing

Buddhists believe that we focus too much on our individual selves, and this applies both to those who are high on themselves, *Oh, I'm so great, look at me, look at me, everyone should revolve around me,* but also to those who are down on themselves, *Oh, I'm no good, I can't do anything right, look at the sacrifices I make for others, I'm not enough.* Both emphasize too much "I."

Now, for some reason, this really struck me. I knew I never felt superior (I secretly congratulated myself for that), but I swung to the opposite spectrum, feeling sorry for myself, swimming laps of negativity in the pool of inferiority. Sometimes I nearly drown in my own *less than* self.

After much introspection and many deep self-cherishing meditations in retreat, a revelation bubbled up from deep within.

I'd led a selfishly selfless life. I would constantly give and give of myself, as I perceived in a selfless way (to men mostly), yet deep down it had been with the unconscious selfish need to be accepted and loved, and this precipitated most of my actions. I was giving to receive. The underlying intentions of my selfless acts were selfish and motivated by "I."

Fully grasping this realization led me to watch and adjust my thought patterns and to be mindful of my intentions before giving of myself. I began making diligent efforts to shift my thoughts from myself to others in all situations. This is likely the teaching that inspired me to help others less fortunate and what grew out of this was: www.ConsciousCreations.world.

Impermanence

I was first introduced to this concept while walking with my friend Fritz on the shore of the Ganges in Rishikesh, India. What then was a new word to me became a topic of everyday discussion amongst my new friends in India. Impermanence is a key Buddhist teaching alongside the concept of attachment. Impermanence is the understanding and acceptance that everything changes. *Everything.*

We may intellectually know this to be true, but much of our internal suffering arises from the hope that we will not have to deal with change in our lives. We expend much mental energy grasping at aspects of our lives that we fear will change. Jealousy is a good example; desperate grasping at another out of fear of abandonment (change in relationship status). When it is truly understood and accepted that all things will change, there is less attachment to a particular outcome. When we achieve this, we become more present in our lives and less obsessed with attachment and, in the case of releasing jealousy, we become more likely to be a sought-after companion. A creative cycle replaces a destructive cycle.

Coming to understand impermanence, one of very few things we can depend on in life, we see how important the present moment is. We don't dwell on the past and we don't obsess about the future; we live in each moment. When we stray from the present, we bring suffering to ourselves. Eckhart Tolle wrote in *A New Earth*, "Why did anxiety, stress, or negativity arise? Because you turned away from the present moment. And why did you do that? You thought something else was more important. You forgot your main purpose. One small error, one misperception, creates a world of suffering" (Tolle 2005, pg. 267). Once we grasp this fully, we can make peace with change that will inevitably come and eventually even embrace it.

Karma

Everyone's heard of karma, *what goes around comes around.* Like The golden rule of the Christian faith, *do unto others as you'd have done unto you,* and the scientific approach of Newton's third law, *for every action there is an equal and opposite reaction,* they all focus on the reciprocity of ethics. Most people in the West view this in a limited capacity, only applying it to this life. For Buddhists though and those who believe in reincarnation, Karma encompasses the cycle of cause and effect across many lifetimes.

My Christian upbringing didn't allow me to believe in reincarnation when I set out into the world, but I did a lot of thinking about this as I traveled and studied philosophies of the East. My interpretation is that the concept of karma and reincarnation encourages believers to live a highly moral existence. As a Christian, I was taught we are all sinners but that God forgives us our trespasses if we are truly repentant and accept Christ as savior; we will be absolved of our transgressions and are told we'll gain entrance to heaven when we die—essentially a get-out-of-jail-free card.

Interestingly, it's said that reincarnation was once a Christian belief but the concept was removed from the Bible because the church believed it allowed for too many lifetimes to be a good person. The concept of sin, and one lifetime that will end in either heaven or hell, was a useful ideology to influence behavior. "The theory of reincarnation is recorded in the Bible. But the proper interpretations were struck from it during the Ecumenical Council meeting of the Catholic Church in Constantinople sometime around 553 A.D., called the Council of Nicea. The Council members voted to strike those teachings from the Bible in order to solidify Church control" (Maclaine, 1983, pg. 234-5).

Believers in reincarnation and karma expect to live many lives until they are worthy of enlightenment and are released from the cycle of birth, death, and rebirth. In my view this encourages deeper personal responsibility and high integrity on the mental, emotional, physical, and spiritual levels in *this life*, as there will be effects crossing multiple life cycles. Consider not only extreme transgressions like killing, adultery, and rape but also everyday transgressions like judgments, lies, jealousy, resentment, passive aggression, accusations, anger, and so on. Each wrong action, thought, or intention toward others or ourselves will bring about a negative consequence—sometimes in this lifetime, sometimes in the next. Similarly, every virtuous action, including thoughts, words, and intentions, will bring about a beneficial result.

Whether you believe in reincarnation or not, consider the possibility that there are soul consequences for every thought, action, and intention. Were we to believe this, we'd be compelled to filter and cleanse the impurities of the mind and turn our thoughts, words, and deeds toward love and compassion.

Love and Compassion

Buddhists view love much differently than we do in the West. They strive to extend love and compassion to all living beings unconditionally with no expectation in return. That's a big ask, no? We may say we love someone, but we attach conditions to that love. I know I did. I'll love you as long as you make me happy or as long as you provide me with _____ or if you complete me in this way. Rarely do we consciously acknowledge our internal conditions connected to the gift of our love, but if we look closely, there are usually underlying motivations. True love doesn't require all that; it extends to another even when receiving nothing in return.

I've thought about this concept at great length, trying to determine how it can be applied in relationships where expectations are necessary in a life shared with another person. I've come to this conclusion: love and compatibility are not necessarily synonymous. Understanding this helped me to release pain, regret, and animosity I harbored for failed relationships. In releasing that, I can still hold love in my heart for people that were once very special in my life, but I do it now with no expectation. I feel that whatever hurts were experienced in past relationships, both parties were doing their best. Everyone acts from his or her level of consciousness. Sometimes in life we hurt those we love and, in turn, are hurt by them. Arguably, there are ways to be compassionate to minimize the hurt we cause but can we ever avoid hurting others if we're being true to ourselves? I don't think so. If we bring awareness to and honor our feelings though, when they arise, we can usually approach potentially hurtful situations with compassion, kindness, and integrity before it reaches the stage of unhealthy toxicity.

Compassion is a lofty ideal. Buddhists teach us to have compassion for all living beings whether it's the ant on the sidewalk or the collector at a tollbooth. So often we get caught up in the "I" of our lives, manipulating our surroundings to bring happiness (get what we want), we forget our attitudes and actions are affecting others.

What if we viewed everyone we came in contact with as if they were our mothers? How would we treat them? This was an example given by Tenzin Palmo, the cave-dwelling nun in the lecture I attended in India. Since Buddhists believe in reincarnation, it's possible that any person we meet could've been our mother in a previous life. It's a farfetched idea to consider, I know, but if it allows us to view *all others with compassion in all situations*, then I think it's a good thing.

Compassion + Loving Kindness = A Better World

There's a saying I like very much from the Dhammapada, a widely read Buddhist text, "One is indeed one's own refuge." You've heard me mention this before in the book. It means, simply, you are your own refuge. You can save yourself. You are your own haven. I've adopted this as my own personal mantra, and it always empowers and reminds me that I can save myself—from myself or any situation—all by changing my mind. I am my own refuge. You are your own refuge. We have to save ourselves.

CHAPTER 23

Tantra Concepts

Your task is not to seek love, but merely
to seek and find the barriers
within yourself that you have built against it.
—Rumi

Working with the Chakras

I was first introduced to the chakra system through my Tantra
school.[1] I'd heard of the chakras before but had no basis for
understanding that these energy centers were real. One day though,
they were presented to me in a time and place where I was open to
it. I think this is how personal development works. One day we may
be closed to something new, and it may not resonate with us, but
then something shifts within, and we are ready to receive it.

Luckily the chakra system is no longer an ancient mystical
concept of the East, so I'll share information from others who
are far more studied on it than I. In *Anatomy of the Spirit,* Caroline
Myss, PhD, writes about the chakras, describing them as energy
centers, and relates them to the Sephirot of the Kabbalah and
Jewish tradition and the sacrament of the Christian tradition, calling
them "the seven sacred truths transcending cultural boundaries"
(Myss 1996, p. 67, 68). David. R. Hawkins, PhD, writes about the

293

levels of consciousness in *Power vs. Force: The Hidden Determinants of Human Behavior,* and although he does not correlate his levels of consciousness to rising through the chakras, the connection is clear to me. When one balances, activates, and rises through the chakras, they are indeed raising their level of consciousness.

> The following is a very brief summary of the spiritual life-lessons represented by the seven chakras (see figure below):
>
> *The first chakra*: lessons related to the material world
> *The second chakra*: lessons related to sexuality, work and physical desire
> *The third chakra*: lessons related to the ego, personality, and self-esteem
> *The fourth chakra*: lessons related to love, forgiveness, and compassion
> *The fifth chakra*: lessons related to will and self-expression
> *The sixth chakra*: lessons related to mind, intuition, insight and wisdom
> *The seventh chakra*: lessons related to spirituality
> (Myss 1996, p. 68, 70)

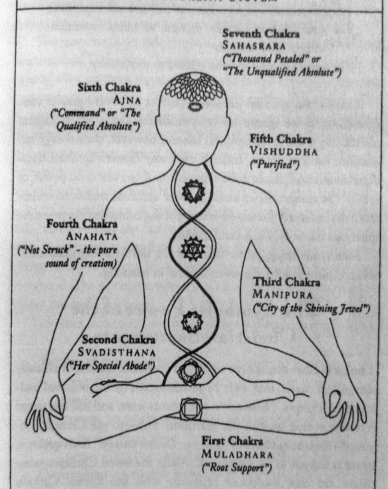

FIGURE 3: SEVEN POWER CENTERS OR CHAKRAS OF THE KUNDALINI SYSTEM

Seventh Chakra
SAHASRARA
("Thousand Petaled" or
"The Unqualified Absolute")

Sixth Chakra
AJNA
("Command" or "The
Qualified Absolute")

Fifth Chakra
VISHUDDHA
("Purified")

Fourth Chakra
ANAHATA
("Not Struck" - the pure
sound of creation)

Third Chakra
MANIPURA
("City of the Shining Jewel")

Second Chakra
SVADISTHANA
("Her Special Abode")

First Chakra
MULADHARA
("Root Support")

The chakras are depicted as lotuses. The spirals indicate the contrasting energies of psyche and spirit: the fiery energies or darker helix contrast with the lighter, spiritual energies and lighter helix, all of which must be brought together in balance.

Source: Joseph Campbell, *The Mythic Image* (Princeton, N.J.: Princeton University Press, 1974)

Tantra teaches that specific yoga poses activate and balance certain chakras. For example, the cobra pose opens the fourth chakra of the heart, the triangle pose activates the third chakra responsible for personal power, and a shoulder stand sends energy to the fifth throat chakra. In Western yoga, this correlation of poses to chakra activation is rarely mentioned; however, this is, in my opinion, why yoga seems to catalyze personal growth and expansion, even though the yogi may not understand the compulsion to make changes in his or her life.

Perhaps this was why I was so struck years earlier after yoga class when my yoga teacher said, "You have to take responsibility for your emotional health." Something opened in me that day, and I was receptive. If she'd said the same words to me over a cappuccino or a glass of wine, I may not have received the message at all; it could've blown right past me instead of propelling me to begin an examination of my life.

So, for the Tantric yogi, as I have experienced, it becomes less about how quickly we move through our vinyasa flow or how soon we can progress to the more difficult poses, and more about becoming conscious of each movement and holding the pose longer with intention to activate and balance the energy of the particular chakra. Five dedicated weeks of study and practice per chakra brought about rapid and substantial development. Most importantly for me, in working on the third chakra, I began to find my personal power and a deep inner strength, and I'm certain it led me to devise the thirty-day Facing Freedom practice. During that period, my self-worth increased, and a quiet confidence and emotional self-sufficiency began to grow—aspects of myself I previously believed I had little control over.

Letting Go of the Stories

Tantra philosophy holds that we should embrace life fully. When we experience sadness, experience it fully; immerse yourself in the sadness, make peace with it, and move on. We so often create and hold onto stories in our minds that perpetuate our own sadness, even sometimes having the sadistic tendency to wallow in it. This comes from our resistance to accept things as they are: *But why can't this work out the way I want it to? It should be this or that way.* Latching onto these stories is what causes us to drift into neurotic and obsessive thought patterns. As a society, we have a very difficult time accepting things *as they are* and instead spend much time and energy wanting things to be different.

When things aren't going our way and we're upset, we obsessively repeat different variations of the same story in our imagination. This brings suffering. If we work to become mindful of the repetitive story and divert ourselves from it, we can diminish the emotional turbulence and suffering that overthinking brings. It takes diligence to bring awareness to thought. It's a discipline that becomes stronger with practice.

The Link between Thought and Emotion

Although Tantra is a spiritual path, it has a psychological approach. One of the great lessons I took from my Tantra teacher Avi is that "emotion has no continuity without thought." I've not just experienced this in theory but in practice. When I work to suspend the thoughts and stories about whatever emotional scenario is playing, I can minimize or eliminate the negative and painful emotions that accompany the thought. Eckhart Tolle confirms, "Emotion in itself is not unhappiness. Only emotion plus an unhappy story is unhappiness" (Tolle 2005, pg. 166). Repetitive thoughts bring about heightened emotions, whether it's sadness, jealousy, greed, anger, or discontent. When thoughts are still, we can be calm and largely without emotional disturbance. Meditation can be a brilliant tool for calming the mind and reducing attachment to certain outcomes and the stories we tell ourselves. In addition, making the conscious choice to simplify our lives will also help to significantly calm the mind.

The Law of Resonance Continued

The aim of the Tantric is to elevate oneself through the chakras, leaving the lower states of individualistic "I" love and transitioning to higher states of universal love—that is, from a place of fear and low resonance/vibrational frequency/energy patterns to high resonance. We can change our resonance or energy pattern by changing our thoughts, intentions, and actions—our consciousness.

David R. Hawkins, MD, PhD, writes in *Power vs. Force:*[2]

> The ability to differentiate between high and low energy patterns is a matter of perception and discrimination that most of us learn by painful trial and error. Failure, suffering, and eventual sickness result from the influence of weak patterns; in contrast, success, happiness, and health proceed from powerful attractor patterns ... Reflection on the many contrasting pairs of qualities (below) can initiate a consciousness-raising process, so that one gradually becomes aware of patterns operating in relationships, business affairs, and all the various interactions that make up the fabric of life.

High Energy Patterns	Low Energy Patterns
Abundant	Excessive
Appreciative	Envious
Confident	Arrogant
Courageous	Reckless
Empathetic	Pitying
Experienced	Cynical
Leading	Coercing
Involved	Obsessed

Noble	Pompous
Observant	Suspicious
Powerful	Forceful
Reliant	Dependent
Responsible	Guilty
Surrendering	Worrying
Trusting	Gullible
(Hawkins 1995,	
pg. 167–169)	

Notice the subtle and preferable differences between, say, high-frequency confidence and low-frequency arrogance. Once we learn to bring awareness to ourselves, our thoughts, and our behaviors, we can align ourselves with high-resonance living.

Our desires, our greed, our attachments, our petty discontent, our intentions, our motivations, and our speech—this is where it would be wise to bring attention in order to raise resonance and change our lives. My chapter early on in the book about The Past is a perfect example. Of course I knew being in an adulterous relationship was wrong, but at the time, I felt unable to keep myself from it. Why? Because I did not understand or know how to handle my emotions and I was caught in the grip of an unconscious pattern.

Upon reflection, related to the role of religion and my upbringing, it seems Christianity taught me *what not to do* with the idea of sin and the Ten Commandments, but it didn't teach me *how not to do it*. Eastern philosophy and psychological self-study did that by teaching me to understand emotions and unconscious behaviors. This is what drives people to hurt one another. Very few wake up in the morning with the intention to bring pain to others, but still we do, and often. Carl Jung said, "Until you make the unconscious conscious, it will direct your life and you will call it fate." Honestly, I don't understand why we're not studying these concepts in school. It makes me angry, really. This is the knowledge we truly need to be better people functioning in society. I spent twelve plus years immersed in the core subjects, English, science, history and math yet I've not once, since leaving school, needed to take the square root of a number. We walk around our entire lives with our minds and no one is teaching us how to deal with them—enter mental health issues, addictions, violence and materialism—the decline of a country.

Pertaining to resonance, it's not only the action that determines our frequency but also the intention behind the action. If we donate money because we feel we should or because it makes us feel better about ourselves, then that gift holds low resonance. If we give from the heart, then the gift is high resonance. If you can absorb this concept of resonance into your consciousness, you're much more likely to become responsible for the state of your mind and your actions, thereby motivated to live a high-resonance life. Once we begin to raise consciousness, we will activate the positive forces of the law of attraction that bring positive experiences. The law of attraction states that we are attracting *something* to us. The quality of our consciousness determines whether we attract positive or negative experiences. If life is not shaping up as we wish, we can ask ourselves if our intentions, thoughts, emotions, words, and actions are that of high or low resonance.

Here's another low-resonance example from my old life. I used to cuss like a sailor, dropping the F-bomb with shocking frequency. The concept of bad words didn't make much sense to me. *What's the big fucking deal?* It's just a word arbitrarily assigned a meaning. I'd grown rather attached to using the word *fuck* as an expressive adjective. *I'm secretly enjoying it now. Shhhhh, don't tell anyone.* Once I understood though that words, intentions, and thoughts hold specific vibrational frequencies, I saw how swearing kept me in low resonance. Energetically speaking, using the word "fuck" holds a negative vibration, whether we say it aloud or in our minds. Not surprisingly, gossip is low resonance, as is violent television or music. *Oh, fuck, not violent television! How will I survive without that?*

Words like "love" and "bliss", of course, hold a positive vibration. *I will cease using the word fuck right now.* See, struck from my vocabulary.

The Environment of the Mind

Scientific evidence now supports the importance of having a healthy environment within the mind. Bruce Lipton, PhD, stem-cell biologist, is leading the frontier in epigenetics, the study of gene expression, and writes about the state of our mind in his book *The Biology of Belief*:

> Your beliefs act like filters on a camera, changing how you see the world. And your biology adapts to those beliefs. When we truly recognize that our beliefs are that powerful, we hold the key to freedom. While we cannot readily change the codes of our genetic blueprints, we can change our minds and, in the process, switch the blueprints used to express our genetic potential … You can filter your life with rose-colored beliefs that will help your body grow or you can use a dark filter that turns everything black and makes your body/mind more susceptible to disease. You can live a life of fear or live a life of love. You have the choice. But I can tell you that if you choose to see a world full of love, your body will respond by growing in health. If you choose to believe that you live in a dark world full of fear, your body's health will be compromised as you physiologically close yourself down in a protection response. (Lipton 2015, pg. 137–138)

The fears he refers to are not life safety related, rather that we are "constantly besieged by multitudes of unresolvable worries about our personal lives, our jobs, and our war-torn global community.

Such worries do not threaten our immediate survival, but they nevertheless can activate the HPA axis, resulting in chronically elevated stress hormones" (Lipton 2015, pg. 155). Simply put, when we are in fear, this suppresses our immune system, making us susceptible to disease, and when we are in love, our bodies are in a state of growth, and it allows us optimal health. "In fact, only 5 percent of cancer and cardiovascular patients can attribute their disease directly to heredity" (Lipton 2015, pg. 48).

Fear takes shape in many ways:

Worry: *Oh, I'm not going to get that promotion, and then I can't buy the new house or get the new car.* Jealousy: *Why aren't you spending more time with me? Don't you love me?* Anger: *Damn—that car cut me off in traffic. Road rage, road rage!*

Love takes shape in many ways:

Compassion: *I'll bet that cashier at the grocery store has a lot going on in her life; that's why she's slow checking me out.* Loving kindness: *I'm going to do something nice for someone today, just because.* Happiness: *I'm going into the world today with a positive attitude.*

I see now and have personally experienced that we have more power and control over our physical health than we could possibly imagine. It begins in the mind. As I became an increasingly experienced meditator and worked to integrate all these philosophical concepts to bring emotional healing and calm to my mind, I noticed my body began to feel different. I intuitively felt that the changes were physically healing and that I was reversing damage I'd caused across decades. I even noticed that my body was assimilating food differently and I was able to maintain a healthy weight with little effort. Imagine my excitement when I was introduced to Bruce Lipton's work in month eighteen of my trip, and my intuition was confirmed by Dr. Lipton's findings.

Please don't take my word for all this. Why not find a Bruce Lipton lecture on YouTube or read his book? His work is of huge significance! If we change our minds, we change our health and our lives!

Compounding Evidence

Dr. Masaru Emoto,[3] a Japanese doctor of alternative medicine, writer, and researcher, studied the effects of thoughts, words, and music on the molecular structure of water and published his results in *Messages from Water.* Dr. Emoto's research shows that water exposed to nurturing stimuli—words like "love" and "thank you," high-resonance music, thoughts, and written text—produced molecules with beautiful, bright, symmetrical crystalline shapes like snowflakes. Whereas, words like "hate" and "Hitler" produced water molecules that were dark, asymmetrical, and ill defined. This has profound implications and is further evidence that our realities are altered by our words, thoughts, deeds, music, movies, and ideas. Essentially, all internal and external stimuli are affecting us positively or negatively.

Dr. Hawkins writes in *Power vs. Force* how our bodies respond negatively to substances even without ingesting them. He used an example of someone holding a packet of artificial sweetener where the subject gave a negative response when tested using kinesiology.

Let's take a moment to ponder these findings. Dr. Emoto proves that words, whether positive or negative, produce chemical changes in water. Consider that our bodies are nearly 70 percent water, we cook and grow our food in water, and our planet is nearly 75 percent water. Dr. Hawkins's findings show that artificial "foods" produce negative responses in human muscle testing. In addition, consider Dr. Bruce Lipton's argument that a positive mind is essential to physical health and a negative mind is promoting disease. These are all highly educated researchers who have taken the risk of departing from mainstream convention of their fields to show us that the state of our minds really matters. The state of our mind matters!

Being vs. Doing

In the USA, we see little value in a still mind, and we may even look down upon it. We are a society that values doing instead of being. Eckhart Tolle writes in *A New Earth*:

> They [people] look upon the present moment as either marred by something that has happened and shouldn't have or as deficient because of something that has not happened but should have. And so they miss the deeper perfection that is inherent in life itself, a perfection that is always already here, that lies beyond what is happening or not happening, beyond form ... The joy of Being, which is the only true happiness, cannot come to you through any form, possession, achievement, person, or event—through anything that happens. That joy cannot *come* to you—ever. It emanates from the formless dimension within you, from consciousness itself and thus is one with who you are. (Tolle 2005, pg. 214)

Our upbringing may tell us to question aspects of life to the nth degree and be skeptical of everything, but is this healthy? Skepticism, by the way, holds a low-energy pattern, says Dr. Hawkins, as it's holding a negative belief. We've overcrowded our lives with the busy-ness of doing and rarely allow ourselves simply to be.

Acceptance over Resistance

In Tantra, we integrate the concept of accepting things *as they are* instead of clinging to how we want them to be. I think this is particularly helpful for us in the West, as we're accustomed to getting what we want in our "have it your way" society. Much of our lives are spent resisting that which is unpleasant yet necessary, and unhappiness comes in our inability to grasp the reality of things as they are. When we resist our own realities, we create our own suffering. If we can come to acknowledge and understand this deeply, finding acceptance in that *which is*, we will experience a monumental internal shift.

CHAPTER 24

Vipassana Insights

Through the portals of silence, the healing sun of wisdom
and peace will shine upon you.
—Paramahansa Yogananda

I had several personal insights in the fourteen-day Vipassana retreat and in the days after that I feel could be universally relatable, informative, or thought-provoking, so I share them here.

Uncontrollable Thoughts

When inside the fourteen days of silence, I witnessed how my mind looped around the same ten to twelve supposedly important topics again and again. Vipassana gave me the rare opportunity to live life for two weeks with absolutely no responsibility; no to-do list, e-mail, phone calls, job, dependents, or even meals to prepare. There was nothing for me to do but eat, meditate, and sleep. My mind should've been free and calm, no?

I found it fascinating—and disturbing—that my mind was still running wild like a monkey. Out of control! My mind could not discriminate between important thoughts needing attention in this moment and unnecessary ones that could wait until I returned to real life after the fourteen days. I had no control over my thoughts.

There was nothing particularly troubling circling my mind, but the repetitive thoughts remained.

I think in the West we have this idea that we should be thinking and problem solving and planning ten steps ahead all the time, and that makes us feel we've accomplished something. Arguably there's a time and place for that type of thinking when planning for an event or a business meeting or a big project. Of course we must use our minds to create, expand, build, learn, and grow business. What I realized though was that even in considering something important, not only did the cycle of thoughts go around a subject once or twice but dozens or hundreds of times depending on the perceived importance or emotional impact of the topic. I encourage you to watch your thoughts and observe when they repeat. Ask yourself, are these repetitive cycles solving any problems? Or are they bringing emotional agitation?

I was also surprised how, as the days progressed and my mind became more still, I found I needed less sleep. See, it's more the mind that creates exhaustion, not the body itself. It's said that many of the monks, nuns, and serious yogis need only several hours of sleep per night, presumably because they have greater mastery of the mind. We need less sleep when the mind is calm, and because the mind is at peace, the sleep we get is of better quality.

Layers of Life

Deep in the silence, I had a vision of dysfunction (shown in the diagram below). I saw how addictions and depression and other various mental afflictions show up in our adult years; however, it's the splintering of self, most often times in our youth, where emotional issues precipitate, later causing the adult dysfunction. This isn't new information. It's well documented by Freud and many others that childhood issues cause adult problems, but the visual for me was striking somehow.

Levels of Childhood Trauma Linked to Adult Dysfunction

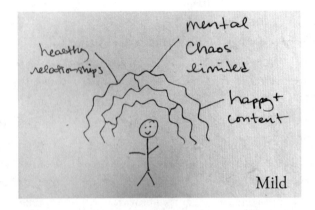

Mild

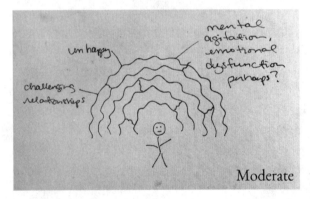

Moderate

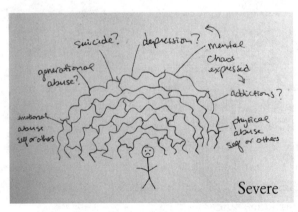

Severe

Journal Entry

When Wisdom Speaks

In the calm, quiet, and sublime stillness, I felt connected to myself and to God, Spirit, or Source in a way I didn't know possible. It lasted only a short while, somewhere between ten and thirty hours. I'm not sure, but I experienced something beyond words.

It's slightly ironic that I felt a connection to God in a Buddhist retreat, as the Buddhists don't believe in God. This is the beauty of silence—it's a catalyst for personal understanding and reordering of the psyche despite one's affiliation with any religious deity. Perhaps the Buddhists would say my connection to God was really my own internal will, and the mental mystical happenings that came in silence allowed my mind to reorder itself. Or maybe when we're silent to this extreme degree, we do have the ability to connect with Source. Maybe God lives inside all of us and my experience was the same whether I consider myself a believer or a nonbeliever, the only difference being how I'd label the experience.

No matter the unknowable "truth," whether it was self or God, I think the profound experience in silence is what's important. It doesn't really matter how I label it. Mental silence came over me, and internal suffering vanished. In that space, I saw how it was the stillness that allowed the true connection with my purest self and with God. Like all the layers of life had shed away, and I was left only with love and internal harmony. Taken from *A Course in Miracles*,[1] "The memory of God comes to the quiet mind. It cannot come where there is conflict, for a mind at war against itself remembers not eternal gentleness" (Schucman 2005, pg. 565).

Days later after leaving the monastery, this visual came to me:

Normal life—Distractions, noise, chaos

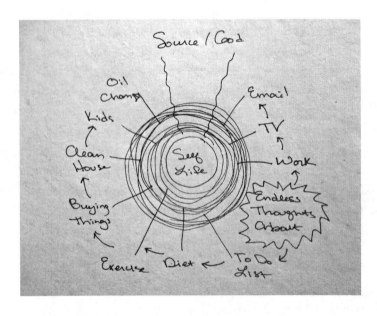

Deep silence—Fewer blockages between me and God

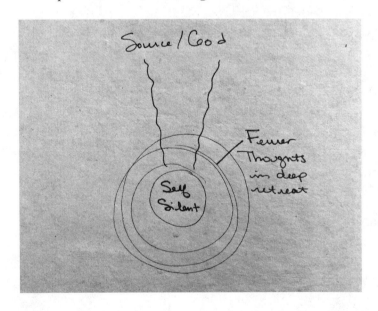

Roadblocks of Religion

I came to question religion on my journey. What is the positive value versus divisive side effect of religion? This has bothered me to no end, how religion seems to separate more than unite us. Although the intention of each religion is pure, humankind has gone and added layers of misinterpretation and ego-driven separations that have brought the world to near destruction. Many wars have been fought, and many men and women have died in the name of religion. It's vexed me and perplexed me how we can kill in the name of God.

I really struggled with the existence of God and religion between months thirteen and fifteen of my trip. I'd recently shed the idea of creationism that had been, for me, previously inseparable from Christianity. God and creationism had been inextricably linked to Christianity, so now what? Did Christianity even make sense for me now that creationism was gone? Does God exist without Christianity? Nothing was clear to me then. I'd seen such vast inequity in the world that crushed me and led me to question faith, asking, if there really was an all-loving God how could He create a world of such disparity? I was also newly alone without the Englishman when I entered Vipassana and new to Chiang Rai, knowing no one … and in this space of vast aloneness I questioned deeply the very existence of God. Yet during that short period of time in Vipassana when I connected with some infinite power, beyond form or any man-made description, I knew God. I'd had a brush with God then and in the lucid dreaming retreat, and I couldn't turn away from that. It was a challenging and lonely time for me, truly—alone in the world and questioning the one thing I'd seen as an unshakable foundation.

Then one night I watched a lecture where a wise Western yogi[2] said, "No one person, no one religion can own God. He is not this or that, He is everything." In that moment everything made sense. Clarity finally came to me. *I had been limiting God by attaching*

Him to one religion, Christianity. I was limiting God. How dare I limit God?

In that spirit, I came to take on more of a spiritual base rather than associating myself with any specific religion. It was a natural transition that came to me in the wake of Vipassana in month fifteen. What I saw was that at the core of all major religions were the base teachings of love and compassion. We get lost in the details of this or that religious text. This is where division among us begins. If we take the teachings back to their root though, there is love and compassion. What else do we need really?

This made me wonder: although meant with good intention, is religion an accelerator or a roadblock to true connection with God?

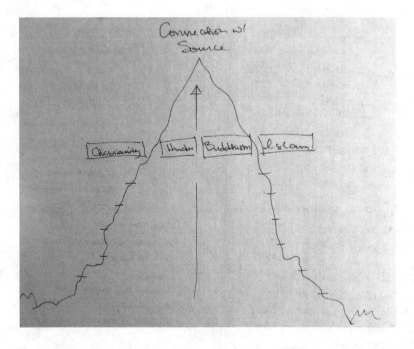

Perhaps formal religions are merely man-made distractions keeping us from true connection with God/Spirit/Source. Could religion itself simply be humankind's need to define ourselves and associate with a formal structure that brings comfort? I was flying solo for a while—on all levels, even without God—I can say it was uncomfortable and awkward and unnatural in a way. But maybe, just maybe to really reach God, all we have to do is step over the roadblocks of these defined religions. Perhaps this formal structure is actually holding us on the mountain at our respective religious designations, leading us to judge and bicker about who's chosen the *right path*. Might that be keeping us from moving toward actual spiritual ascension? These are the mysteries of the spiritual universe. Only God knows.

Teachers

I am eternally grateful for these special people and teachers of diverse nationalities who significantly impacted me on my journey while abroad and still today.

Aharoni, N.	Israel
Artola, S.	Nicaragua
Bell, J.	Scotland
Bernhardson, G.	Norway
Boas, T.	Brazil
Boyle, S.	Australia
Cibrian, S.	Mexico
De Deus, J.	Brazil
Fritz, J.	Germany
Harvey, F.	America
Iribauer, C.	Austria
Kanuri, V.	India
Marino, M.	America
Nicel, Venerable J.	Canada
Oliveira, C.	Sweden
Palmo, T.	England
Pawlyn, J.	England
Shaw, V.	England
Soni, R.	India
Straus, L.	Scotland
Svensson, G.	Australia
Wegener, M.	Germany
Yariv, U.	Israel

Notes and References

Introduction

[1] Lao Tzu (6th century BC) was one of the most famous Chinese philosophers. Not much is known of the details of his life, and some have thought he was not a real person. He was the author of a book called *Tao Te Ching, The Way of Life*, a work of about 81 stories with a consistent theme or moral.

According to this book, Tao ("the Way") does not change and it is the universal truth. His Taoism has been enormously influential in China. Lao Tzu is also known as the main source of Taoism (or Daoism). His name translates as "Old Master" in English.
—en.wikipedia.org/wiki/Laozi

The Catalyst

[1] *Shavasana, Savasana* or Corpse Pose is an asana. Shavasana is a pose usually done at the end of a yoga practice in which practitioners lie flat on their backs with the heels spread as wide as the yoga mat and the arms at the sides of the body, palms facing upward.
—en.wikipedia.org/wiki/Shavasana

[2] The term "dark night (of the soul)" in Roman Catholic spirituality describes a spiritual crisis in the journey towards union with God, like that described by St. John of the Cross, OCD.

St. John of the Cross, (1542 - 1591), was a major figure of the Counter-Reformation, a Spanish mystic and a Roman Catholic saint. John of the Cross is known for his writings. Both his poetry and his studies on the growth of the soul are considered the summit of mystical Spanish literature and one of the peaks of all Spanish literature.

—en.wikipedia.org/wiki/John_Of_The_Cross

Just the Past

[1] Caroline Myss, Ph.D. talks extensively in her book, *Anatomy of the Spirit,* about the mind, body and spirit connection. In the Foreword, C. Norman Shealy, M.D., Ph.D. explains, "Caroline Myss will intrigue, provoke, and inspire you with her views on spirituality and your personal responsibility for your own health… Herein lies the foundation for medicine of the twenty-first century."

Jewels on the Ganges

[1] Traditionally, an ashram is a spiritual hermitage or a monastery in Indian religions. According to S.S. Chandra, the term means "a step in the journey of life". In contrast, according to George Weckman, the term *ashram* connotes a place where one strives towards a goal in a disciplined manner. Such a goal could be ascetic, spiritual, yogic or any other.

—en.wikipedia.org/wiki/ashram

[2] Aarti also spelled arti, arati, arathi, aarthi is a Hindu religious ritual of worship, a part of puja, in which light from wicks soaked in ghee (purified butter) or camphor is offered to one or more deities. Aartis also refer to the songs sung in praise of the deity, when lamps are being offered.

—en.wikipedia.org/wiki/Aarti

Satsang in South Asian religions is being in the company of the truth or the good, by sitting together with a guru or a group of spiritual students.

—en.wikipedia.org/wiki/satsang

Anthony Paul Moo-Young, known as Mooji, was born on 29 January 1954 in Port Antonio, Jamaica. In 1969, he moved to the UK and lived in Brixton, London. Anthony worked in London's 'West End' as a street portrait artist for many years, then as a painter and a stained glass artist, and later as a teacher at Brixton College. For a long time, he was well known as Tony moo, but is now affectionately known as Mooji by the many seekers and friends who visited him.

Mooji is a direct disciple of Sri Harilal Poonja, the renowned advaita master, or Papaji, as his followers call him. In 1987, a chance meeting with a Christian mystic was to be a life-changing encounter for Mooji. It brought him, through prayer, into the direct experience of the Divine within. Within a short period, he experienced a radical shift in consciousness so profound that outwardly, he seemed, to many who knew him, to be an entirely different person. As his spiritual consciousness awakened, a deep inner transformation began which unfolded in the form of many miraculous experiences and mystical insights.

—mooji.org/biography/

Banged Up Abroad (rebadged as *Locked Up Abroad* in America and *Jailed Abroad* in India for the National Geographic Channel) is a British documentary/ docudrama television series created by Bart Layton that was produced for Channel 5 and that premiered in March 2006. Most episodes feature stories of people who have been arrested while travelling abroad, usually for trying to smuggle illegal drugs, although some episodes feature people who were either kidnapped or captured while they were either travelling or living in other countries.

—en.wikipedia.org/wiki/Banged_Up_Abroad

[6] *The Innocents Abroad* is a travel book by American author Mark Twain published in 1869 which humorously chronicles what Twain called his "Great Pleasure Excursion" on board the chartered vessel *Quaker City* through Europe and the Holy Land with a group of American travelers in 1867. It was the best-selling of Twain's works during his lifetime, as well as one of the best-selling travel books of all time.

[7] In Hinduism, the river Ganges is considered sacred and is personified as a goddess Gangā. She is worshiped by Hindus who believe that bathing in the river caused the remission of sins and facilitates Moksha (liberation from the cycle of life and death), and that the water of the Ganges is considered very pure.
—en.m.wikipedia.org/wiki/Ganges_in_Hinduism

[8] A Swami is an ascetic or yogi who has been initiated into the religious monastic order, founded by some religious teacher.
—en.m.wikipedia.org/wiki/Swami

[9] Alan Watts was a British philosopher, writer, and speaker, best known as an interpreter and populariser of Eastern philosophy for a Western audience.
—en.m.wikipedia.org/wiki/Alan_Watts

[10] Affluenza, a portmanteau of *affluence* and *influenza*, is a term used by critics of consumerism. It is thought to have been first used in 1954 but it gained legs as a concept with a 1997 PBS documentary of the same name and the subsequent book, Affluenza: The All-Consuming Epidemic (2001, revised in 2005, 2014). These works define affluenza as "a painful, contagious, socially transmitted condition of overload, debt, anxiety, and waste resulting from the dogged pursuit of more". The term "affluenza" has also been used to refer to an inability to understand the consequences of one's actions because of financial privilege.
—en.wikipedia.org/wiki/Affluenza

The Path to Silence

[1] *Cave in the Snow: Tenzin Palmo's Quest for Enlightenment.* The book and movie details the journey of Tenzin Palmo.
—Cave in the Snow (Mackenzie, 1998)

[2] In 1976 Diane Perry, by then known by her Tibetan name, Tenzin Palmo, secluded herself in a remote cave, 13,200 feet up in the Himalayas, cut off from the world by mountains and snow. There she engaged in twelve years of intense Buddhist meditation. She faced unimaginable cold, wild animals, near-starvation, and avalanches; she grew her own food and slept in a traditional wooden meditation box, three-feet-square—she never lay down. Her goal was to gain Enlightenment as a woman.
—Cave in the Snow (Mackenzie, 1998)

[3] Realizing the woman about to give the lecture was the same brave woman I'd just seen on the movie, *Cave in the Snow,* I pulled out my phone and recorded the entire lecture. I somehow sensed that whatever she was about to say would change me. I listen to her lecture regularly for inspiration.
—Palmo Lecture, Dharamsala, India 4.4.14

[4] Phillip Calvin McGraw (born September 1, 1950), known as Dr. Phil, is an American television personality, author, psychologist, and the host of the television show Dr. Phil, which debuted in 2002. McGraw first gained celebrity status with appearances on The Oprah Winfrey Show in the late 1990s.
—en.wikipedia.org/Phil_McGraw

[5] Originally from Australia, Glen has been a student and practitioner of Tibetan Buddhism since 1995 and graduated from the seven-year *Masters Program in Advanced Buddhist Studies of Sutra and Tantra* at the Lama Tzong Khapa Institute (Pomaia, Italy) in 2004.

Since 2005 he has taught and led meditation retreats in India, Europe, North America and Australia with a teaching style emphasizing clarity and stressing the integration of philosophical view, meditation and daily life conduct.

—glensvensson.org

6   The Donnalley Family Bible, A Psalm of David, Psalm XXIII
Holy Bible, King James Version, The Crusade Analytical Study Edition

7   *The Tibetan Book of Living and Dying*, Sogyal Rinpoche
Revised and Updated. Copyright 2002 by Rigpa Fellowship
Pg. 47, The Nature of the Mind: "The still revolutionary insight of Buddhism is that *life and death are in the mind, and nowhere else.* Mind is revealed as the universal basis of experience—the creator of happiness and the creator of suffering, the creator of what we call life and what we call death."

8   Journal entry by Eryn Donnalley taken 4.9.14 from Buddhist teachings in silent retreat. Instructor, Venerable Joan Nicell, Dharamsala, India.
Four noble truths: 1) The truth of suffering, find the cause, recognize the suffering. 2) The truth of the cause of suffering. 3) The truth of the end of suffering. 4) The truth of the path to the end of suffering.

I Climbed a Mountain

1   The Tibetan diaspora is a term used to refer to the communities of Tibetan people living outside their original homeland of Tibet. Tibetan emigration has three separate stages. The first stage was in 1959 following the 14th Dalai Lama's escape to Dharamsala in India, in fear of persecution from the People's Liberation Army. The second stage occurred in the 1980s, when China opened Tibet

to foreigners. The third stage began in 1996 and continues today although with less frequency.

Not all emigration from Tibet is permanent; today some parents in Tibet send their children to communities in the diaspora to receive a traditional Tibetan education. The 2009 census registered about 128,000 Tibetans in exile, with the most numerous part of the community living in India, Nepal, and Bhutan. However, in 2005 and 2009 there were estimates of up to 150,000 living in exile.
—en.wikipedia.org/wiki/Tibetan_diaspora

[2] Ladies, listen up. Condoms. It is our responsibility to protect ourselves in this department. Men, it seems, are happy to engage in sexual activity with no serious consideration to protection against STD's and pregnancy. We must value ourselves enough to hold the line.

[3] Vipassanā (Pāli) in the Buddhist tradition means insight into the true nature of reality, namely as the Three marks of existence: impermanence, suffering or unsatisfactoriness, and the realization of non-self.
—en.wikipedia.org/wiki/Vipassanā

Delhi Premonitions

[1] David R. Hawkins, Ph.D. author of *Power vs. Force: The Hidden Determinants of Human Behavior* is Director of the Institute for Spiritual Research, Inc. He is a widely known authority within the field of consciousness research. He writes and teaches from the unique perspective of an experienced clinician, scientist, and teacher.
—Power vs. Force, Copyright 1995 Published by Hay House, Inc.

Narrow Minds

[1] Elisabeth Kübler-Ross (July 8, 1926 – August 24, 2004) was a Swiss-American psychiatrist, a pioneer in near-death studies and

the author of the groundbreaking book On Death and Dying (1969), where she first discussed her theory of the five stages of grief.

Pocket Watches

1   Oprah Winfrey paraphrased her guest, Gerald G. Jampolsky from the January 4, 1990 episode on forgiveness. During that show, Jampolsky asserted that the secret to happiness was forgiveness, which he described in a way Oprah hadn't heard before. "It really means *letting go of the past that we thought we wanted.*"
—google.com/amp/m.huffpost.com/us/entry/us_58546579 e4b0b3ddfd8cdeb0/amp

2   Conscious Lifestyle Magazine published the article titled: *The Art of Shifting Your Reality: 4 Deep Practices for Clearing Emotional Blockages and Harnessing the Power of Your Subconscious Mind* by Joseph Drumheller, spiritual healer and author. Quote taken from the *Human Suffering and the Power of the Mind* section
—consciouslifestylemag.com/subconscious-mind-power/

Half a Hippy

1   *This Is Your Brain on Drugs* was a large-scale US anti-narcotics campaign by Partnership for a Drug-Free America (PDFA) launched in 1987, that used three televised public service announcements (PSAs) and a related poster campaign.

The 30-second version of the first PSA, from 1987, shows a man (played by John Roselius) in a starkly furnished apartment who asks if there is anyone out there who still doesn't understand the dangers of drug abuse. He holds up an egg and says, "This is your brain," before motioning to a frying pan and adding, "This is drugs." He then cracks open the egg, fries the contents, and says,

"This is your brain on drugs." Finally he looks up at the camera and asks, "Any questions?"
—en.wikipedia.org/wiki/This_Is_Your_Brain_on_Drugs

2   Stanislav Grof (born July 1, 1931, in Prague, Czechoslovakia) is one of the founders of the field of transpersonal psychology and a pioneering researcher into the use of altered states of consciousness for purposes of healing, growth, and insight.

"In one of my early books I suggested that the potential significance of LSD and other psychedelics for psychiatry and psychology was comparable to the value the microscope has for biology or the telescope has for astronomy. My later experience with psychedelics only confirmed this initial impression. These substances function as unspecific amplifiers that increase the cathexis (energetic charge) associated with the deep unconscious contents of the psyche and make them available for conscious processing. This unique property of psychedelics makes it possible to study psychological undercurrents that govern our experiences and behaviors to a depth that cannot be matched by any other method and tool available in modern mainstream psychiatry and psychology. In addition, it offers unique opportunities for healing of emotional and psychosomatic disorders, for positive personality transformation, and consciousness evolution."
—en.wikiquote.org/wiki/Stanislav_Grof

3   Portugal decriminalized the use of all drugs in 2001. Weed, cocaine, heroin, you name it—Portugal decided to treat possession and use of small quantities of these drugs as a public health issue, not a criminal one. The drugs were still illegal, of course. But now getting caught with them meant a small fine and maybe a referral to a treatment program—not jail time and a criminal record.
—washingtonpost.com/news/wonk/wp/2015/06/05/why-hardly-anyone-dies-from-a-drug-overdose-in-portugal/?utm_term=.76b0d35b4dd6

1   Wayne Dyer, American philosopher, self-help author and motivational speaker was interviewed by Oprah Winfrey on Super Soul Sunday regarding his remote surgery from John of God.
    Part I—youtu.be/smjWQninbUY
    Part II— youtu.be/F8SclCQFh1Y

2   Dr. Fred Harvey, The Harvey Center for Integrative Medicine— Triple Board Certified in Internal Medicine, Geriatric Medicine and Functional Medicine
    — harveycenter.com/about/meet-the-team.html

3   Caroline Myss is a five-time New York Times best-selling author and internationally renowned speaker in the fields of human consciousness, spirituality and mysticism, health, energy medicine, and the science of medical intuition.
    — myss.com/about-caroline-myss/

4   João Teixeira de Faria is living proof of a unique form of mediumship in which benevolent spirits, aka disembodies entities or angels, use his body to perform seemingly miraculous healing, including both physical and psychic surgery. When João is acting as a host (to one spirit at a time) he is called 'the Entity', and referred to, more formally as João de Deus (John of God).
    —friendsofthecasa.info/index.php?page=joao-teixeira-de-faria

5   Jeffrey D. Rediger, MD, is medical director for the McLean SouthEast Adult Psychiatric Programs and an instructor in psychiatry at Harvard Medical School. He has a Master of Divinity degree from Princeton Theological Seminary and publishes in the fields of medicine, psychiatry and spirituality.
    — mcleanhospital.org/biography/jeffrey-rediger

6   Susan Casey interviewed by Oprah Winfrey
    —youtu.be/Vaf5MhqoDmk

[7] The Casa de Dom Inácio (the house of St. Ignatius Loyola) is a spiritual healing centre in Abadiânia, central Brazil.
—friendsofthecasa.info/

[8, 9] Dr. Jeff Rediger interviewed by Oprah Winfrey
—youtu.be/Vaf5MhqoDmk

[10] Sadly, the repaired vision of my loved one diminished over time, and she has not yet been cured from her rare health disorder; however, at a doctor's appointment following the channeled healings, her doctor reported good news. He said, rather boldly, while looking at her then most recent blood work, "Well, this is the first time I can say I don't think this thing is going to kill you." We live in hope and pray that someday she will be well, whether by miracle cure, energy healing, or some new treatment.

[11] Dr. Jeff Rediger interviewed by Oprah Winfrey
—youtu.be/Vaf5MhqoDmk

[12] Dhammapada is a collection of sayings of the Buddha in verse form and one of the most widely read and best known Buddhist scriptures. Verses 379 and 380 included here.
—tipitaka.net/tipitaka/dhp/verseload.php?verse=379

[13] Over eighteen months after leaving Brazil, I made concerted efforts to naturally heal my thyroid through yoga, meditation, diet, emotional healing, raising my vibrational frequency and believing fully in my body's natural ability to heal itself. This all took place after I went through intensive self-study and emotional healing (which also continued during the eighteen months). I feel strongly that addressing the emotional realm was the catalyst and that physical healing wouldn't have been possible without it. Please consult with your doctor before attempting to reduce medications yourself.

Detour to Humility

1 Study says that "White extremists have killed more Americans in the U.S. than Jihadists since 9/11."
—time.com/3934980/right-wing-extremists-white-terrorism-islamist-jihadi-dangerous/

2 [2] The Dalai Lama's *Amazing proclamation to woman*
—huffingtonpost.com/ariane-de-bonvoisin/the-dalai-lamas-amazing-p_b_324760.html

3 MV *Liemba*, formerly *Graf Goetzen* or *Graf von Goetzen*, is a passenger and cargo ferry that runs along the eastern shore of Lake Tanganyika. The Marine Services Company Limited of Tanzania sails her, with numerous stops to pick up and set down passengers, between the ports of Kigoma, Tanzania and Mpulungu, Zambia.

Graf von Goetzen was built in 1913 in Germany, and was one of three vessels the German Empire used to control Lake Tanganyika during the early part of the First World War. Her captain had her scuttled on 26 July 1916 in Katabe Bay during the German retreat from Kigoma. In 1924, a British Royal Navy salvage team raised her and in 1927 she returned to service as *Liemba*. *Liemba* is the last vessel of the German Imperial Navy still actively sailing anywhere in the world.
—en.wikipedia.org/wiki/MV_Liemba

4 *This column will change your life: the guru who didn't believe in gurus*
—theguardian.com/lifeandstyle/2013/aug/10/stop-minding-psychology-oliver-burkeman

5 The Rwandan genocide, also known as the genocide against the Tutsi was a genocidal mass slaughter of Tutsi in Rwanda by members of the Hutu majority government. An estimated 500,000–1,000,000 Rwandans were killed during the 100-day

period from April 7 to mid-July 1994, constituting as many as 70% of the Tutsi population.

—en.wikipedia.org/wiki/Rwandan_genocide

[6] *Think you can't live without plastic bags? Consider this: Rwanda did it*

—theguardian.com/commentisfree/2014/feb/15/rwanda-banned-plastic-bags-so-can-we

[7] Azizi Life began in 2008 as an initiative of the Christian nonprofit, Food for the Hungry. Through a business development program, we met a number of artisan cooperatives. What we saw is that the artisans had skills, organization and leadership. They had vision for the future. They were from impoverished communities, but had a means to rise up. The problem was this: although the artisans could sell their crafts to their neighbors or through a middleman, the income they earned was insufficient to support their families. In some cases, they didn't even cover the cost of the raw materials!

Azizi Life was begun to honor the initiatives and work of the artisans and serve as a bridge to customers around the world.

From the very beginning, we had a vision: to build a family of businesses which would partner with local efforts for poverty alleviation and community development.

— azizilife.com/story/

Monastery in the Forest

[1] The Vipassanā movement, also called the Insight Meditation Movement, refers to a number of branches of modern Theravāda Buddhism, which stress insight into the three marks of existence as the main means to attain awakening and become a stream-enterer.

Thai Forest Tradition: This is a tradition of Buddhist monasticism within Thai Theravāda Buddhism, which was in part a reaction against this perceived dilution in Buddhism. Practitioners inhabit

remote wilderness and forest dwellings as spiritual practice training grounds. It is widely known among Thai people for its orthodoxy, conservatism, and strict adherence to monastic rules (vinaya).
—en.wikipedia.org/wiki/Vipassana_movement

2 The Eight Precepts are for upāsakas and upāsikās who wish to practice Buddhism more strictly than through adherence to the five precepts. The eight precepts focus both on avoiding morally bad behavior, as do the five precepts, and on leading a more ascetic life.

The Buddha gave teachings on how the eight precepts are to be practiced,[23] and on the right and wrong ways of practicing the eight precepts.[24]

1. I undertake to abstain from causing harm and taking life (both human and non-human).
2. I undertake to abstain from taking what is not given (for example stealing, displacements that may cause misunderstandings).
3. I undertake to abstain from sexual activity.
4. I undertake to abstain from wrong speech: telling lies, deceiving others, manipulating others, using hurtful words.
5. I undertake to abstain from using intoxicating drinks and drugs, which lead to carelessness.
6. I undertake to abstain from eating at the wrong time (the right time is after sunrise, before noon).
7. I undertake to abstain from singing, dancing, playing music, attending entertainment performances, wearing perfume, and using cosmetics and garlands (decorative accessories).
8. I undertake to abstain from luxurious places for sitting or sleeping, and overindulging in sleep.
 —en.wikipedia.org/wiki/Five_Precepts

3 Vāsanā is a behavioral tendency or karmic imprint which influences the present behavior of a person. It is a technical term in Indian religions, particularly Buddhist philosophy and Advaita Vedanta.

Keown (2004) defines the term generally within Buddhism as follows:

"Vāsanā (Skt.). Habitual tendencies or dispositions, a term, often used synonymously with bīja ('seed'). It is found in Pāli and early Sanskrit sources but comes to prominence with the Yogācāra, for whom it denotes the latent energy resulting from actions which are thought to become 'imprinted' in the subject's storehouse-consciousness (ālaya-vijñāna). The accumulation of these habitual tendencies is believed to predispose one to particular patterns of behavior in the future."
—en.wikipedia.org/wiki/Vāsanā

Raising Resonance

[1] A visa run is the journey towards a neighboring country where a foreigner (whether tourist or professional) needs to apply a visa to stay legally in the kingdom. Due to the government's complicated visa laws and provisions, a *falang* (Thai term which means foreigner) is rendered to apply for it outside the country upon the visa's expiration.
—thaiembassy.com/thailand/visa-run-malaysia.php

[2] The First Thai–Lao Friendship is a bridge over the Mekong, connecting Nong Khai province and the city of Nong Khai in Thailand with Vientiane Prefecture in Laos; the city of Vientiane is approximately 20 km (12 mi) from the bridge.
—en.wikipedia.org/wiki/Thai%E2%80%93Lao_Friend ship_Bridge

[3] *The Shawshank Redemption* is a 1994 American drama film written and directed by Frank Darabont, and starring Tim Robbins and Morgan Freeman. Adapted from the Stephen King novella Rita Hayworth and Shawshank Redemption, the film tells the story of Andy Dufresne, a banker who is sentenced to life in Shawshank

State Penitentiary for the murder of his wife and her lover, despite his claims of innocence. During his time at the prison, he befriends a fellow inmate, Ellis Boyd "Red" Redding, and finds himself protected by the guards after the warden begins using him in his money-laundering operation.

4   The *Yoga Sūtras of Patañjali* are 196 Indian sutras (aphorisms). The *Yoga Sutras* were compiled prior to 400 CE by Sage Patañjali, taking materials about yoga from older traditions. Scholars consider the *Yoga Sūtras of Patañjali* formulations to be one of the foundations of classical Yoga philosophy of Hinduism.

5   Excerpt from *Power vs. Force*, David R. Hawkins, Ph.D. "The levels of consciousness ("energy fields") are calibrated according to their measurable effect. With each progressive rise in the level of consciousness, the "frequency" or "vibration" of energy increases. Thus, higher consciousness radiates a beneficial and healing effect on the world." (New Foreword, xxxvii)

6   Tantra denotes the esoteric traditions of Hinduism and Buddhism that co-developed most likely about the middle of 1st millennium CE. The term *tantra*, in the Indian traditions, also means any systematic broadly applicable "text, theory, system, method, instrument, technique or practice. In Hinduism, the tantra tradition is most often associated with its goddess tradition called Shaktism, followed by Shaivism and Vaishnavism.

Tantra literally means "loom, warp, weave". The connotation of the word tantra to mean an esoteric practice or religious ritualism is a colonial era European invention. The term is based on the metaphor of weaving, states Ron Barrett, where the Sanskrit root *tan* means the warping of threads on a loom. It implies "interweaving of traditions and teachings as threads" into a text, technique or practice.

In modern era scholarship, Tantra has been studied as an esoteric practice and ritualistic religion, sometimes referred to as Tantrism. There is wide gap between what Tantra means to its followers, and what Tantra has been represented or perceived as since colonial era writers began commenting on Tantra. Many definitions of Tantra have been proposed ever since, and there is no universally accepted definition of Tantra.

—en.wikipedia.org/wiki/Tantra

7   Tantra is a millenary science that refers to the life of man and to his spiritual evolution… Tantra is an assembly of practical methods that gradually guide the aspirant towards a spiritual state and realization helping him successfully surpass the limitations that were self-imposed in the process of personality development… Tantra is directly oriented towards Truth and does not lose itself in sterile formalisms that protect and amplify the meaningless labyrinth of the ego.

—Natha Yoga Center 2008, Intensive Tantra Course Material, Year 1 Course 1

8   When practiced in a couple, Tantra is a kind of meditation in two, which springs from the union of the feminine and masculine principles, and is fueled by the sexual energy. It is an invitation to discover the sacred dimension of the erotic encounters and the means to make the body, soul and consciousness vibrate in unison.

At its essence, Tantra is not a technique, but love; a prayer; the relaxation of the heart to the point of generating a space where the man and the woman merge with each other.

—tantrayogathailand.com/what-tantra-is-and-what-it-is-not/

9   Tapas is a Sanskrit word that means "to heat". It also connotes certain spiritual practices in Indian religions. In Jainism, it refers to asceticism (austerities, body mortification); in Buddhism to spiritual practices including meditation and self-discipline;[4]

and in the different traditions within Hinduism it refers to a spectrum of practices ranging from asceticism, inner cleansing to self-discipline.
—en.wikipedia.org/wiki/Tapas_(Sanskrit)

10 Sir David R. Hawkins, M.D., Ph.D. is a nationally renowned psychiatrist, physician, researcher, spiritual teacher and lecturer. The uniqueness of his contribution to humanity comes from the advanced state of spiritual awareness known as "Enlightenment," "Self–Realization," and "Unio Mystica."Rarely, if ever, has this spiritual state occurred in the life of an accomplished scientist and physician. Therefore, Dr. Hawkins is uniquely qualified to present a spiritual path that is scientifically compelling to modern society.
—veritaspub.com/about_us.php

11 The Law of Resonance is the Universal Law which determines the various vibratory patterns or frequencies which are determined and projected based on various thoughts, beliefs and emotions and the resulting projected frequency which activates the Law of Attraction ensuring that this resonance or projected energy can only harmonize with energies that vibrate or resonate at a similar harmonious vibratory frequency which determine and create your physical results.
—lawsoftheuniverse.weebly.com/uncommonmisc-laws.html

12 Wayne Dyer is interviewed by Oprah Winfrey where they discuss his departure from the movie, *The Secret.*
—youtu.be/V4zhQ3M892E

13 John Kehoe combines the most up-to-date scientific discoveries with mystical teachings from our major religions to create a vision of the quantum warrior and the possibilities of our future as a species. With great insight he reveals the extraordinary mysteries of consciousness and the universe.
—learnmindpower.com/store/books/quantum-warrior-the-future-of-the-mind/

Mirrors

[1] Possible link of breast cancer to the use of antiperspirant
—www.cancer.gov/about-cancer/causes-prevention/risk/myths/
antiperspirants-fact-sheet

Facing Freedom

[1] George Ohsawa (born Yukikazu Sakurazawa) managed to revert his incurable diseases at the age of 18 by following the principles of what is now known as macrobiotic diet. After George Ohsawa managed to cure his diseases completely, he started to write various articles and books about these principles, the result being the birth of the macrobiotic diet. What is commonly known as the Ohsawa diet is a short period of time when only "neutral" foods are consumed, in order to allow the body to regulate itself.

There are multiple reports of people being completely cured from diseases by undertaking this diet. Since any illness is the expression of an energy imbalance, restoring the correct yin-yang balance allows the body to heal. Eliminating toxins clears the burden from the body, enabling it to function better and more efficiently. The Ohsawa diet has a strong detoxification effect; therefore it can be used as such.

The Ohsawa diet lasts for 10 days and can be repeated if necessary, after a pause of at least a week. There are only 4 foods allowed: wheat, rice, millet and buckwheat – and salt.
—alkalinedietexposed.com/my-10-day-oshawa-diet-experiment/

[2] Who am I? Mooji gives a satsang on this question.
—youtu.be/9QIpxP_glO0

[3] Eckhart Tolle is a German-born resident of Canada, best known as the author of The Power of Now and A New Earth: *Awakening to your Life's Purpose*. In 2011, he was listed by Watkins Review as

the most spiritually influential person in the world. In 2008, a *New York Times* writer called Tolle "the most popular spiritual author in the United States".

Tolle has said that he was depressed for much of his life until he underwent, at age 29, an "inner transformation". He then spent several years wandering "in a state of deep bliss" before becoming a spiritual teacher.

—en.wikipedia.org/wiki/Eckhart_Tolle

Messages From Beyond

[1] According to halakha (Jewish religious law), Shabbat is observed from a few minutes before sunset on Friday evening until the appearance of three stars in the sky on Saturday night.

—en.wikipedia.org/wiki/Shabbat

[2] A hijab is a veil traditionally worn by Muslim women in the presence of adult males outside of their immediate family, which usually covers the head and chest.

—en.wikipedia.org/wiki/Hijab

[3] On 12 June 2014, three Israeli teenagers were kidnapped at the bus/ hitchhiking stop at the Israeli settlement of Alon Shvut in Gush Etzion, in the West Bank, as they were hitchhiking to their homes.

The Israel Defense Forces initiated *Operation Brother's Keeper* in search of the three teenagers. As part of the operation, in the following 11 days Israel arrested around 350 Palestinians, including nearly all of Hamas' West Bank leaders.

On 30 June, search teams found the bodies of the three missing teenagers in a field north-west of Hebron. They had apparently been shot dead shortly after the abduction.

—en.wikipedia.org/wiki/2014_kidnapping_and_murder_ of_Israeli_teenagers

[4] A lucid dream is a dream during which the dreamer is aware of dreaming. During lucid dreaming, the dreamer may be able to exert some degree of control over the dream characters, narrative, and environment.

—en.wikipedia.org/wiki/Lucid_dream

[5] Stephen LaBerge (born 1947) is an American psycho-physiologist specializing in the scientific study of lucid dreaming. In 1967 he received his Bachelor's Degree in mathematics. He began researching lucid dreaming for his Ph.D. in Psychophysiology at Stanford University, which he received in 1980. He developed techniques to enable himself and other researchers to enter a lucid dream state at will, most notably the MILD technique (mnemonic induction of lucid dreams), which was necessary for many forms of dream experimentation. In 1987, he founded The Lucidity Institute, an organization that promotes research into lucid dreaming, as well as running courses for the general public on how to achieve a lucid dream.

—en.wikipedia.org/wiki/Stephen_LaBerge

[6] In the Discovery Channel documentary, *Beyond Human Limits*, Pam Reynold's gives the account of her near death experience. Pam describes seeing the white light, "I asked what was the nature of the light? Is the light God? It was communicated to me, "no, the light is not God. The light is what happens when God breathes." At that point, I remembered thinking, I'm standing in the breath of God."

—youtu.be/Bu1ErDeQ0Zw

Living on in Love

[1] Auras explained
—gaia.com/article/how-to-see-auras-for-beginners

The Siggy Effect

[1]   Burning in Northern Thailand, Burma, Laos, Cambodia and Southern China is an annual problem and seems to be getting worse. Air quality in the burning season is among the worst in Thailand. On bad days, visibility is severely limited. On really bad days, it is common to experience eye irritation and breathing discomfort. The worst months are February and March.
—guidetothailand.com/thailand-weather/thailand-burning-season.php

Individuation

[1]   Carl Gustav Jung (26 July 1875—6 June 1961) was a Swiss psychiatrist and psychoanalyst who founded analytical psychology. His work has been influential not only in psychiatry but also in anthropology, archaeology, literature, philosophy and religious studies.

Among the central concepts of analytical psychology is individuation—the lifelong psychological process of differentiation of the self out of each individual's conscious and unconscious elements. Jung considered it to be the main task of human development. He created some of the best known psychological concepts, including synchronicity, archetypal phenomena, the collective unconscious, the psychological complex, and extraversion and introversion.
—en.wikipedia.org/wiki/Carl_Jung

[2]   Jung considered personality to be an achievement, not something given. Moreover, it was essentially an achievement of the second half of life. In the first half of life, a person is, and should be, concerned with emancipating himself from parents and with establishing himself in the world as a spouse, parent and effective contributor. In the modern world, especially, a certain one-sidedness might be

needed to fulfill these conventional demands; but, once a person had done so, then he could and should look inwards. Jung called the journey toward wholeness the "process of individuation," and it is toward the study of this process that the thrust of his later work is directed.

—The Essential Jung, Selected writings introduced by Anthony Storr (1983, pg. 19)

Closing Thoughts

[1] Conscious business enterprises and people (also sometimes referred to under the label conscious capitalism) are those that choose to follow a business strategy, in which they seek to benefit both human beings and the environment. The Conscious Business movement in the US, which emerged from the theory of corporate social responsibility, pushes for "values-based" economic values where values represent social and environmental concerns at both global and local scales. This effort is related to not-just-for-profit business models, conscious consumerism, and socially responsible investing.
—en.wikipedia.org/wiki/Conscious_business

Petals of the Lotus

[1] All concepts in this chapter were first introduced to me at Tushita Meditation Center in Dharamsala, India in April of 2014 from the Tibetan Buddhism lineage, specifically the Mahāyāna tradition. Most theories in this chapter I was later reintroduced to through general study of Eastern philosophy, Tantra and Thai Buddhism in the Theravada tradition.

Tantra Concepts

[1] Tantra Teachings are from the Mahasiddha Yoga School in Thailand, also known as Natha Yoga Center in Europe.
—tantrayogathailand.com

A trademark of Dr. Hawkins's research is his pioneering, internationally–known and applied "Map of Consciousness," presented in the ever–popular book Power vs. Force (1995), translated into over twenty–five languages. The "Map of Consciousness" incorporates findings from quantum physics and nonlinear dynamics, thereby confirming the classical "stages" of spiritual evolution found in the world's sacred literature as actual "attractor fields."

These spiritual levels had been delineated by saints, sages, and mystics; yet there had never been a scientific framework by which to understand the inner terrain. The "Map of Consciousness" is clinically sophisticated in its depiction of each level's emotional tone, view of God, and view of life. For example, "Fear" views God as punitive, whereas "Love" views God as loving.

The "Map of Consciousness" illumines heretofore unknown aspects of consciousness. With each progressive rise in the level of consciousness, the "frequency" or "vibration" of energy increases. Thus, higher consciousness radiates a beneficial and healing effect on the world, verifiable in the human muscle response which stays strong in the presence of love and truth. In contrast, non–true or negative energy fields which "calibrate" below the level of integrity induce a weak muscle response. This stunning discovery of the difference between "power" and "force" has influenced numerous fields of human endeavor: business, advertising, education, psychology, medicine, law, and international relations.
—veritaspub.com/about_us.php

³ Masaru Emoto (22 July 1943—17 October 2014) was a Japanese author, researcher, photographer and entrepreneur, who claimed that human consciousness has an effect on the molecular structure of water. Emoto's conjecture evolved over the years, and his early work explored his belief that water could react to positive thoughts and words, and that polluted water could be cleaned through prayer and positive visualization.

Since 1999, Emoto published several volumes of a work entitled Messages from Water, which contain photographs of ice crystals and their accompanying experiments.

—en.m.wikipedia.org/wiki/Masaru_Emoto

Vipassana Visions

[1] *A Course in Miracles* is a book scribed and edited by Helen Schucman, with portions transcribed and edited by William Thetford, containing a curriculum to bring about what it calls a "spiritual transformation". Schucman believed that the "inner dictation" came from Jesus.

—en.wikipedia.org/wiki/A_Course_in_Miracles

[2] It's unfortunate but I'm not able to locate the lecture on YouTube to cite this quote properly. The man was a Caucasian, Western yogi, I believe American, but I'm not certain. I wrote the text in my journal, but at the time had no idea that I'd use it in my book.

Suggested Reading List

A New Earth: Awakening to Your Life's Purpose
Eckhart Tolle

Anatomy of the Spirit: The Seven Stages of Power and Healing
Caroline Myss, PhD

Power vs. Force: The Hidden Determinants of Human Behavior
David R. Hawkins, MD, PhD

Biology of Belief: Unleashing the Power of Consciousness, Matter & Miracles
Bruce H. Lipton, PhD

Quantum Warrior: The Future of the Mind
John Kehoe

Understanding Our Mind
Thich Nhat Hanh

The Essential Jung: Selected Writings
Introduced by Anthony Storr

Cave in the Snow: Tenzin Palmo's Quest for Enlightenment
Vicki Mackenzie

About the Author

Eryn Donnalley is an author, artist, life coach, and dedicated change-agent who inspires others to find their highest selves. After working sixteen years in the construction and development industry, she felt called to find a more authentic, creative path. Her incredible solo journey, recounted in Facing Freedom, sparked an awakening that reinvigorated her to live life more fully with purpose and meaning. Through her travels she came to understand the invaluable healing power of intentional silence, a concept largely unfamiliar in the West, and that creativity is a vehicle to explore our greatest potential.

The author is inspired and motivated by the wisdom of His Holiness the 14th Dalai Lama, "I believe that to meet the challenge of our times, human beings will have to develop a greater sense of universal responsibility. Each of us must learn to work not for his or her self, family or nation, but for the benefit of all mankind... Those who have something to offer should come forward. Now is the time."

Although Eryn currently resides in Colorado, she considers herself a nomad at heart and dedicates her life to seeking truth, knowledge, and wisdom from all corners of the globe.

A portion of the royalties from the sale of this book will be donated to special needs individuals and reputable charity organizations at home and abroad.